Tier 2

# INTERVENTION

Grades K-2

# Phonemic Awareness

TEACHER'S EDITION

A

*The McGraw-Hill Companies*

**Macmillan/McGraw-Hill**

Published by Macmillan/McGraw-Hill, of McGraw-Hill Education, a division of The McGraw-Hill Companies, Inc., Two Penn Plaza, New York, New York 10121.



Printed in the United States of America

2 3 4 5 6 7 8 9 HES 14 13 12 11 10

# Table of Contents



## Sound Awareness, Rhyme, and Beginning Sounds

### Section 1 — 2



### Section 2 — 18



## Syllables and Ending Sounds

### Section 3 — 40

## Section 4 62



# Medial Sounds

## Section 5 78



# Blending and Segmenting

## Section 6 100

## Section 7 120



# Substitution, Deletion, Addition, and Reversals

## Section 8 140



## Section 9 162

# Using *Phonemic Awareness Intervention*

## Purpose and Use

*Treasures* provides a set of strategic intervention materials, one set for each of the key technical skill domains of beginning reading (phonemic awareness and phonological awareness, phonics and decoding, oral reading fluency, vocabulary, and reading comprehension skills). Each set of materials contains over ninety 15-minute lessons. These lessons

- focus on children in Kindergarten through Grade 2 who need reteaching and practice in one or more of the technical skills (e.g., phonemic awareness);
- provide explicit, sequential, and systematic needs-based instruction of standards taught in the target grade or previous grade that have not been mastered by children;
- connect to the basic program and key instructional routines used there;
- are designed for efficient and effective use in tutorials or small groups;
- can be administered by a teacher or teacher's aide but are also great for after-school programs and one-on-one tutoring sessions;
- contain a periodic review for determining attainment of skills taught after approximately every ten lessons.

## Contents and Resources

*Phonemic Awareness Intervention* organizes instruction and practice on two-page spreads for ease of use. A short, 15-minute lesson provides targeted instruction in a discrete skill. A Practice Reproducible provides targeted practice.

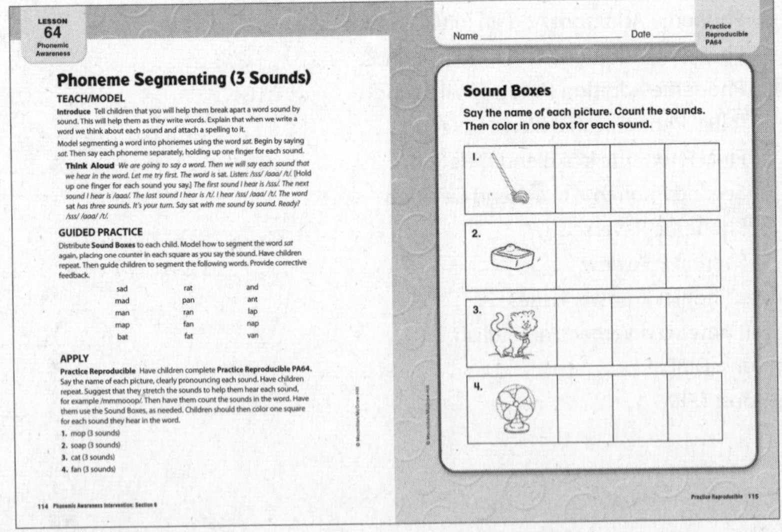

LESSON 64 Phonemic Awareness

**Phoneme Segmenting (3 Sounds)**

TEACH/MODEL

**Introduce** Tell children that you will help them break apart a word sound by sound. This will help them as they write words. Explain that when we write a word we think about each sound and attach a spelling to it.

Model segmenting a word into phonemes using the word *sat*. Begin by saying *sat*. Then say each phoneme separately, holding up one finger for each sound.

**Think Aloud** *We are going to say a word. Then we will say each sound that we hear in the word. Let me try first. The word is* sat. *Listen: /sss/ /aaa/ /t/.* [Hold up one finger for each sound you say.] *The first sound I hear is /sss/. The next sound I hear is /aaa/. The last sound I hear is /t/. I hear /sss/ /aaa/ /t/. The word* sat *has three sounds. It's your turn. Say* sat *with me sound by sound. Ready? /sss/ /aaa/ /t/.*

GUIDED PRACTICE

Distribute **Sound Boxes** to each child. Model how to segment the word *sat* again, placing one counter in each square as you say the sound. Have children repeat. Then guide children to segment the following words. Provide corrective feedback.

| | | |
|---|---|---|
| sad | rat | and |
| mad | pan | ant |
| man | ran | lap |
| map | fan | nap |
| bat | fat | van |

APPLY

**Practice Reproducible** Have children complete **Practice Reproducible PA64.** Say the name of each picture, clearly pronouncing each sound. Have children repeat. Suggest that they stretch the sounds to help them hear each sound, for example /mmmooop/. Then have them count the sounds in the word. Have them use the Sound Boxes, as needed. Children should then color one square for each sound they hear in the word.

1. mop (3 sounds)
2. soap (3 sounds)
3. cat (3 sounds)
4. fan (3 sounds)

114 Phonemic Awareness Intervention: Section 6

Name ______ Date ______ Practice Reproducible PA64

**Sound Boxes**

**Say the name of each picture. Count the sounds. Then color in one box for each sound.**

1.

2.

3.

4.

Practice Reproducible 115

Sample Lesson

Additional materials used with the instruction in the *Phonemic Awareness Intervention* include the following manipulatives:

- Sound Boxes (Elkonin boxes) to help children orally segment words
- Word-Building Cards for more sophisticated phonemic awareness tasks

Sound Boxes

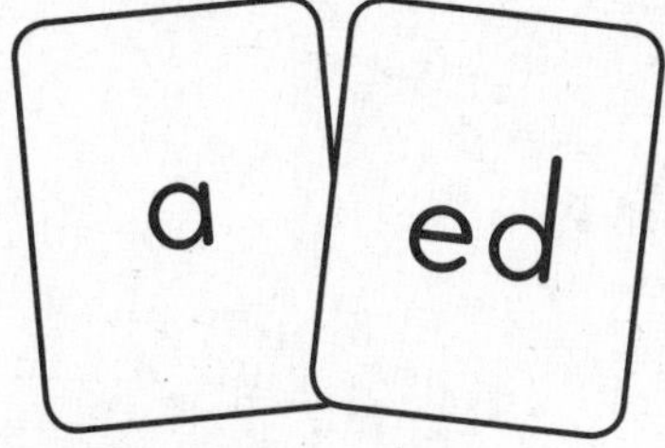


Word-Building Cards

## Assessment

**Placement** To place children into the *Phonemic Awareness Intervention* scope and sequence, use their results from the various types of phonemic awareness tasks, such as rhyming, blending, segmenting, and manipulating sounds found in the *Treasures* progam.

Each section in *Phonemic Awareness Intervention* focuses on a small set of phonemic awareness skills. You can place children in one of the following ways:

- You can teach a discrete lesson or a discrete group of lessons as a prescription for specific skills that children have not yet mastered.
- You can provide sequential and systematic instruction over a longer period of time, perhaps as a regular part of additional instruction that you provide a group of struggling readers.

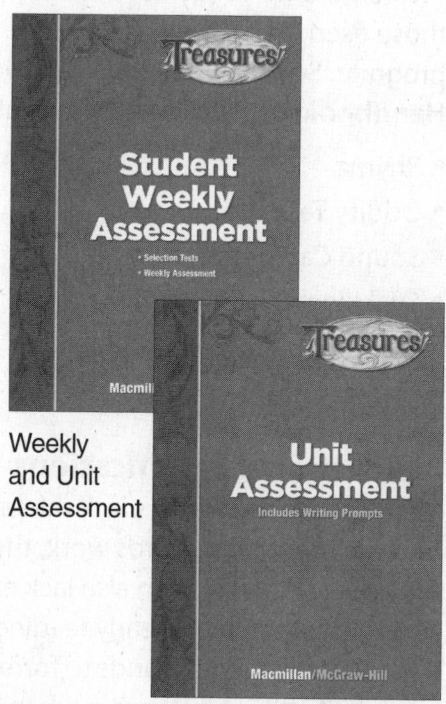


Weekly and Unit Assessment

**Monitoring Progress** Use the skill review provided at the end of each section in *Phonemic Awareness Intervention*.

- These reviews appear after about every ten lessons.
- Use the results to determine which children are ready to move on and which need to repeat the sequence of lessons.

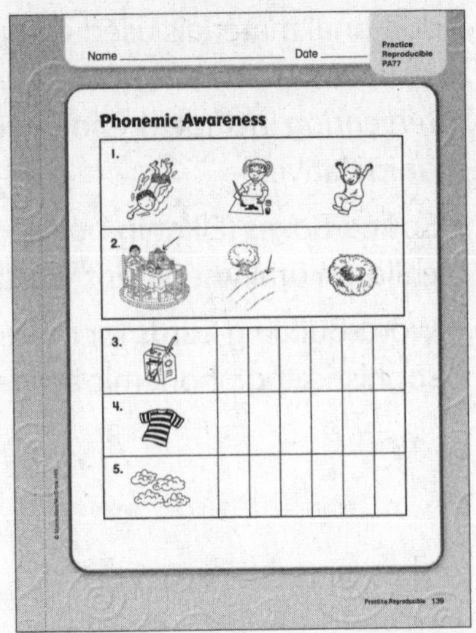


Sample Review

## Instructional Routines

The instructional routines used in the *Phonemic Awareness Intervention* are consistent with those used in the *Treasures* core program. See the **Instructional Routine Handbook** for details on these routines:

- Rhyme
- Oddity Tasks
- Sound Categorization
- Oral Blending
- Oral Segmentation
- Manipulation

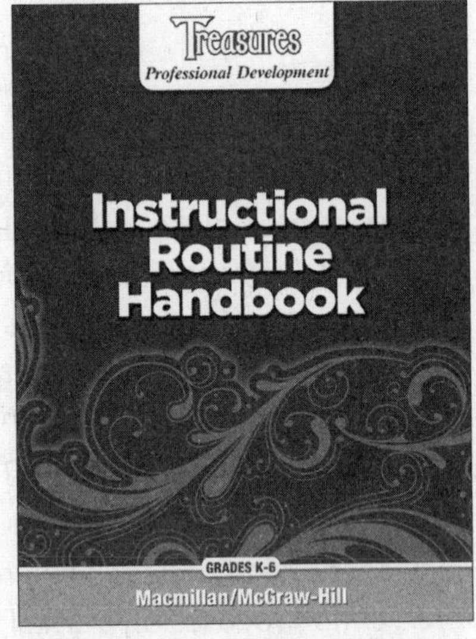


Instructional Routine Handbook

## Instructional Modifications

Many struggling readers lack the prerequisite phonemic awareness skills to understand how words work, thereby rendering phonics instruction less effective. Some children also lack mastery of the phonemic awareness tasks strongly connected to early reading and writing. For example, children who cannot orally blend sounds to form words will struggle with decoding a word in print. Children who struggle when orally segmenting a word into its constituent sounds will struggle with spelling words when writing. These children need more time and practice to master these essential building blocks of reading. The lessons in *Phonemic Awareness Intervention* are ideal for these children.

- Other children who may require more time and instruction are English learners, due to the nontransferable sounds from their primary language.
- In addition, speakers of African American Vernacular English (AAVE) may have some articulation issues with specific sounds and require additional support.

- Throughout the lessons, information on transferable and nontransferable skills is noted. Also noted are sounds that will be most problematic for English learners and speakers of AAVE.

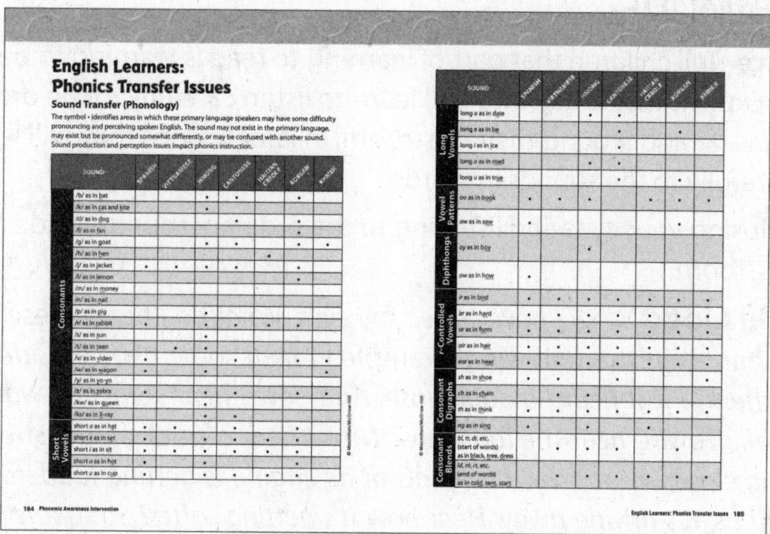

**English Learners: Phonics Transfer Issues**

**Sound Transfer (Phonology)**

The symbol • identifies areas in which these primary language speakers may have some difficulty pronouncing and perceiving spoken English. The sound may not exist in the primary language, may exist but be pronounced somewhat differently, or may be confused with another sound. Sound production and perception issues impact phonics instruction.

| | Sound | Spanish | Vietnamese | Hmong | Cantonese | Haitian Creole | Korean | Khmer |
|---|---|---|---|---|---|---|---|---|
| Consonants | /b/ as in bat | | | • | • | | • | |
| | /k/ as in cat and kite | | | • | | | | |
| | /d/ as in dog | | | | • | | • | |
| | /f/ as in fan | | | | | | • | |
| | /g/ as in goat | | | • | • | | • | • |
| | /h/ as in hen | | | | | • | | |
| | /j/ as in jacket | • | • | • | • | | • | |
| | /l/ as in lemon | | | | | | • | |
| | /m/ as in money | | | | | | | |
| | /n/ as in nail | | | | | | | |
| | /p/ as in pig | | | • | | | | |
| | /r/ as in rabbit | • | | • | • | • | • | |
| | /s/ as in sun | | | • | | | | |
| | /t/ as in teen | | • | • | | | | |
| | /v/ as in video | • | | | • | | • | • |
| | /w/ as in wagon | • | | • | | | | • |
| | /y/ as in yo-yo | | | | | | | |
| | /z/ as in zebra | • | | • | • | | • | • |
| | /kw/ as in queen | | | • | | | | |
| | /ks/ as in X-ray | | | • | • | | | |
| Short Vowels | short *a* as in hat | • | • | | • | | • | |
| | short *e* as in set | • | | • | • | • | • | |
| | short *i* as in sit | • | • | • | • | • | • | |
| | short *o* as in hot | • | | • | | | • | |
| | short *u* as in cup | • | | • | • | • | • | |

© Macmillan/McGraw-Hill

184 Phonemic Awareness Intervention

| | Sound | Spanish | Vietnamese | Hmong | Cantonese | Haitian Creole | Korean | Khmer |
|---|---|---|---|---|---|---|---|---|
| Long Vowels | long *a* as in date | | | • | • | | | |
| | long *e* as in be | | | | • | | • | |
| | long *i* as in ice | | | | • | | | |
| | long *o* as in road | | | • | • | | | |
| | long *u* as in true | | | | • | | • | |
| Vowel Patterns | *oo* as in book | • | • | • | | • | • | • |
| | *aw* as in saw | • | | | | | • | |
| Diphthongs | *oy* as in boy | | | • | | | | |
| | *ow* as in how | • | | | | | | |
| *r*-Controlled Vowels | *ir* as in bird | • | • | • | • | • | • | • |
| | *ar* as in hard | • | • | • | • | • | • | • |
| | *or* as in form | • | • | • | • | • | • | • |
| | *air* as in hair | • | • | • | • | • | • | • |
| | *ear* as in hear | • | • | • | • | • | • | • |
| Consonant Digraphs | *sh* as in shoe | • | • | | • | | | • |
| | *ch* as in chain | | • | • | | | | |
| | *th* as in think | • | • | • | • | • | • | • |
| | *ng* as in sing | • | | • | | • | | |
| Consonant Blends | *bl, tr, dr,* etc. (start of words) as in black, tree, dress | | • | • | • | | • | |
| | *ld, nt, rt,* etc. (end of words) as in cold, tent, start | | • | • | • | • | • | • |

© Macmillan/McGraw-Hill

English Learners: Phonics Transfer Issues 185

English Learners: Phonics Transfer Issues

## Research and Guiding Principles

Research has shown that phonemic awareness

- is the ability to hear, identify, and manipulate the individual sounds in spoken words;
- can be developed through a number of tasks, such as identifying phonemes, categorizing phonemes, blending phonemes to form words, segmenting words into phonemes, deleting or adding phonemes to form new words, and substituting phonemes to make new words;
- involves the sounds in spoken language, whereas phonics involves the relationship between sounds and spellings in written language;
- is only one type of phonological awareness (meaning awareness of word parts, ranging from the phoneme to larger chunks such as the syllable);
- can be taught and learned;
- helps children learn to read and comprehend text, as well as spell;
- is taught most effectively when children are taught to manipulate phonemes by using the letters of the alphabet (Early tasks such as rhyming and blending onsets/rimes are primarily oral while later tasks, such as oral segmentation, combine oral and written components);
- is taught most effectively when it focuses on only one or two types of phoneme manipulation, rather than several types.

LESSON
1
Phonemic Awareness

# Sound Awareness: Listening

## TEACH/MODEL

**Introduce** Tell children that part of learning to read is learning to be a careful listener. Explain that today they will learn to listen carefully to the ordinary sounds inside and around their classroom. In later lessons they will learn to listen carefully to the sounds in words.

Model closing your eyes and listening to the ordinary sounds inside and around your classroom.

**Think Aloud** *Now I have closed my eyes. What do I hear?* [Describe what you hear, as in the following example.] *I hear some birds outside. Do you hear them? I just heard a door close. And now I hear someone walking down the hall. Do you hear the footsteps? Now I hear a truck on the street. It's getting closer. Hear how the sound of its engine is getting louder? Now it has passed us. It's driving away. Hear how it's getting softer? So that is how I listen when I want to hear the sounds around me.*

## GUIDED PRACTICE

Have children sit with closed eyes and listen for a few minutes. Then ask individuals to talk about the different sounds they hear. Promote active listening by prompting them with questions about the details of the sounds they hear. Children might hear sounds such as these:

| | | |
|---|---|---|
| a dog barking | someone breathing | people talking |
| water dripping | a clock ticking | cars on a busy road |
| a bug buzzing | their heart beating | a horn honking |
| wind blowing | a lawnmower | a siren |

## APPLY

**Activity** Ask children to close their eyes and listen for a few minutes at home. Then ask them to tell an adult what they hear.

# Sound Awareness: Sequence

## TEACH/MODEL

**Introduce** Remind children that part of learning to read is learning to be a careful listener. Explain that they will be listening to tell the difference between sounds in their classroom. Tell them that in later lessons they will learn to listen for the different sounds in words.

Coach a child to make two sounds, such as tapping a pencil or dropping a book. Then model closing your eyes and listening to tell the difference between these sounds.

> **Think Aloud** *Now I have closed my eyes. Now I am going to listen to the first sound.* [Have a child make the first sound.] *What did I hear? Let me think about this sound.* [Describe what you hear.] *I heard a quick click-click-click. That sounded like a pencil tapping. Okay. Now I am going to listen to the second sound.* [Have child make the second sound.] *Now what did I hear? Let me think about this second sound. I heard a thud. It went whump! That sounded like a book dropping on a desk. So that is how I listen when I want to tell the difference between sounds.*

## GUIDED PRACTICE

Have children sit with closed eyes. First, make a single sound, and have children identify it. Then make two different sounds, and have children identify each. Finally, try making three sounds in a row and have children identify each. Make sure children do not call out the answer before you ask for a response. Also, alternate between calling on the whole group and calling on individuals. This gives everyone a chance to think about what they hear. Spend extra time working with children who have difficulty identifying sounds.

You might use sounds such as these. Remind children not to look at what you are doing.

| | | |
|---|---|---|
| ripping paper | clapping your hands | closing a window |
| crumpling paper | snapping your fingers | closing a door |
| writing on a chalkboard | stomping your foot | opening a drawer |
| using scissors | biting an apple | turning on a computer |

## APPLY

**Activity** Have children make sounds for a partner to figure out. Guide partners to identify two to three different sounds in a sequence.

# Sound Awareness: Source

## TEACH/MODEL

**Introduce** Tell children that learning to listen carefully will help them as they read words. Explain that today they will learn to listen to animal sounds and decide where in the classroom they hear them. In later lessons, they will learn to listen carefully to the sounds in words and decide where in the word they hear them.

Model making an animal sound repeatedly, such as a cat meowing. Then sit in a special chair in the center of the classroom and close your eyes. Tell a child to go to one of the four corners of the room and make this animal sound. Model identifying the location of the sound.

> **Think Aloud** *I have closed my eyes and begun to listen very carefully. I hear the meow sound. Do you hear it? Where is it coming from?* [Identify the source of the sound, as in the following example.] *I know that the meowing is coming from inside this classroom, but where exactly is it coming from? I think that it is coming from a spot behind me, but which side of the room is it coming from? I will listen carefully again and see if I can tell. Now I know!* [Point to the spot.] *The meowing sound is coming from the block corner near the windows.*

## GUIDED PRACTICE

Repeat this routine with the animal sounds below, directing children to produce them repeatedly from spots of their choosing in the classroom. Have other children listen carefully from the special chair with their eyes closed, identifying each sound and its source. Promote active listening by prompting them with questions about the source of the animal sounds they hear. Provide children with corrective feedback as necessary. Spend extra time with children who have difficulty identifying sounds.

| | | |
|---|---|---|
| oinking | cawing | hooting |
| hissing | chirping | baaing |
| barking | clucking | roaring |
| buzzing | cock-a-doodle-dooing | mooing |

## APPLY

**Activity** Ask children to participate in a similar activity outdoors, having them close their eyes, listen carefully, and identify sounds they hear and where they are coming from.

# Sound Awareness: Nonsense

## TEACH/MODEL

**Introduce** Tell children that learning to listen carefully to sentences and the words in them will help them as they read words. Tell them that they will listen to parts of nursery rhymes that they may have heard before. They will listen for and name words that are wrong or that do not make sense. In later lessons, they will learn to think carefully about the words that they read in sentences.

Model saying the first line of a familiar nursery rhyme, such as "Mary had a little lamb, its fleece was white as snow." Then say it again, but this time substitute an incorrect word, such as *green* for *white*. Have children repeat the line. Model listening carefully and identifying the incorrect word.

**Think Aloud** *I have closed my eyes and listened very carefully. I have heard this sentence before, but something in it does not make sense. I know that snow and a sheep's fleece are white, but I heard the color word* green *used to describe them in the sentence. The word* green *does not make sense. The sentence should be,* "Mary had a little lamb, its fleece was white as snow."

## GUIDED PRACTICE

One by one, read aloud the lines from familiar nursery rhymes below. Then read each line with an incorrect or nonsensical word or words in it. Have children listen carefully to each line, identify the incorrect word or words, and repeat the line correctly. Promote active listening by having them say how they determined which word did not make sense. Provide corrective feedback as necessary.

| | ***With an Incorrect or Nonsense Word*** |
|---|---|
| *Little Boy Blue, come blow your horn.* | *Little Boy Blue, come blow your* **corn**. |
| *Jack and Jill up went up the hill.* | *Jack and Jill went up the* **pill**. |
| *Little Bo Peep has lost her sheep.* | *Little Bo Peep has* **shop her least**. |
| *Rain, rain, go away, come again another day.* | *Rain, rain, go away, come again another* **play**. |
| *Humpty Dumpty sat on a wall.* | *Humpty Dumpty* **wat on a sall**. |

## APPLY

**Activity** Using the lines above or lines from other familiar rhymes and poems, conduct similar activities. Transpose words or word parts, add or delete a word, add a nonsense word, or change the order of several words. Then have children identify and explain what you changed.

# Sound Awareness: Remembering

## TEACH/MODEL

**Introduce** Tell children that learning to listen carefully to directions and remembering them in the correct order will help them when they read. Explain that today they will play a game in which they listen to sets of directions and then try to follow them in the same order that they heard them.

Say some simple two-step direction, such as this: *Walk to the door. Then knock on it.* Have children repeat the directions. Then model following them.

> **Think Aloud** *I remember that the directions had two parts: walking to the door and knocking on the door. I recall that the first step of the directions told me to walk to the door, so I will do that first. I won't run or hop, but I will walk to the door. I recall that the second step of the directions told me to knock on the door, so I will do that second. I won't slap or pound on the door, but I will knock on it, using my knuckles.*

## GUIDED PRACTICE

Continue the game, using the two-step directions in the box below or others similar to them. Have a child listen carefully to a set of directions, repeat them, and then follow the steps in the correct order. Promote active listening by prompting the child to listen for the two steps in each set of directions and to recall the order in which he or she heard the steps. Provide corrective feedback as necessary.

- Stand beside your desk. Then wave to the class.
- Hop to the chalkboard. Then draw a circle on it.
- Get a red crayon. Then bring it to a classmate.
- Hold up a pencil. Then use it to draw a square in the air.
- Open a book. Then show the class a picture in it.
- Sit on the floor. Then count to ten.
- Take off one shoe. Then pretend that it is a cell phone.
- Crawl over to a classmate. Then tell the classmate how old you are.

## APPLY

**Activity** Instruct children to ask a family member to say sets of two-step directions so that they can demonstrate how well they are able to listen, recall the steps, and follow them in the correct order.

# Identify Rhyme

## TEACH/MODEL

**Introduce** Tell children that learning about rhymes will help as they read words. Explain that words rhyme when they have the same ending sounds. Say: *The words* hop *and* top *rhyme because they both end in the sounds /op/. Listen:* [Say each word, stretching out the ending sounds] */h/ /ooop/,* hop; */t/ /ooop/,* top. [Have children repeat, stretching out the ending sounds.] *The words* top *and* tip *do not rhyme. Listen: /t/ /ooop/,* top; */t/ /iiip/,* tip. [Have children repeat.] *The words* top *and* tip *have different ending sounds: /op/ and /ip/.*

Say two more rhyming words: *man* and *pan*. Stretch out the ending sounds. Have children repeat the words and say the ending sounds. Then model generating a third word that rhymes with the first two.

**Think Aloud** *I have listened very carefully to the two rhyming words. They are* man *and* pan. Man *and* pan *rhyme because they both end in /an/. Listen:* [Stretch out the ending sounds] */m/ /aaannn/, man; /p/ /aaannn/,* pan. *Both* man *and* pan *have the same ending sounds, /an/. Now I will think of another word that ends in /an/. I know. The word /f/ /aaan/* fan *ends in /an/, so* fan *must rhyme with* man *and* pan. [Have children repeat.]

## GUIDED PRACTICE

One at a time, say each pair of rhyming words below. Have individual children listen to and repeat the words and say the ending sounds common to both. Then help them generate a word that rhymes with the first two. Provide children with corrective feedback as necessary.

| | | |
|---|---|---|
| cap, map (tap, lap) | dog, fog (log, frog) | tug, rug (mug, hug) |
| tag, bag (wag, rag) | top, hop (pop, stop) | sun, run (fun, bun) |
| bad, mad (sad, dad) | hot, cot (not, spot) | nut, hut (shut, mutt) |
| cat, rat (sat, mat) | lock, rock (sock, dock) | rub, tub (cub, stub) |

## APPLY

**Activity** Have partners take turns saying two rhyming words. After one child says the words, the other one then tries to generate as many additional words as possible that rhyme with the first two.

# Identify Rhyme

## TEACH/MODEL

**Introduce** Say: *Learning about rhymes will help as you read words.* Explain that words rhyme when they have the same ending sounds. Say: *The words* sat *and* mat *rhyme because they both end in the sounds /at/. Listen: /s/ /aaat/,* sat; */m/ /aaat/,* mat. [Have children repeat, stretching out the ending sounds.] *The words* mat *and* map *do not rhyme. Listen: /m/ /aaat/,* mat; */m/ /aaap/,* map. [Have children repeat.] *The words* mat *and* map *have different ending sounds: /at/ and /ap/.*

Say three words, and model identifying which two rhyme. Emphasize the difference between words that rhyme and words that only have the same consonant sound at the end. Stretch out the ending sounds as you say each word.

**Think Aloud** *Now I am going to say three words: /m/ /aaad/,* mad; */s/ /aaad/,* sad*; /s/ /eeed/,* said. [Have children repeat.] *Which words have the same ending sounds?* Mad *and* sad *do. They rhyme because they both end with the /ad/ sounds: /m/ /aaad/,* mad, *and /s/ /aaad/,* sad. *The other word ends with the /ed/ sounds* [Stretch out the ending sounds]: */s/ /eeed/,* said. *Now I will say three other words: /k/ /ē/,* key; */k/ /ôl/,* call, *and /s/ /ē/,* see. *Which of these words have the same ending sounds?* Key *and* see *do.* Call *has different ending sounds, /ôl/.*

## GUIDED PRACTICE

Have children identify word pairs that rhyme. Say each set of three words below to children, one word at a time. Stretch out the ending sounds in each word. Ask children which two words rhyme.

said, red, hit
sip, rip, rope
bell, wall, well
hug, tug, dig
pan, pin, tin
drip, drop, stop

Provide corrective feedback. Spend extra time working with children who confuse words that rhyme with words that have the same final consonant.

## APPLY

**Practice Reproducible** Have children complete **Practice Reproducible PA7.** Say the names of the three pictures in each row, clearly pronouncing the sounds in each name: (1. sock, fan, clock 2. soap, rope, hat 3. boat, coat, pig 4. can, car, man 5. mouse, house, book). Have children repeat. Help them stretch the ending sounds to decide which words rhyme, for example /s/ /oook/, *sock*. Then have children circle the two pictures that stand for words that rhyme.

**Answer Key: 1.** *sock, clock* **2.** *soap, rope* **3.** *boat, coat* **4.** *can, man* **5.** *mouse, house*

Name ________________________ Date __________

Practice Reproducible PA7

# Rhymes

**Look at each picture. Circle the two pictures that stand for words that rhyme.**

| | | | |
|---|---|---|---|
| 1. |  | 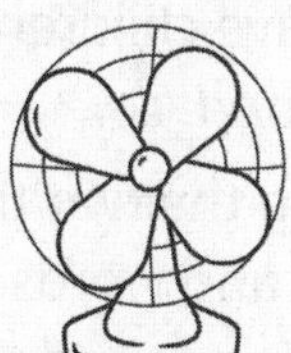 | 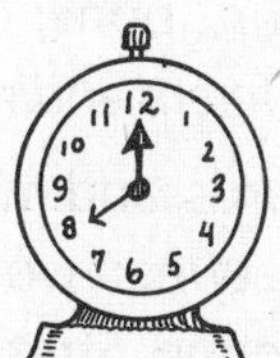<br> |
| 2. |  |  | 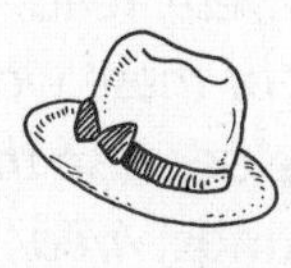 |
| 3. | 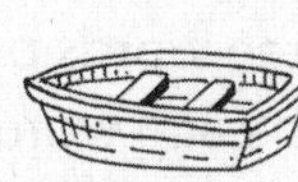 |  |  |
| 4. |  |  |  |
| 5. |  |  | 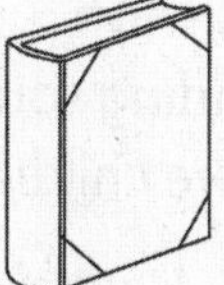 |

# Identify Rhyme

## TEACH/MODEL

**Introduce** Tell children that learning about rhymes will help as they read words. Explain that words rhyme when they have the same ending sounds. Say: *The words* bone *and* phone *rhyme because they both end in the sounds /ōn/. Listen:* [Stretch out the ending sounds] */b/ /ōn/,* bone; */f/ /ōn/,* phone. [Have children repeat.] *The words* bone *and* bike *do not rhyme. Listen:* [Stretch out the ending sounds] */b/ /ōn/,* bone; */b/ /ik/,* bike. [Have children repeat.] *The words* bone *and* bike *have different ending sounds: /ōn/ and /īk/.*

Say three words, and model identifying the two that rhyme. Emphasize the difference between words that rhyme and words that end with only the same consonant sound. Stretch out the ending sounds as you say each word.

> **Think Aloud** *Now I am going to say three words* [Stretch out the ending sounds]: */r/ /ēd/,* read*; /f/ /ēd/,* feed*; /r/ /ōd/,* road. [Have children repeat.] *Which two of these words have the same ending sounds?* Read *and* feed *do. They rhyme because they both end with the /ēd/ sounds:* [Stretch out the ending sounds] */r/ēd/,* read, *and /f/ /ēd/,* feed. *The other word,* road, *ends with the /ōd/ sound:* [Stretch out the ending sound] */r/ /ōd/,* road.

## GUIDED PRACTICE

Have children identify word pairs that rhyme. Say each set of three words below to children, one word at a time. Stretch out the ending sounds in each word. Ask children which two words rhyme.

| | | |
|---|---|---|
| make, late, date | peel, pail, seal | time, lime, line |
| side, ride, weed | rode, toad, hide | broke, joke, black |

## APPLY

**Practice Reproducible** Have children complete **Practice Reproducible PA8.** Say the names of the three pictures in each row, clearly pronouncing the sounds in each picture name: (1. gate, skate, game 2. hook, throw, book 3. kite, nine, vine 4. rake, snake, wave 5. van, comb, pan). Have children repeat. Suggest that they stretch the ending sounds to decide which words rhyme, for example /g/ /āt/, *gate.* Then have children circle the two pictures whose names rhyme.

**Answer Key: 1.** *gate, skate* **2.** *hook, book* **3.** *nine, vine* **4.** *rake, snake* **5.** *van, pan*

Name ______________________ Date __________



# Rhymes

**Look at each picture. Circle the two pictures whose names rhyme.**

| | | | |
|---|---|---|---|
| 1. |  |  | 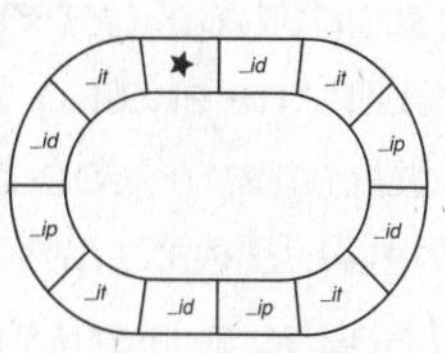 |
| 2. | 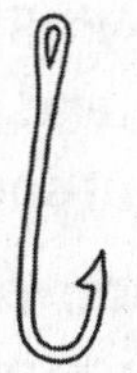 |  | 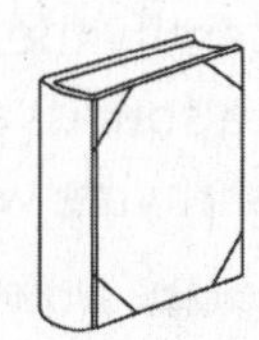 |
| 3. |  |  | 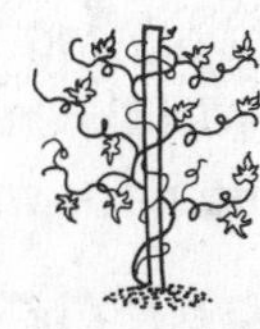 |
| 4. |  |  |  |
| 5. |  |  |  |

# Phoneme Categorization: Rhyme (Oddity Task)

## TEACH/MODEL

**Introduce** Tell children that learning about rhymes will help as they read words. Explain that words rhyme when they have the same ending sounds, such as */ot/* in *cot* and *not*. Say: *The words* cot *and* not *rhyme because they both end in the sounds /ot/. Listen: /k/ /ooot/, cot; /n/ /ooot/,* not. [Have children repeat, stretching out the ending sounds.] Then say: *The word* cap *does not rhyme with* cot *and* not. *Listen: /k/ /ooot/, cot; /n/ /ooot/,* not; */k/ /aaap/,* cap. [Have children repeat.] *The word* cap *ends in /ap/. These ending sounds are not the same as those in* cot *and* not, *so* cap *does not rhyme with them.*

Model identifying a word that does not rhyme. Say three words, two of which rhyme, and identify the word that does not rhyme with the other two. Stretch out the ending sounds as you say each word. Help children understand that one word does not rhyme with the other two because it ends in different sounds.

**Think Aloud** *Now I am going to say three words: /b/ /aaak/,* back; */p/ /aaak/,* pack; */l/ /iiik/,* lick. [Have children repeat, stretching out the ending sounds.] *Which of these words end in the same sounds?* Back *and* pack *do. They rhyme because they both end with the /ak/ sounds: /b/ /aaak/,* back; */p/ /aaak/,* pack. *The other word,* lick, *ends with the /ik/ sounds: /l/ /iiik/,* lick. *The word* lick *does not rhyme with* back *and* pack *because it has different ending sounds.*

## GUIDED PRACTICE

Have children identify the word in each group below that does not rhyme. Say the three words in each group, stretching the ending sounds. First, have children identify the two words that do rhyme. Next, have them identify the word that does not rhyme with the other two. Last, have them pronounce the different ending sounds. Provide corrective feedback as necessary.

| | | |
|---|---|---|
| hop, top, let | cut, sat, nut | pat, pot, sat |
| hum, pen, drum | ten, fit, hit | tin, bun, pin |

## APPLY

**Practice Reproducible** Have children complete **Practice Reproducible PA9.** Say the names of the three pictures in each row, clearly pronouncing the sounds in each name: (1. mix, ring, swing 2. net, nest, jet 3. clock, ox, sock 4. cat, fan, man 5. sun, cup, run). Have children repeat, stretching the ending sounds to identify rhyming words. Then have them circle the picture whose name does **not** rhyme.

**Answer Key: 1.** *mix* **2.** *nest* **3.** *ox* **4.** *cat* **5.** *cup*

# Rhymes

**Look at each picture. Circle the picture whose name does NOT rhyme.**

| | | | |
|---|---|---|---|
| 1. |  | 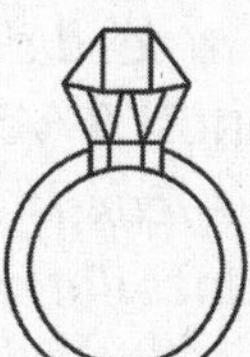 |  |
| 2. |  |  |  |
| 3. |  |  |  |
| 4. |  |  |  |
| 5. |  |  |  |

# Phoneme Categorization: Rhyme (Oddity Task)

## TEACH/MODEL

**Introduce** Tell children that learning about rhymes will help as they read words. Say: *Words rhyme when they have the same ending sounds, such as /ōt/ in* coat *and* boat. *Listen:* [Stretch out the ending sounds] */k/ /ōt/,* coat; */b/ /ōt/,* boat. [Have children repeat.] Then say: *The word* seed *does not rhyme with* coat *and* boat. *Listen:* [Stretch out the ending sounds] */k/ /ōt/,* coat; */b/ /ōt/,* boat; */s/ /ēd/,* seed; [Have children repeat.] Seed *ends in /ēd/. These ending sounds are not the same as those in* coat *and* boat, *so* seed *does not rhyme with them.*

Model identifying a word that does not rhyme. Say three words, two of which rhyme, and identify the word that does not rhyme with the other two. Stretch out the ending sounds as you say each word.

> **Think Aloud** *Now I am going to say three words:* [Stretch out the ending sounds] */b/ /āk/,* bake; */t/ /āk/,* take; */b/ /īk/,* bike. [Have children repeat.] *Which of these words end in the same sounds?* Bake *and* take *do. They rhyme because they both end with the /āk/ sounds:* [Stretch out the ending sounds] */b/āk/,* bake; */t/ /āk/,* take. *The other word,* bike, *ends with the /īk/ sounds:* [Stretch out the ending sounds] */b/ /īk/,* bike. *The word* bike *does not rhyme with* bake *and* take *because it has different ending sounds.*

## GUIDED PRACTICE

Have children identify the word in each set below that does not rhyme. Say the three words in each set, one word at a time. Stretch out the ending sounds. First, have children identify the two words that do rhyme. Next, have them identify the word that does not rhyme with the other two. Last, have children pronounce the different ending sounds. Provide correctice feedback.

| | | |
|---|---|---|
| rain, joke, pain | peek, rake, leak | tube, soon, tune |
| night, bite, seat | soap, soup, hope | feed, meat, need |

## APPLY

**Practice Reproducible** Have children complete **Practice Reproducible PA10.** Say the names of the three pictures in each row, clearly pronouncing the sounds in each picture name (1. wave, lake, rake 2. skate, face, gate 3. comb, goat, boat 4. write, slide, kite 5. feet, read, eat). Have children repeat, stretching the ending sounds. Then have children circle the picture whose name does **not** rhyme.

**Answer Key: 1.** *wave* **2.** *face* **3.** *comb* **4.** *slide* **5.** *read*

Name ______________________________ Date ____________



# Rhymes

**Look at each picture. Circle the picture whose name does NOT rhyme.**

1.

2.

3.

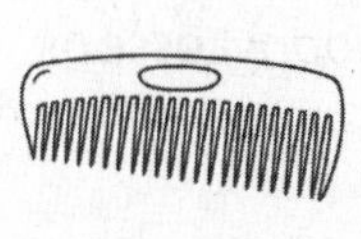

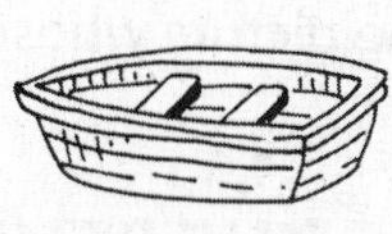

4.

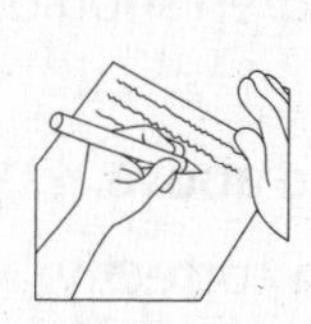

5.

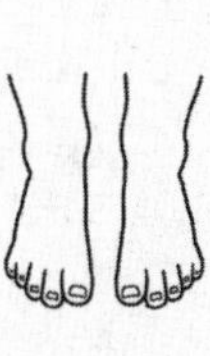

# Review

## PREPARING THE REVIEW

- Make one copy of **Practice Reproducible PA11** for each child.
- Write the child's name and today's date at the top of the review.

## ADMINISTERING THE REVIEW

- Administer the review to one child at a time.
- Follow these instructions for each item. Each phonemic awareness skill was taught in the lessons indicated in parentheses.

1. Identify each picture: **dog, cat,** and **log.** Then ask children to circle the two pictures whose names ***do*** rhyme. (Answer: *dog, log*; Lessons 7–8)
2. Identify each picture: **key, hat,** and **cat.** Then ask children to circle the two pictures whose names ***do*** rhyme. (Answer: *hat, cat*; Lessons 7–8)
3. Identify each picture: **four, ball,** and **door.** Then ask children to circle the two pictures whose names ***do*** rhyme. (Answer: *four, door;* Lessons 7–8)
4. Identify each picture: **lock, clock,** and **cow.** Then ask children to circle the one picture whose name ***does not*** rhyme. (Answer: *cow;* Lessons 9–10)
5. Identify each picture: **moon, house,** and **mouse.** Then ask children to circle the one picture whose name ***does not*** rhyme. (Answer: *moon;* Lessons 9–10)

## SCORING THE REVIEW

- Total the number of items answered correctly.
- Use the Percentage Table below to identify a percentage. Children should get at least 80 percent correct.
- Analyze each child's errors, using the lesson numbers provided above.
- Reteach those skills for which the child did not answer an item correctly.

| Percentage Table | |
|---|---|
| **5 correct** 100% | **2 correct** 40% |
| **4 correct** 80% | **1 correct** 20% |
| **3 correct** 60% | **0 correct** 0% |

Name ____________________ Date __________

Practice Reproducible PA11

# Phonemic Awareness Review

1.   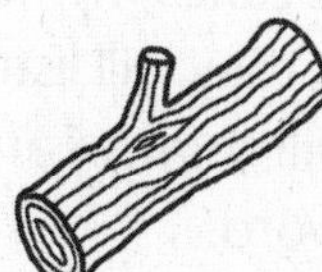

2.   

3. 4 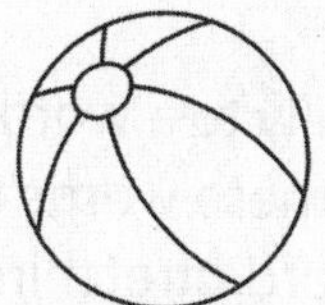 

4.   

5.   

# Generate Rhyme

## TEACH/MODEL

**Introduce** Tell children that learning about rhymes will help as they learn to read words. Say: *Words that end with the same sounds, such as /ooop/ in* hop *and* stop, *are called rhyming words. Listen: /h/ /ooop/,* hop; */st/ /ooop/,* stop. Tell children that they will listen for the sounds that end a word and say the sounds. Then they will think of another word that rhymes, or ends with the same sounds as the first word.

Model listening carefully to a word and then thinking of another word that rhymes with it. Begin by saying the word *nap*. Repeat the word, name the sounds that end it, and then generate another word that rhymes with the first one.

> **Think Aloud** *I just heard the word* nap. Nap *ends with the sounds /aaap/. Listen:* [Stretch out the ending sounds] nap, */n/ /aaap/. Now I will think of another word that ends in /aaap/. I know. The word* cap *also ends in /aaap/. Listen:* [Stretch out the ending sounds] */k/ /aaap/, so* cap *rhymes with* nap.

## GUIDED PRACTICE

Have children practice listening carefully to a word and then thinking of another word that rhymes with it. Say each of these words to children, one set at a time. Have individual children repeat the word, stretching out the ending sounds, and then think of a word that rhymes with the first one. Provide children with corrective feedback as necessary.

| | | |
|---|---|---|
| said (bed, red) | dip (nip, rip) | mug (bug, hug) |
| beg (egg, leg) | mill (pill, will) | fun (sun, bun) |
| pet (let, set) | dot (hot, cot) | wag (tag, bag) |
| when (men, pen) | fog (hog, dog) | Dan (pan, tan) |

## APPLY

**Practice Reproducible** Have children complete **Practice Reproducible PA12.** Say the name of the picture in each row, clearly pronouncing each sound (1. wig 2. rug 3. hat 4. bed). Have children repeat. Suggest that they stretch the ending sounds to help them think of another word that rhymes, for example /w/ /iiig/, wig. Then in each row, have children draw a picture of something whose name rhymes with the name of the picture that they see.

**Answer Key:** Drawings will vary, but the name of each one must rhyme with that of the picture in the row.

Name ______________________ Date __________

Practice Reproducible PA12

# Rhymes

**Say each picture name. Then draw a picture of something whose name rhymes with it.**

| | |
|---|---|
| **1.**  | |
| **2.** 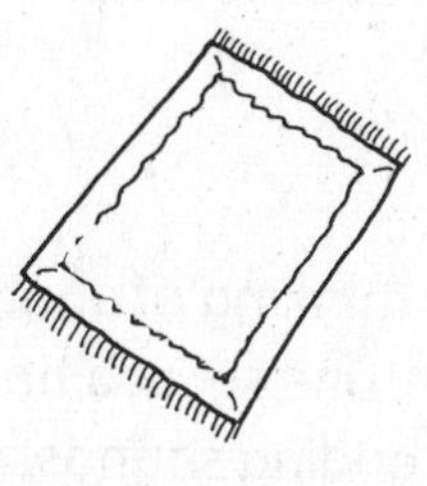 | |
| **3.**  | |
| **4.**  | |

# Generate Rhyme

## TEACH/MODEL

**Introduce** Tell children that learning about rhymes will help as they learn to read words. Say: *Words that end with the same sounds, such as /ōp/ in* hope *and* rope, *are called rhyming words. Listen: /h/ /ōp/,* hope; */r/ /ōp/,* rope. Tell children that today they will listen for the sounds that end a word and say the sounds. Then they will think of another word that rhymes, or ends with the same sounds as the first word.

Model listening carefully to a word and then thinking of another word that rhymes with it. Begin by saying the word *night.* Repeat the word, name the sounds that end it, and then generate another word that rhymes with the first one.

> **Think Aloud** *I just heard the word* night. Night *ends with the sounds /īt/. Listen*: [Stretch the ending sounds] night, */n/ /īt/. Now I will think of another word that ends in /īt/. I know. The word* bite *also ends in /īt/. Listen* [Stretch out the ending sounds]: */b/ /īt/, so* bite *rhymes with* night.

## GUIDED PRACTICE

Have children practice listening carefully to a word and then thinking of another word that rhymes with it. Say each of these words to children, one set at a time. Have individual children repeat the word, stretching out the ending sounds, and then think of a word that rhymes with the first one. Provide children with corrective feedback as necessary.

| | | |
|---|---|---|
| make (bake, take) | hide (ride, lied) | leap (deep, keep) |
| sail (mail, tail) | pile (mile, smile) | bone (cone, phone) |
| mean (green, bean) | broke (joke, soak) | made (played, grade) |

## APPLY

**Practice Reproducible** Have children complete **Practice Reproducible PA13.** Say the name of the picture in each row, clearly pronouncing each sound (1. egg 2. sled 3. key 4. goat). Have children repeat. Suggest that they stretch the ending sounds in each picture name to help them think of another word that rhymes. Then in each row, have children draw a picture of something whose name rhymes with that of the picture that they see.

**Answer Key:** Drawings will vary, but the name of each one must rhyme with that of the picture in the row.

Name ____________________ Date __________

Practice Reproducible PA13

## Rhymes

**Say each picture name. Then draw a picture of something whose name rhymes with it.**

| | |
|---|---|
| **1.** 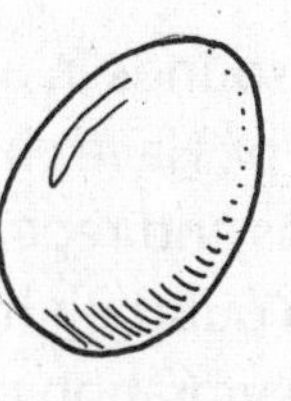 | |
| **2.** 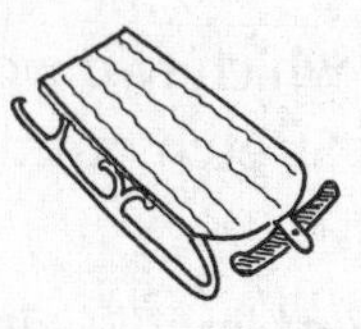 | |
| **3.**  | |
| **4.**  | |

LESSON 14
Phonemic Awareness

# Phoneme Identity: Beginning Sounds

## TEACH/MODEL

**Introduce** Tell children that listening carefully for the sound that begins a word will help them as they learn to read. Explain that the sound they hear first in a word, such as /f/ in *fun,* is called its beginning sound. Tell children that today they will name pictures and listen for the sound that begins each picture name.

**Contrasting Phonemes** Explain to children that the different sounds in a word are formed differently in their mouths. Say the sounds /g/ and /p/. Have children repeat. Now ask them to put their hands in front of their mouths and repeat both sounds. Which sound makes a puff of air? (/p/) Have them put their hands on their throats and repeat both sounds. Which sound makes a vibration in their throat? (/g/) Finally, ask them to describe what their lips and tongue do as they make each sound. Repeat with other contrasting sounds, such as /m/ and /f/.

Model listening carefully to three words and then identifying which two words have the same beginning sound. Say three words together. Stretch out the beginning sound as you say each word.

> **Think Aloud** *I am going to say three words. Listen: /lll/ /ip/,* lip; */lll/ /āt/,* late; */sss/ /ip/,* sip. [Have children repeat.] *Which have the same beginning sound?* Lip *and* late *do. They both begin with the /lll/ sound. Listen: /lll/ /ip/,* lip, *and /lll/ /ate/,* late. *The other word begins with the /sss/ sound. Listen: /sss/ /ip/,* sip.

## GUIDED PRACTICE

Say these words to children, one set at a time. Have individual children say each word, repeat its beginning sound, and then name the two words in each row that begin with the same sound. Provide corrective feedback as necessary.

| | | |
|---|---|---|
| sat, sign, mix | zip, new, next | pat, pan, give |
| mat, mine, road | vet, mile, vote | toad, pile, take |

## APPLY

**Practice Reproducible** Have children complete **Practice Reproducible PA14.** Say the name of the three pictures in each row, clearly pronouncing the beginning sound in each (1. rug, fan, rope 2. net, nest, fox 3. ten, king, kite 4. bag, sock, bug). Have children repeat. They can stretch out the beginning sound (rug, /rrr/ /ug/) or repeat it (/k/, /k/, /k/ /k īt/). Then have children draw a circle around the two pictures in each row whose names begin with the same sound.

**Answer Key: 1.** *rug, rope* **2.** *net, nest* **3.** *king, kite* **4.** *bag, bug*

Name ______________________ Date __________



# Beginning Sounds

**Say each picture name. Draw a circle around the two pictures in each row whose names begin with the same sound.**

**1.**

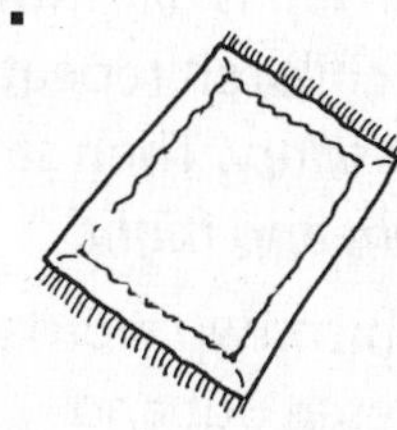

**2.**

**3.**

**4.**

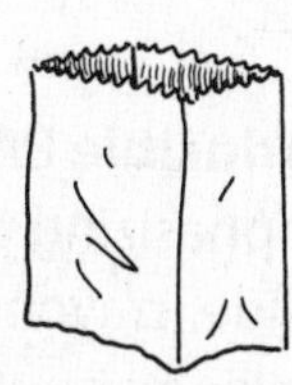

# Phoneme Identity: Beginning Sounds

## TEACH/MODEL

**Introduce** Explain that today children will name pictures and listen for the sounds that begin each picture name.

**Consonant Blends** Explain that some words begin with a single sound and that some words begin with two sounds. Say the word *lap*, stretching the beginning sound /lll/. Have children repeat. Say: *The beginning sound in* lap is */lll/.* Now say *slap*, stretching out the /sss/ and the /lll/, /sss/ /lll/ /ap/. Have children repeat. Say: *There are two sounds at the beginning of* slap, */sss/ and /lll/, /ssslllap/.* Then say *lap* and *slap* several times. Have children repeat. Repeat with *right* and *fright.*

Model listening carefully to three words and then identifying which two words have the same beginning sounds. Say three words together. Stretch out and emphasize the sounds at the beginning of each word.

> **Think Aloud** *Listen to three words: /sss/ /lll/ /id/,* slid; */sss/ /lll/ /ō/,* slow; */fff/ /rrr/ /ī/,* fry. [Have children repeat.] *Which of these words begin with the same two sounds?* Slap *and* slow *do. They both begin with these two sounds /sss/ and /lll/: /sss/ /lll/ /id/,* slid, *and /sss/ /lll/ /ō/,* slow. *The other word begins with these two sounds: /fff/ and /rrr/: /fff/ /rrr/ /ī/,* fry. *Listen to three other words: /g/ /rrr/ /āp/,* grape; */g/ /rrr/ /ab/,* grab; */k/ /lll/ /ap/,* clap. [Have children repeat.] *Which words begin with the same sounds?* Grape *and* grab. Clap *begins with /klll/.*

## GUIDED PRACTICE

Say one set of words at a time. Have individual children say each word, repeat its beginning sounds, and then name the two words that begin with the same sounds. Provide corrective feedback.

| | | |
|---|---|---|
| freeze, fry, snake | snow, slip, snap | crab, black, blue |
| brag, brain, crow | plow, plan, flip | crawl, clay, crow |

## APPLY

**Practice Reproducible** Have children complete **Practice Reproducible PA15.** Say the names of the three pictures in each row, stretching or emphasizing the two beginning consonant sounds (1. frog, friends, skate 2. sled, slide, crayons 3. plant, clock, cloud 4. drum, crab, draw). Have children repeat, thinking about the position of their lips and tongue. Then have children circle the two pictures in each row whose names begin with the same consonant blend.

**Answer Key: 1.** *frog, friends* **2.** *sled, slide* **3.** *clock, cloud* **4.** *drum, draw*

Name ____________________ Date __________



# Beginning Sounds

**Say each picture name. Draw a circle around two pictures in each row whose names begin with the same sounds.**

1.

2.

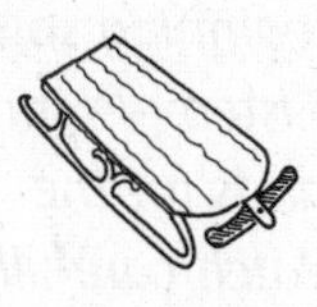

3.

4.

LESSON
16
Phonemic Awareness

# Phoneme Isolation: Beginning Sounds

## TEACH/MODEL

**Introduce** Tell children that listening carefully for the sound that begins a word and then matching it to the letter that stands for the sound will help them as they learn to read. Tell children that today they will name pictures and listen for the sound that begins each picture name. Then they will name and write the letter that stands for the beginning sound.

**Teach Sound-Spellings** Tell children that the sound they hear first in a word, such as /mmm/ in *mitt*, is called its beginning sound. Teach the sound-spellings for *M*, *S*, and *F*. Say: *Listen as I say the word* mitt: */mmm/ /it/.* [Have children repeat.] *The sound at the beginning of* mitt *is /mmm/. The /mmm/ sound is spelled with the letter* M. Model writing *M* on the board. Repeat for *S* and *F*.

Model identifying the beginning sound in a word and then writing the letter that stands for that sound. Leave the letters *M*, *S*, and *F* displayed on the board.

**Think Aloud** *I am going to say a word and listen for the beginning sound:* man, */mmm/ /an/,* man. Man *begins with the /mmm/ sound. Listen: /mmm/ /an/,* man. [Have children repeat.] *I know that the letter* M *stands for the /mmm/ sound, so I will write the letter* M *to spell the sound. Watch carefully.* [Write *M* slowly and carefully several times.]

## GUIDED PRACTICE

Have children practice identifying the beginning sound in a word and then writing the letter that stands for that sound. One at a time, say the words in each column below. Have individual children listen to and repeat each word, say its beginning sound several times, and then name and write the letter that stands for it. Provide children with corrective feedback and assistance as needed.

| | | | |
|---|---|---|---|
| fin | sail | make | save |
| man | five | feed | sing |

## APPLY

**Practice Reproducible** Have children complete **Practice Reproducible PA16.** Say the name of each picture, clearly pronouncing the beginning sound (1. sun 2. fish 3. soap 4. mop). Have children repeat. Have them repeat the beginning sound in each picture name, thinking about the position of their lips and tongue. Help children name and write the letter that stands for each beginning sound.

**Answer Key: 1.** *S* **2.** *F* **3.** *S* **4.** *M*

Name ____________________ Date __________



# Beginning Sounds

**Trace each letter. Then say each picture name and the sound that begins it. Then write the letter that stands for the beginning sound.**

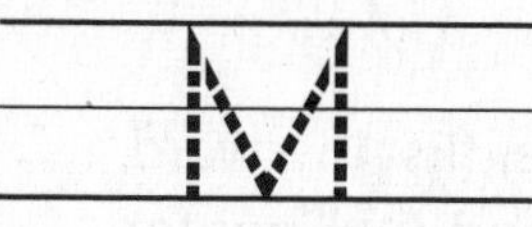

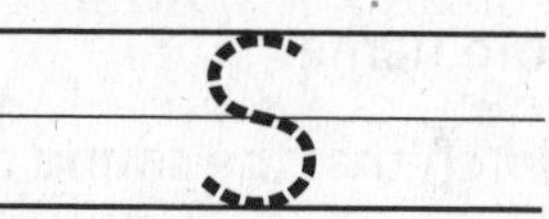

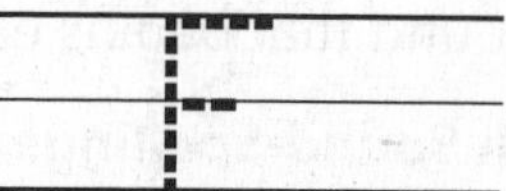

| | |
|---|---|
| **1.**  | |
| **2.**  | |
| **3.** | |
| **4.** 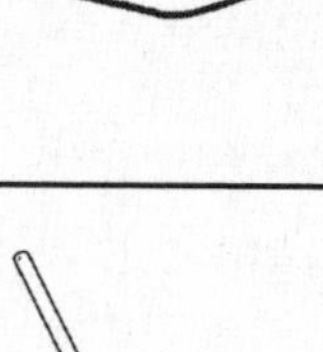 | |

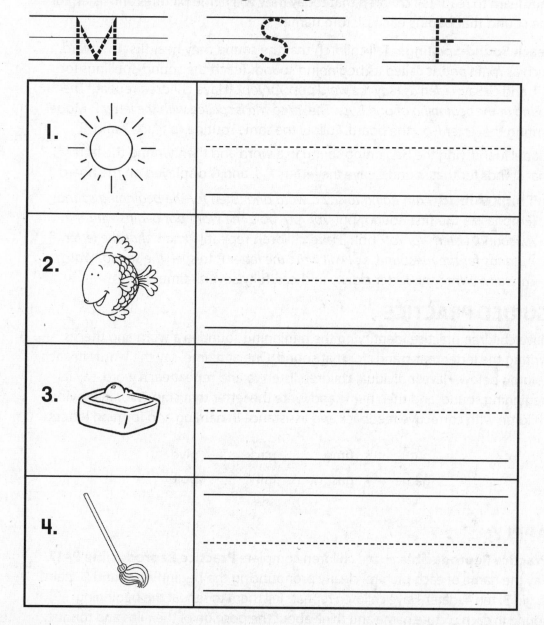

# Phoneme Isolation: Beginning Sounds

## TEACH/MODEL

**Introduce** Tell children that listening carefully for the sound that begins a word and then matching it to the letter that stands for the sound will help them as they learn to read. Tell children that today they will name pictures and listen for the sound that begins each picture name.

**Teach Sound-Spellings** Tell children that the sound they hear first in a word, such as /p/ in *pop,* is called its beginning sound. Teach the sound-spellings for *P, T,* and *G*. Say: *Listen as I say the word* pop: */p/ /op/.* [Have children repeat.] *The sound at the beginning of* pop *is /p/. The /p/ sound is spelled with the letter* P. Model writing the letter *P* on the board. Follow the same routine to teach *T* and *G*.

Model identifying the beginning sound in a word and then writing the letter that stands for that sound. Leave the letters *P, T,* and *G* displayed on the board.

> **Think Aloud** *I am going to say a word and listen for the beginning sound:* [Emphasize the first sound] pot, */p/ /ot/,* pot. *The word pot begins with the /p/ sound. Listen: /p/ /ot/* pot. [Have children repeat.] *I know that the letter* P *stands for the /p/ sound, so I will write the letter* P *to spell the sound. Watch carefully.* [Write the letter slowly and carefully several times.]

## GUIDED PRACTICE

Have children practice identifying the beginning sound in a word and then writing the letter that stands for that sound. One at a time, say the words in each column below. Have individual children listen to and repeat each word, say its beginning sound, and then name and write the letter that stands for it. Provide children with corrective feedback and assistance in naming and forming letters.

| | | | |
|---|---|---|---|
| pat | time | pack | give |
| game | gas | tail | pole |

## APPLY

**Practice Reproducible** Have children complete **Practice Reproducible PA17.** Say the name of each picture, clearly pronouncing the beginning sound (1. paint 2. girl 3. ten 4. gate). Have children repeat. Tell them to repeat the beginning sound in each picture name and think about the position of their lips and tongue. Help children name and write the letter that stands for each beginning sound.

**Answer Key: 1.** *P* **2.** *G* **3.** *T* **4.** *G*

Name ______________________ Date __________



# Beginning Sounds

**Trace each letter. Then say each picture name and the sound that begins it. Then write the letter that stands for the beginning sound.**

P 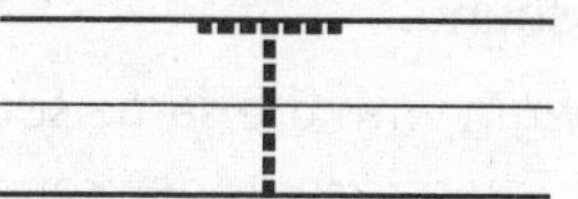 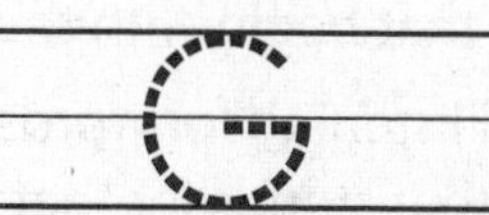

| | |
|---|---|
| 1. 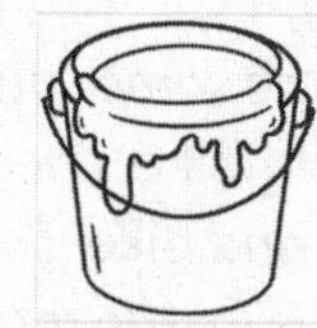 | |
| 2.  | |
| 3.  | |
| 4.  | |

# Alliteration

## TEACH/MODEL

**Introduce** Tell children that listening carefully for words that begin with the same sound and then naming the letter that stands for the sound will help them as they learn to read. Explain that in some stories and poems, they will often hear many words that begin with the same sound, such as /p/ in *Pam put a penny in the piggy bank.* Tell children that today they will listen for words in a poem that begin with the same sound.

Model listening for words that begin with the same sound and then circling the letter that stands for that sound. Say this sentence several times, emphasizing the /b/ sound at the beginning of words. Then write the sentence on the board.

*Bob bought a big bike.*

**Think Aloud** *A lot of the words in this sentence begin with the same sound. I am going to read this sentence again. Listen:* Bob bought a big bike. *I hear four words that begin with the same sound:* Bob, bought, big, *and* bike. *Each of them begins with the /b/ sound. I know that the letter* B *stands for the /b/ sound, so watch carefully as I circle the* B *in the four words that begin with the /b/ sound.*

## GUIDED PRACTICE

One at a time, write each sentence below and read it aloud several times, emphasizing the beginning sound in words that begin with the same sound. Have children repeat the sentence, say the words that begin with the same sound, and produce that sound. Help children identify and circle the letter that stands for the sound in each word that begins with it. Provide corrective feedback.

*Ted took his tools to town.*
*Felix found a fallen feather.*
*Lucy loves to lick lollipops.*

## APPLY

**Practice Reproducible** Have children complete **Practice Reproducible PA18.** Read the poem aloud several times, emphasizing words that begin with /s/ in the first stanza and words that begin with /h/ in the second stanza. Then slowly read the first stanza again line by line. Have children identify words that begin with the same sound. Help children say the sound and circle the *s* at the beginning of each word. Repeat with the *h* words in the second stanza.

**Answer Key: Stanza 1.** *Silly, Sam, saw, sock, sitting, sweet, Sue's, sock, soaked, said, Sam, Sue, soaked, sock* **Stanza 2.** *Helpful, Hal, heard, How, had, hoped, Helpful, Hal, had, he, hung, her, high*

Name ______________________ Date __________



## Beginning Sounds

**Listen to the poem. In each part, listen for words that begin with the same sound. In each word that begins with the same sound, circle the letter that stands for it.**

Silly Sam saw a sock,

While sitting on sweet Sue's dock.

"That sock is soaked," said Sam to Sue,

"Does that soaked sock belong to you?"

Helpful Hal heard Sue cry,

"How I had hoped that it would dry!"

Helpful Hal knew what had to be done,

So, he hung her sock high in the sun.

# Alliteration

## TEACH/MODEL

**Introduce** Tell children that listening carefully for words that begin with the same sound and then naming the letter that stands for the sound will help them as they learn to read. Explain that in some stories and poems, they will hear many words that begin with the same sound, such as /j/ in *Jim jokes with Jenny.* Tell children that today they will listen for words in a poem that begin with the same sound.

Model listening for words that begin with the same sound and then circling the letter that stands for that sound. Say this sentence several times, emphasizing the /f/ sound at the beginning of words. Then write the sentence on the board.

*Fred found Fran's fork.*

**Think Aloud** *All of the words in this sentence begin with the same sound. I am going to read the sentence again. Listen:* Fred found Fran's fork. *I hear four words that begin with the same sound:* Fred, found, Fran's, *and* fork. *Each of them begins with the /f/ sound. I know that the letter* F *stands for the /f/ sound, so watch carefully as I circle the* F *in the four words that begin with the /f/ sound.*

## GUIDED PRACTICE

Write each sentence below and read it aloud several times, emphasizing the beginning sound in words that begin with the same sound. Have children repeat the sentence, say the words that begin with the same sound, and produce that sound. Help children identify and circle the letter that stands for the sound in each word that begins with it. Provide corrective feedback.

*Mom made my mask.*
*Nan never needs noodles.*
*Rick ran to the river.*

## APPLY

**Practice Reproducible** Have children complete **Practice Reproducible PA19.** Read the poem aloud several times, emphasizing words that begin with /l/ in the first stanza and words that begin with /d/ in the second stanza. Then slowly read the first stanza again line by line. Have children identify words that begin with the same sound. Help them say the sound and circle the *l* at the beginning of each word they correctly name. Repeat with the /d/ words in the second stanza.

**Answer Key: Stanza 1.** *Larry, loves, leap, logs, Like, lively, little, Laura, loves, lazy, lie, lovely, leaves* **Stanza 2.** *Danny, doesn't, dare, dig, dirt, Dot, Dora, doesn't, dare, Dad's, dreaded*

# Beginning Sounds

**Listen to the poem. In each part, listen for words that begin with the same sound. In each word that begins with the same sound, circle the letter that stands for it.**

Larry loves to leap off logs,
Like a lively little frog.

Laura loves to be lazy and lie
In lovely leaves, piled up high.

Danny doesn't dare to dig
In the dirt with Dot, the pig.
Dora doesn't dare to try
Her dad's dreaded pickle pie.

LESSON
20
Phonemic Awareness

# Phoneme Categorization: Beginning Sounds (Oddity Task)

## TEACH/MODEL

**Introduce** Tell children that listening carefully for the sound that begins a word will help them as they learn to read, write, and spell. Explain that the sound they hear first in a word, such as /m/ in *mop,* is called its beginning sound. Tell children that today they will name some pictures and listen for the beginning sound in each picture name. Then they will decide which picture name does not begin with the same sound as the other two.

Model listening to three words and identifying which word does not have the same beginning sound. If children need help identifying beginning sounds, use **Sound Boxes.** Have them drag a counter into the first box of a Sound Box with each of the three words.

> **Think Aloud** *I am going to say three words:* fan, fog, *and* nap. *Two of these words begin with the same sound. Listen:* [Stretch the beginning sound] fan, */fff/ /an/;* fog, */fff/ /og/.* Fog *and* fan *begin with the /fff/ sound. Then say:* Nap *begins with a different sound. Listen:* [Stretch the beginning sound] nap, */nnn/ /ap/.* Nap *does not begin with /fff/ like* fan *and* fog. Nap *begins with /nnn/.*

## GUIDED PRACTICE

Have children practice listening to three words and identifying which word does not have the same beginning sound. One at a time, say the three words in each row below. Have individual children listen to and repeat each word, say its beginning sound, and then name the word in each row that does not begin with the same sound as the others. Provide corrective feedback as necessary.

| | | |
|---|---|---|
| not, new, road | lip, go, get | pail, time, tell |
| sat, said, mix | vine, box, vet | lift, sit, leg |

## APPLY

**Practice Reproducible** Have children complete **Practice Reproducible PA20.** Say the names of the pictures in each row, clearly pronouncing the beginning sound in each picture name (1. mop, map, six 2. zipper, cow, zebra 3. king, ten, kite 4. box, goat, bag). Have children repeat. Tell them to say the beginning sound in each picture name and think about the position of their lips and tongue as they do so. Then have children circle the picture in each row whose name does **not** begin with the same sound as the other two.

**Answer Key: 1.** *six* **2.** *cow* **3.** *ten* **4.** *goat*

Name ______________________ Date __________



# Beginning Sounds

**Say each picture name and the sound that begins it. Circle the picture in each row whose name does NOT begin with the same sound as the other two.**

| | | | |
|---|---|---|---|
| 1. | 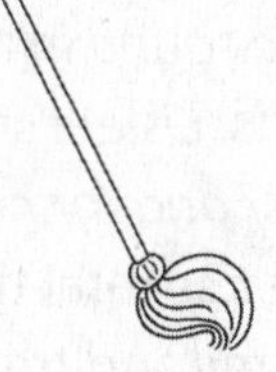 | 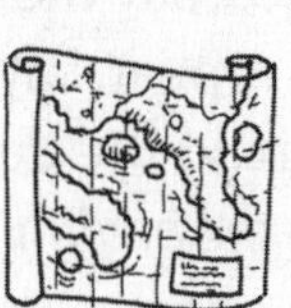 |  |
| 2. | 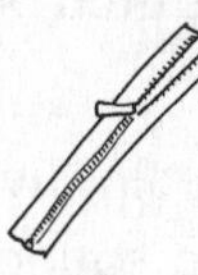 |  |  |
| 3. |  | 10 |  |
| 4. |  |  |  |

# Phoneme Categorization: Beginning Sounds (Oddity Task)

## TEACH/MODEL

**Introduce** Explain that today children will name pictures and listen for the sounds that begin each picture name. Then they will decide which picture name does not begin with the same sounds as the other two.

**Consonant Blends** Review that some words begin with a single sound and that some words begin with two sounds. Say the word *nap,* stretching the beginning sound /nnn/. Have children repeat. Say: *The beginning sound in* nap *is /nnn/.* Now say the word *snap,* stretching the beginning sounds. *Listen:* snap, */sss/ /nnn/ /ap/. There are two sounds at the beginning of* snap, */sss/ and /nnn/, /sssnnnap/.* Have children repeat. Then say *nap* and *snap* together several times. Have children repeat. Follow the same routine with *lo* and *flow; rail* and *trail.*

Model listening carefully to three words and then identifying which word does not have the same beginning sounds. Say three words together. Stretch out and emphasize the sounds at the beginning of each word.

> **Think Aloud** *I am going to say three words:* stop, stick, *and* train. *Two words begin with the same sounds. Listen:* [Stretch the beginning sounds] stop, */ssst/ /op/;* stick, */ssst/ /ik/.* Stop *and* stick *begin with the /ssst/ sound.* Then say: Train *begins with different sounds. Listen:* [Stretch the beginning sound] train, */trrr/ /ān/.* Train *does not begin with /ssst/ like* stop *and* stick. Train *begins with /trrr/.*

## GUIDED PRACTICE

Say the three words in each group below. Have children listen to and say each word, blend and stretch its two beginning sounds, and then name the word that does not begin with the same sounds. Provide corrective feedback.

| | | |
|---|---|---|
| fry, free, plate | snow, glass, glow | flip, flag, brag |
| crack, cream, black | grow, play, plum | snip, stone, snap |

## APPLY

**Practice Reproducible** Have children complete **Practice Reproducible PA21.** Say the names of the pictures in each row, clearly pronouncing and blending the two beginning consonant sounds (1. sled, sleep, truck 2. swim, plant, swing 3. play, draw, dress 4. slide, frog, friends). Have children repeat, thinking about the position of their lips and tongue. Then have them circle the picture in each row whose name does **not** begin with the same consonant blend as the others.

**Answer Key: 1.** *truck* **2.** *plant* **3.** *play* **4.** *slide*

# Beginning Sounds

**Say each picture name and blend the two sounds that begin it. Circle the picture in each row whose name does NOT begin with the same consonant blend as the other two.**

**1.**

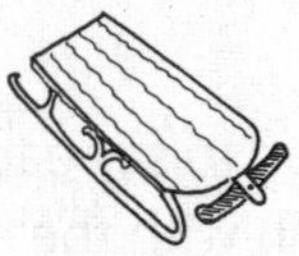

**2.**

**3.**

**4.**

# Review

## PREPARING THE REVIEW

- Make one copy of **Practice Reproducible PA22** for each child.
- Write the child's name and today's date at the top of the review.

## ADMINISTERING THE REVIEW

- Administer the review to one child at a time.
- Follow these instructions for each item. Each phonemic awareness skill was taught in the lessons indicated in parentheses.

1. Identify the picture: **rug.** Ask students to say the picture name and then draw a picture whose name rhymes with it. (Possible Drawings: *tug, bug, hug, mug;* Lessons 12–13)
2. Identify each picture: **gate, can,** and **goat.** Then ask children to say each picture name and circle the two pictures whose names begin with the same sound. (Answer: *gate, goat;* Lessons 14–15; Lessons 18–19)
3. Identify each picture: **swing, crayons,** and **crab.** Then ask children to say each picture name and circle the two pictures whose names begin with the same sounds. (Answer: *crayons, crab;* Lessons 14–15)
4. Identify the picture: **fish.** Then ask children to write the letter that stands for the sound that begins the picture name. (Answer: *F*; Lessons 16–17)
5. Identify the picture: **girl.** Then ask children to write the letter that stands for the sound that begins the picture name. (Answer: *G*; Lessons 16–17)

## SCORING THE REVIEW

- Total the number of items answered correctly.
- Use the Percentage Table below to identify a percentage. Children should get at least 80 percent correct.
- Analyze each child's errors, using the lesson numbers provided above.
- Reteach those skills for which the child did not answer an item correctly.

| Percentage Table | | | |
|---|---|---|---|
| **5 correct** | 100% | **2 correct** | 40% |
| **4 correct** | 80% | **1 correct** | 20% |
| **3 correct** | 60% | **0 correct** | 0% |

Name ______________________ Date __________



# Phonemic Awareness Review

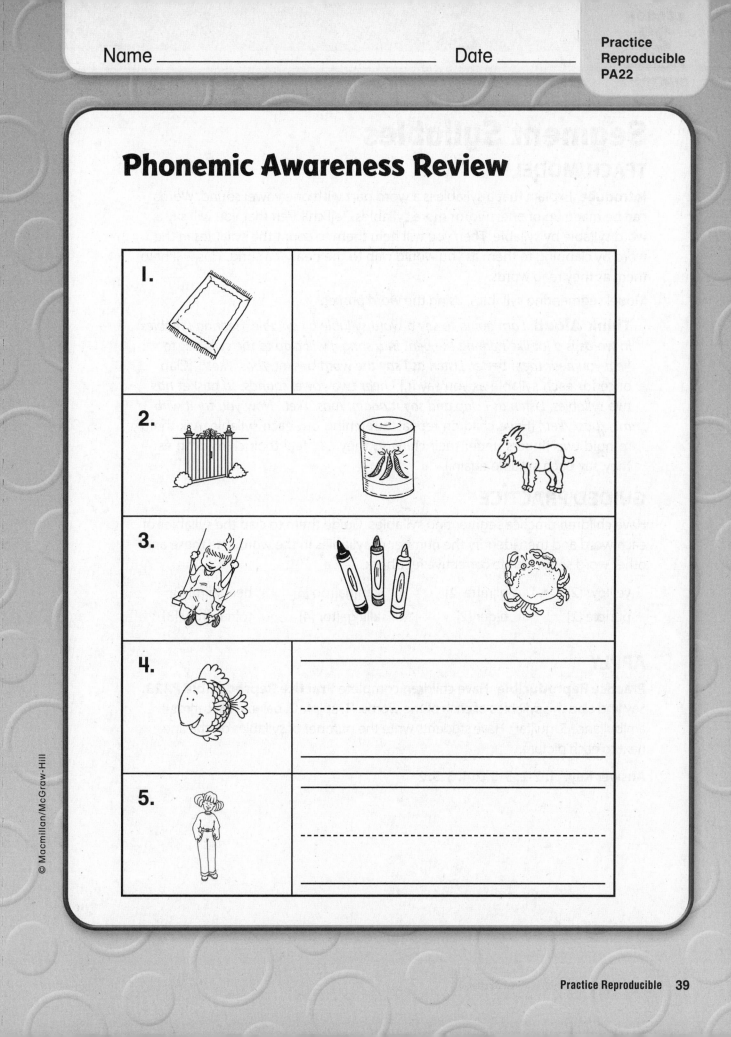

| | |
|---|---|
| 1. 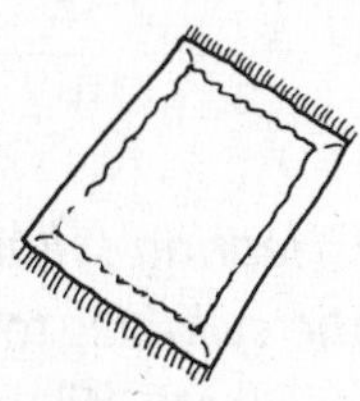 | |
| 2. 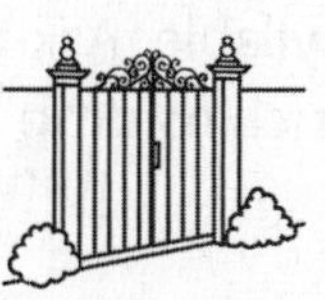 | 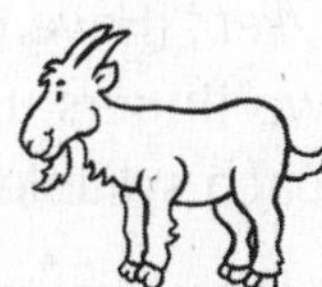 |
| 3. 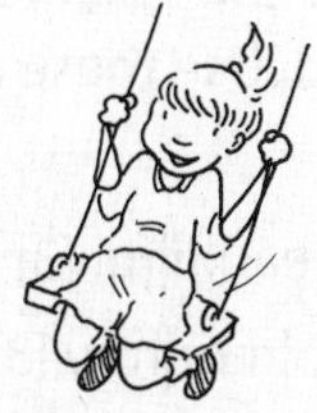 | 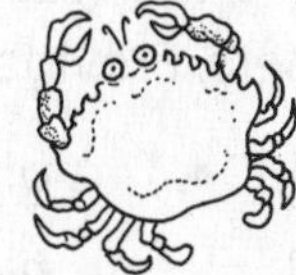 |
| 4. 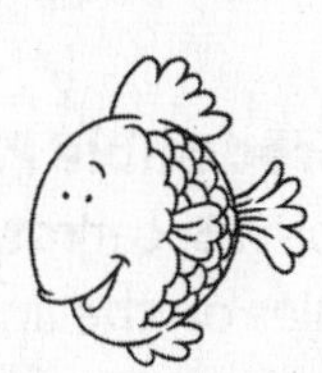 | |
| 5. 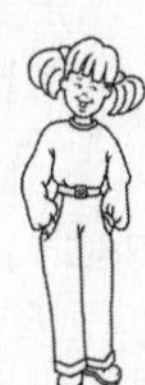 | |

# Segment Syllables

## TEACH/MODEL

**Introduce** Explain that a syllable is a word part with one vowel sound. Words can be made up of one, two, or more syllables. Tell children that you will say a word syllable by syllable. Then you will help them to count the syllables in the word by clapping to them as you would clap to the beat of a song. This will help them as they read words.

Model segmenting syllables, using the word *basket*.

> **Think Aloud** *I am going to say a word syllable by syllable. Hearing syllables in words is a lot like hearing the beat in a song. I will clap to the syllables to help you hear them better. Listen as I say the word* basket, */bas/ /ket/.* [Clap once for each syllable as you say it.] *I hear two vowel sounds, so* basket *has two syllables. Listen as I clap and say it again, /bas/ /ket/. Now you try it with me, /bas/ /ket/.* [Have children repeat, stretching out each syllable. Ask them to hold two fingers under their chins so they can feel their chins drop as they say each syllable again.]

## GUIDED PRACTICE

Have children practice segmenting syllables. Guide them to clap the syllables of each word and then identify the number of syllables in the word. Use these and other word sets. Provide corrective feedback.

| | | | |
|---|---|---|---|
| yel\|low [2] | gi\|raffe [2] | kan\|ga\|roo [3] | beau\|ti\|ful [3] |
| pur\|ple [2] | ti\|ger [2] | al\|li\|ga\|tor [4] | to\|mor\|row [3] |

## APPLY

**Practice Reproducible** Have children complete **Practice Reproducible PA23.** Say and clap the syllables of each of the words: (1. ap|ple 2. ba|na|na 3. car|rot 4. am|bu|lance 5. gui|tar). Have students write the number of syllables on the line next to each picture.

**Answer Key: 1.** 2 **2.** 3 **3.** 2 **4.** 3 **5.** 2

# Counting Syllables

**Say the name of each picture. Then count the syllables in each picture name. Write the number of syllables on the line next to each picture.**

| | |
|---|---|
| 1.  | ____________ |
| 2.  | ____________ |
| 3.  | ____________ |
| 4.  | ____________ |
| 5.  | ____________ |

# Segment Syllables

## TEACH/MODEL

**Introduce** Explain that a syllable is a word part with one vowel sound. Words can be made up of one or more syllables. Tell children that you will say a word syllable by syllable. Then you will help them to count the syllables in the word by clapping to them as you would clap to the beat of a song. This will help them as they read words.

Model segmenting syllables, using the word *rectangle.*

> **Think Aloud** *I am going to say a word syllable by syllable. Hearing syllables in words is a lot like hearing the beat in a song. I will clap to the syllables to help you hear them better. Listen as I say the word* rectangle, */rek/ /tan/ /gəl/.* [Clap once for each syllable as you say it.] *I hear* rectangle *has three syllables, or vowel sounds. Listen as I clap and say it again, /rek/ /tan/ /gəl/. Now you try it with me, /rek/ /tan/ /gəl/.* [Have children repeat, stretching out each syllable. Ask them to hold two fingers under their chins so they can feel their chins drop as they say each syllable again.]

## GUIDED PRACTICE

Have children practice segmenting syllables. Guide children to clap the syllables of each word and then identify the number of syllables in the word. Use these and other word sets. Provide corrective feedback.

| | | | |
|---|---|---|---|
| tri\|an\|gle [3] | fur\|ni\|ture [3] | rib\|bon [2] | waste\|bas\|ket [3] |
| cir\|cle [2] | win\|ter [2] | rain\|drop [2] | tel\|e\|vi\|sion [4] |

## APPLY

**Practice Reproducible** Have children complete **Practice Reproducible PA24.** Say and clap the syllables of each of the words (1. muf|fin 2. piz|za 3. mon|key 4. cray|ons 5. oc|to|pus). Have students write the number of syllables on the line next to each picture.

**Answer Key: 1.** 2 **2.** 2 **3.** 2 **4.** 2 **5.** 3

# Counting Syllables

**Say the name of each picture. Then count the syllables in each picture name. Write the number of syllables on the line next to each picture.**

| | |
|---|---|
| **1.**  | ______ |
| **2.** 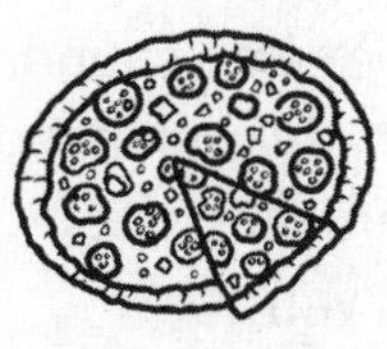 | ______ |
| **3.**  | ______ |
| **4.**  | ______ |
| **5.**  | ______ |

# Phoneme Identity: Ending Sounds

## TEACH/MODEL

**Introduce** Explain to children that the sound they hear last in a word, such as /l/ in *roll*, is called its ending sound. Say: *Listen:* [Stretch out the ending sound] */rōlll/* roll. [Have children say the word, repeating the ending sound.] Tell children that they will name pictures and listen for the sound that ends each picture name. Then they will decide which picture names end with the same sound.

**Contrasting Phonemes** Explain to children that the different sounds in a word are formed differently in their mouth. Say the sounds /g/ and /p/. Have children repeat. Now ask them to put their hands in front of their mouths and repeat both sounds. Which sound makes a puff of air? (/p/) Then ask them to put their hands on their throats and repeat both sounds. Which sound makes a vibration in their throat? (/g/) Finally, ask them to tell what their lips and tongue do as they make each sound. Repeat with other contrasting sounds, such as /m/ and /f/.

Say three words, and model identifying which two end with the same sound. Stretch out or repeat the ending sound as you say each word. If children need help identifying an ending sound, use **Sound Boxes.** Have them drag one counter into the last box of a Sound Box with each of the three words.

> **Think Aloud** *Now I am going to say three words: /busss/, bus; /thummm/,* thumb; */grasss/,* grass. [Have children repeat.] *Which of these words have the same ending sound?* Bus *and* grass *do. They both end with the /s/ sound: /busss/,* bus, *and /grasss/,* grass. [Have children repeat.] *The word* thumb *ends with the /m/* sound: */thummm/,* thumb. *Let's say* bus *and* thumb *again, listening and paying attention to how we pronounce the ending sounds /s/ and /m/ differently: /busss/,* bus; */thummm/,* thumb. [Have children repeat.]

## GUIDED PRACTICE

Say these words to children. Have children practice identifying which word pairs end in the same sound. Provide corrective feedback.

| | | |
|---|---|---|
| man, top, soap | fall, shell, sheep | wheel, duck, snake |
| ten, kite, sun | beach, big, frog | cat, frog, get |

## APPLY

**Practice Reproducible** Have children complete **Practice Reproducible PA25.** Say the names of the pictures in each row: (1. log, leaf, rug 2. bug, man, nine 3. truck, rope, lock 4. nut, cat, mop). Have children circle the two pictures in each row with the same ending sound.

**Answer Key: 1.** *log, rug* **2.** *man, nine* **3.** *truck, lock* **4.** *nut, cat*

Name ______________________ Date __________ Practice Reproducible PA25

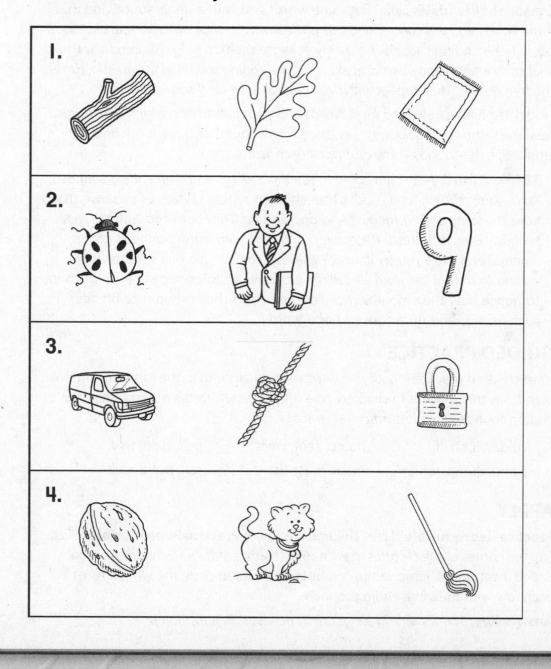

# Ending Sounds

**Say each picture name. Draw a circle around the two pictures in each row whose names end with the same sound.**

1.

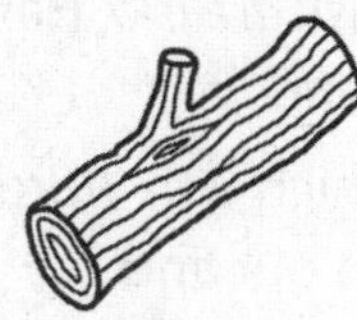 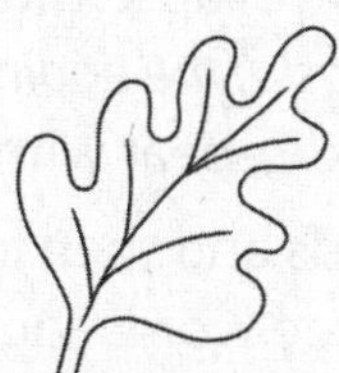 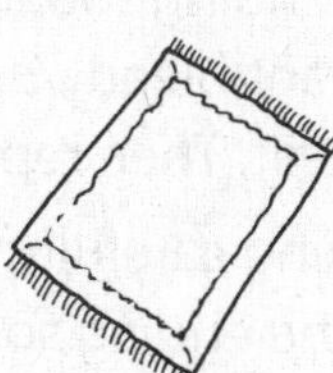

2.

3.

4.

  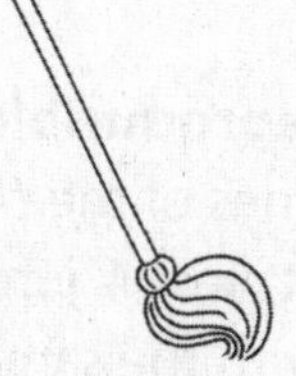

# Phoneme Identity: Ending Sounds

## TEACH/MODEL

**Introduce** Tell children that today they will listen for the ending sounds in words. Explain that they will name pictures and listen for the sound that ends each picture name. Then they will decide which picture names end with the same sounds. This will help them to read and write words.

**Consonant Blends** Explain that some words end with a single sound and that some words end with two sounds. Say: *The word* ask *ends with two sounds. Listen:* [Stretch the ending sounds and slowly collapse them to help children hear the final consonant blend] */asssk/, /assk/, /ask/; the ending sounds of* ask *are /sk/.* Have children repeat. Then repeat with *desk*. Repeat with *sand* and *found*.

Model listening carefully to three words and then identifying which two words have the same ending sounds. Say three words together. Stretch out and emphasize the sounds at the ending of each word.

> **Think Aloud** *Now I am going to say three words and their ending sounds: /and/,* and; */elf/,* elf; */end/,* end. [Have children repeat.] *Which of these words have the same ending sounds?* And *and* end *do. They both end with the /nd/ sounds. Listen as I stretch the ending sounds of both words: /annnd/,* and; */ennnd/,* end. *Now you try it.* [Have children repeat.] *Now let's stretch the ending sounds of the word* elf: */ellllfff/,* elf. [Have children repeat. Prompt them to notice how their mouths move differently as they pronounce blends such as /nd/ and /lf/ at the end of a word.]

## GUIDED PRACTICE

Have children practice identifying which word pairs end in the same consonant blend. Say these words to children, one set at a time. Stretch out or repeat the ending sounds. Provide corrective feedback.

| | | |
|---|---|---|
| cold, self, shelf | bump, sent, want | belt, bald, told |
| camp, dump, sand | mask, must, list | salt, front, melt |

## APPLY

**Practice Reproducible** Have children complete **Practice Reproducible PA26.** Say the names of the pictures in each row: (1. ant, paint, bat 2. hand, yarn, corn 3. sled, nest, vest 4. jump, lamp, comb). Have children circle the two pictures in each row with the same ending sounds.

**Answer Key: 1.** *ant, paint* **2.** *yarn, corn* **3.** *nest, vest* **4.** *jump, lamp*

Name ______________________ Date __________



# Ending Sounds

**Say each picture name. Draw a circle around the two pictures in each row whose names end with the same sounds.**

1.

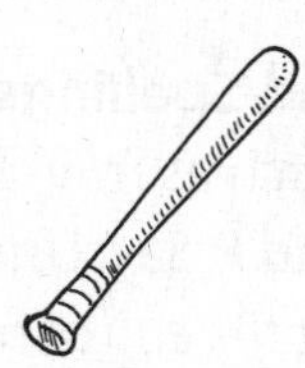

2.

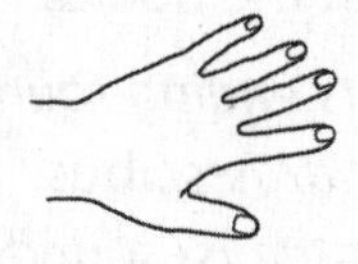

3.

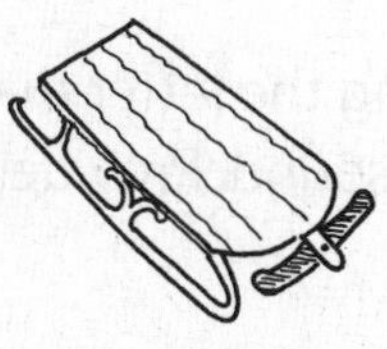

4.

# Phoneme Isolation: Ending Sounds

## TEACH/MODEL

**Introduce** Tell children that listening carefully for the sound that ends a word and then matching it to the letter that stands for the sound will help them as they learn to read. Tell children that today they will name pictures and listen for the sound that ends each picture name. Then they will name and write the letter that stands for the end sound. This will help them to write words.

**Teach Sound-Spellings** Tell children that the sound that they hear at the end of a word, such as /t/ in *bat*, is called its ending sound. Teach the sound-spellings for *T, S, G,* and *P.* Say: *Listen as I say the word* bat: */b/ /a/ /t/.* [Have children repeat.] *The sound at the end of* bat *is /t/. The /t/ sound is spelled with the letter* T. Model writing the letter *T* on the board. Follow the same routine with the word *bus* to teach *S,* the word *hug* to teach *G,* and the word *hop* to teach *P.*

Model identifying the ending sound in a word and then writing the letter that stands for that sound. Leave the letters *T, S, G,* and *P* displayed on the board.

> **Think Aloud** *Now I am going to say a word and listen for its ending sound:* bus, */busss/. The word* bus *ends with the /s/ sound. Listen: /b/ /u/ /sss/,* bus. [Have children repeat.] *Now I know that the letter* S *stands for the /s/ sound, so I will write the letter* S *to spell the sound. Watch carefully.* [Write *S* slowly and carefully several times.]

## GUIDED PRACTICE

Have children practice identifying the ending sound and writing the letter that spells it. Say each word, stretching out or repeating its ending sound. Provide corrective feedback.

| | | | |
|---|---|---|---|
| top | hiss | tag | grip |
| kite | get | miss | hat |

## APPLY

**Practice Reproducible** Have children complete **Practice Reproducible PA27.** Say the name of each picture: (1. log 2. mop 3. mouse 4. nut). Have children repeat the name and write the letter that represents the ending sound they hear.

**Answer Key: 1.** *G* **2.** *P* **3.** *S* **4.** *T*

## Ending Sounds

**Trace each letter below. Then say the name of each picture. Say each ending sound. Then write the letter that stands for the ending sound.**

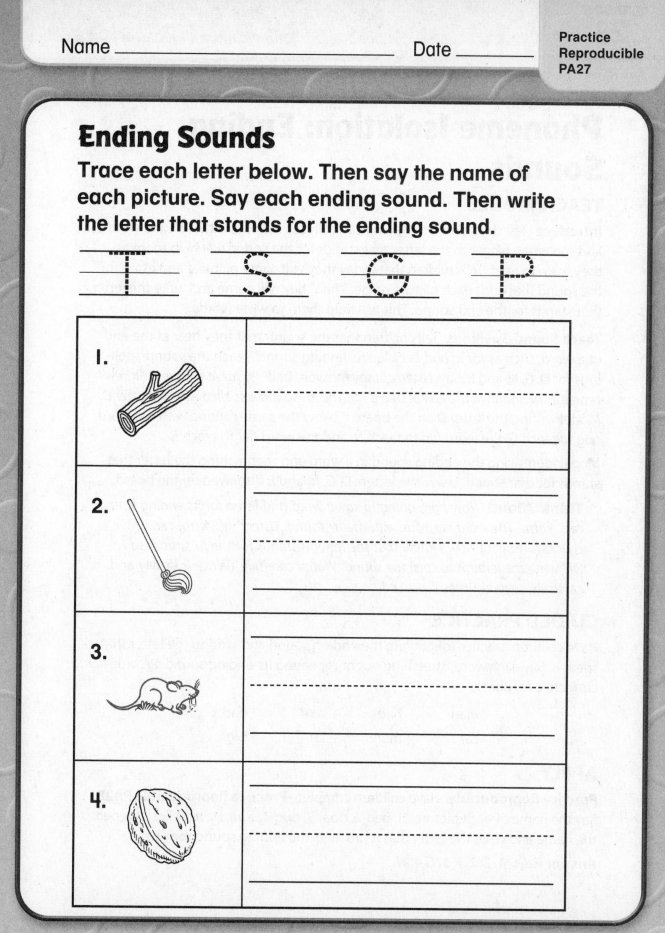

T 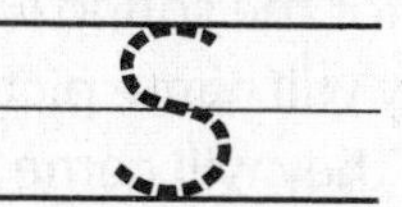 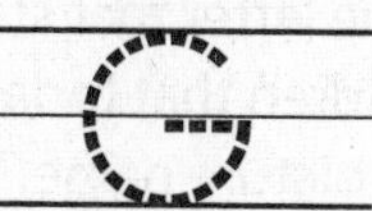 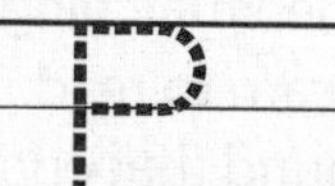

| | |
|---|---|
| 1. 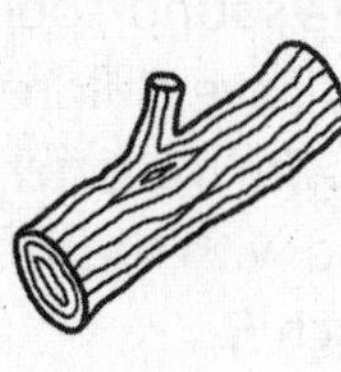 | |
| 2. 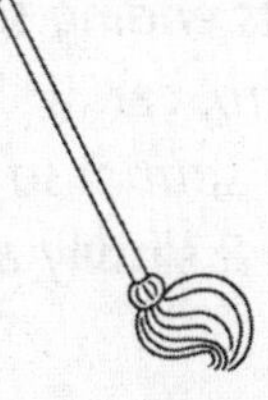 | |
| 3.  | |
| 4.  | |

# Phoneme Isolation: Ending Sounds

## TEACH/MODEL

**Introduce** Tell children that listening carefully for the sound that ends a word and then matching it to the letter that stands for the sound will help them as they learn to read. Tell children that today they will name pictures and listen for the sound that ends each picture name. Then they will name and write the letter that stands for the end sound. This will help them to write words.

**Teach Sound-Spellings** Tell children that the sound that they hear at the end of a word, such as /d/ in *bad*, is called its ending sound. Teach the sound-spellings for *D, G, N,* and *R*. Say: *Listen as I say the word* bad: */b/ /a/ /d/.* [Have children repeat.] *The sound at the end of* bad *is /d/. The /d/ sound is spelled with the letter* D. Model writing the letter *D* on the board. Follow the same routine with the word *hug* to teach *G,* the word *fun* to teach *N,* and the word *her* to teach *R*.

Model identifying the ending sound in a word and then writing the letter that stands for that sound. Leave the letters *D, G, N,* and *R* displayed on the board.

**Think Aloud** *Now I am going to say a word and listen for its ending sound:* car, */karrr/. The word* car *ends with the /r/ sound. Listen: /k/ /arrr/,* car. [Have children repeat.] *Now I know that the letter* R *stands for the /r/ sound, so I will write the letter* R *to spell the sound. Watch carefully.* [Write *R* slowly and carefully several times.]

## GUIDED PRACTICE

Have children practice identifying the ending sound and writing the letter that spells it. Say each word, stretching out or repeating its ending sound. Provide corrective feedback.

| | | | |
|---|---|---|---|
| man | bad | ran | had |
| car | more | far | big |

## APPLY

**Practice Reproducible** Have children complete **Practice Reproducible PA28.** Say the name of each picture: (1. bed 2. door 3. bug 4. sun). Have children repeat the name and write the letter that represents the ending sound they hear.

**Answer Key: 1.** *D* **2.** *R* **3.** *G* **4.** *N*

Name ____________________ Date __________



## Ending Sounds

**Trace each letter below. Then say the name of each picture. Say each ending sound. Then write the letter that stands for the ending sound.**

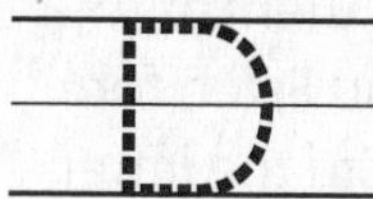
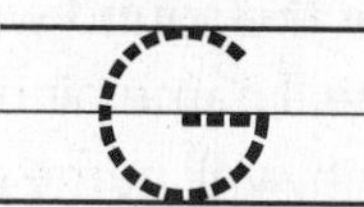

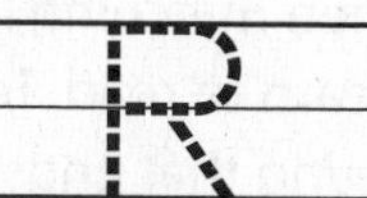

| | |
|---|---|
| 1.  | |
| 2.  | |
| 3.  | |
| 4.  | |

# Phoneme Isolation: Ending Sounds

## TEACH/MODEL

**Introduce** Tell children that listening carefully for the sound that ends a word and then matching it to the letter that stands for the sound will help them as they learn to read. Tell children that today they will name pictures and listen for the sound that ends each picture name. Then they will name and write the letter that stands for the end sound. This will help them to write words.

**Teach Sound-Spellings** Tell children that the sound that they hear at the end of a word, such as /l/ in *call*, is called its ending sound. Teach the sound-spellings for *L, P, N,* and *F*. Say: *Listen as I say the word* call: */k/ /ô/ /l/.* [Have children repeat.] *The sound at the end of* call *is /lll/. The /l/ sound is spelled with the letter* L. Model writing the letter *L* on the board. Follow the same routine with the word *hop* to teach *P*, the word *fun* to teach *N*, and the word *sniff* to teach *F*.

Model identifying the ending sound in a word and then writing the letter that stands for that sound. Leave the letters *L, P, N,* and *F* displayed on the board.

> **Think Aloud** *Now I am going to say a word and listen for its ending sound:* pin, */pin/. The word* pin *ends with the /n/ sound. Listen: /p/ /in/,* pin. [Have children repeat.] *Now I know that the letter* N *stands for the /n/ sound, so I will write the letter* N *to spell the sound. Watch carefully.* [Write *N* slowly and carefully several times.]

## GUIDED PRACTICE

Have children practice identifying the ending sound and writing the letter that spells it. Say each word, stretching out or repeating its ending sound. Provide corrective feedback.

| | | | |
|---|---|---|---|
| hill | in | map | cup |
| up | stuff | pan | stiff |

## APPLY

**Practice Reproducible** Have children complete **Practice Reproducible PA29.** Say the name of each picture: (1. fan 2. leaf 3. jeep 4. ball). Have children repeat the name and write the letter that represents the ending sound they hear.

**Answer Key: 1.** *N* **2.** *F* **3.** *P* **4.** *L*

Name ______________________ Date __________



# Ending Sounds

**Say the name of each picture. Say each ending sound. Then write the letter that stands for the ending sound.**

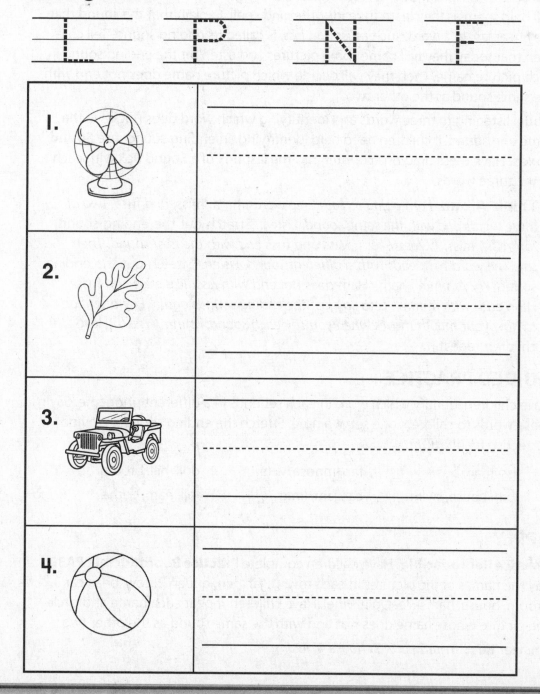

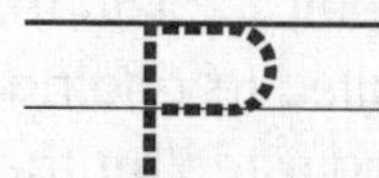

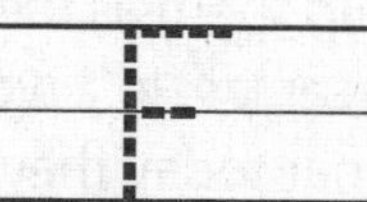

| | |
|---|---|
| **1.**  | |
| **2.** 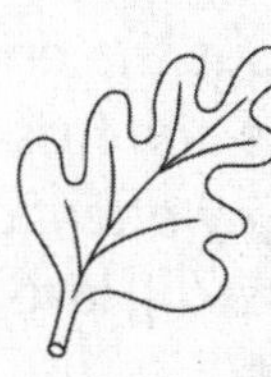 | |
| **3.**  | |
| **4.** 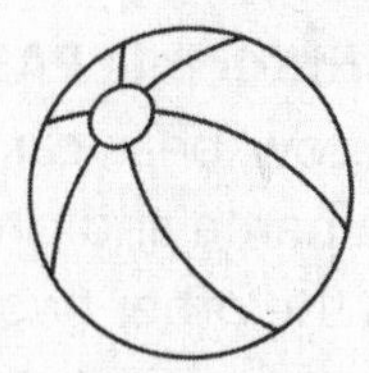 | |

# Phoneme Categorization: Ending Sounds (Oddity Task)

## TEACH/MODEL

**Introduce** Tell children that listening carefully for the sound that ends a word will help them as they learn to read, write, and spell. Explain that the sound that they hear last in a word, such as /sss/ in *kiss,* is called its ending sound. Tell children that today they will name some pictures and listen for the ending sound in each picture name. Then they will decide which picture name does not end with the same sound as the other two.

Model listening to three words and identifying which word does not have the same end sound. If children need help identifying an ending sound, use **Sound Boxes.** Have them drag one counter into the last box of a Sound Box with each of the three words.

**Think Aloud** *I am going to say three words:* ham, miss, *and* fuss. *Two of these words end with the same sound. Listen:* [Stretch out the ending sound] */m/ /isss/,* miss; */f/ /usss/,* fuss. Miss *and* fuss *end with the /sss/ sound. Then say: The word* ham *ends with a different sound. Listen:* [Stretch out the ending sound] */h/ /ammm/,* ham. Ham *does not end with /sss/ like* miss *and* fuss. Ham *ends with /mmm/. Let's say just the ending sounds again. Pay attention to how your mouth moves when you say each sound: /mmm/; /sss/.* [Have children repeat.]

## GUIDED PRACTICE

Have children identify which word in each set ends in a different phoneme. Say these words to children, one set at a time. Stretch the ending sounds. Provide corrective feedback.

| | | |
|---|---|---|
| kiss, man, bus | fan, moose, win | doll, hill, broom |
| gum, house, swim | car, jam, lime | tall, ham, game |

## APPLY

**Practice Reproducible** Have children complete **Practice Reproducible PA30.** Say the names of the pictures in each row: (1. jar, pen, queen 2. cow, bear, car 3. broom, house, ham 4. leaf, pin, vine). Have children repeat each name and circle the picture whose name does **not** end with the same sound as the other two.

**Answer Key: 1.** *jar* **2.** *cow* **3.** *house* **4.** *leaf*

Name ______________________ Date __________



# Ending Sounds

**Say each picture name and the sound that ends it. Circle the picture in each row whose name does NOT end with the same sound as the other two.**

| |
|---|
| **1.** |
| **2.** |
| **3.** |
| **4.** |

# Phoneme Categorization: Ending Sounds (Oddity Task)

## TEACH/MODEL

**Introduce** Tell children that listening carefully for the sound that ends a word will help them as they learn to read, write, and spell. Explain that the sound that they hear last in a word, such as /d/ in *mad,* is called its ending sound. Tell children that today they will name some pictures and listen for the ending sound in each picture name. Then they will decide which picture name does not end with the same sound as the other two.

Model listening to three words and identifying which word does not have the same end sound.

> **Think Aloud** *I am going to say three words:* lip, cat, *and* cup. *Two of these words end with the same sound. Listen:* [Emphasize the ending sound] */l/ /ip/,* lip*; /k/ /up/,* cup. Lip *and* cup *end with the /p/ sound.* Then say: *The word* cat *ends with a different sound. Listen:* [Emphasize the ending sound] */k/ /at/,* cat. Cat *does not end with /p/ like* lip *and* cup. Cat *ends with /t/. Let's say just the ending sounds again. Pay attention to how your mouth moves when you say each sound: /p/; /t/.* [Have children repeat.]

## GUIDED PRACTICE

Have children identify which word in each set ends in a different phoneme. Say these words to children, one set at a time. Repeat the ending sounds. Provide corrective feedback.

| | | |
|---|---|---|
| bat, feet, bus | can, coat, sun | hat, soap, mop |
| glass, cake, duck | gate, man, pet | leg, dog, sat |

## APPLY

**Practice Reproducible** Have children complete **Practice Reproducible PA31.** Say the names of the pictures in each row: (1. bike, bag, book 2. dog, egg, duck 3. cat, jeep, kite 4. hook, cat, gate). Have children repeat each name and circle the picture whose name does **not** end with the same sound as the other two.

**Answer Key: 1.** *bag* **2.** *duck* **3.** *jeep* **4.** *hook*

Name ______________________ Date __________

Practice Reproducible PA31

# Ending Sounds

**Say each picture name and the sound that ends it. Circle the picture in each row whose name does NOT end with the same sound as the other two.**

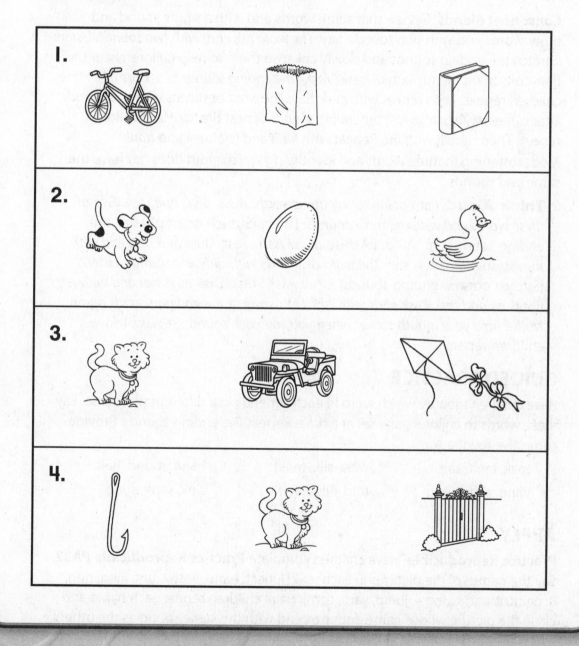

1.

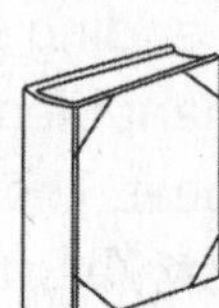

2.

3.

4.

# Phoneme Categorization: Ending Sounds (Oddity Task)

## TEACH/MODEL

**Introduce** Tell children that listening carefully for the sounds that end a word will help them as they learn to read, write, and spell. Tell children that they will name pictures and listen for the ending sounds in each picture name. Then they will decide which picture name does not end with the same sounds.

**Consonant Blends** Review that some words end with a single sound and other words end with two sounds. Say: *The word* ask *ends with two sounds. Listen:* [Stretch the ending sounds and slowly collapse them to help children hear the final consonant blend] */asssk/, /assk/, /ask/; the ending sounds of* ask *are /sk/.* Have children repeat. Then repeat with *desk*. Say: *The word* best *ends with two sounds. Listen: /bessst/, /besst/, /best/; the ending sounds of* best *are /st/.* Have children repeat. Then repeat with *fist*. Repeat with *fault* and *felt, sunk* and *honk*.
Model listening to three words and identifying which word does not have the same end sounds.

> **Think Aloud** *I am going to say three words:* dust, disk, *and* rest. *Two of these words end with the same sounds. Listen:* [Stretch or emphasize the ending sounds] */d/ /u/ /ssst/,* dust; */r/ /e/ /ssst/,* rest. Dust *and* rest *end with the /st/ sounds.* Then say: *The word* disk *ends with different sounds. Listen:* [Stretch out the ending sounds] */d/ /i/ /sssk/,* disk. Disk *does not end with /st/ like* dust *and* rest. Disk *ends with /sk/. Let's say just the ending sounds again. Notice how your mouth moves when you say each sound: /st/; /sk/.* [Have children repeat.]

## GUIDED PRACTICE

Have children identify which word in each set ends in a different phoneme. Say these words to children, one set at a time. Repeat the ending sounds. Provide corrective feedback.

| | | |
|---|---|---|
| milk, fault, salt | west, silk, most | hand, round, halt |
| wing, taste, lung | told, filled, felt | sink, sunk, sung |

## APPLY

**Practice Reproducible** Have children complete **Practice Reproducible PA32.** Say the names of the pictures in each row (1. nest, hand, vest 2. ant, king, ring 3. paint, plant, swing 4. jump, yarn, corn). Have children repeat each name and circle the picture whose name does **not** end with the same sound as the others.

**Answer Key:** **1.** *hand* **2.** *ant* **3.** *swing* **4.** *jump*

Name ______________________ Date __________



# Ending Sounds

**Say each picture name and blend the two sounds that end it. Circle the picture in each row whose name does NOT end with the same consonant blend as the other two.**

**1.**

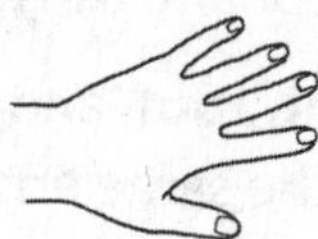
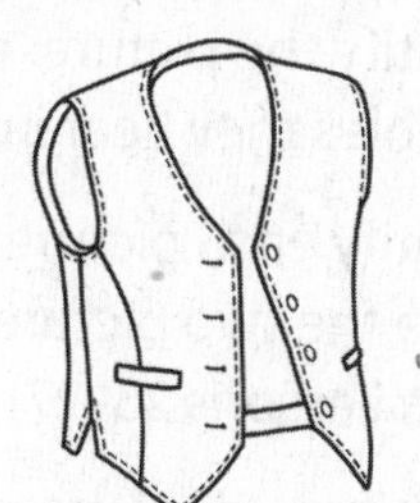

**2.**

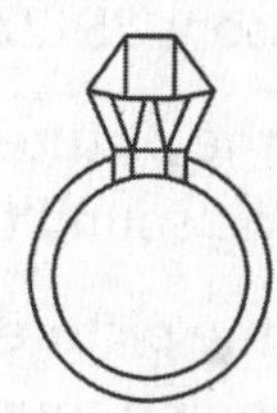

**3.**

**4.**

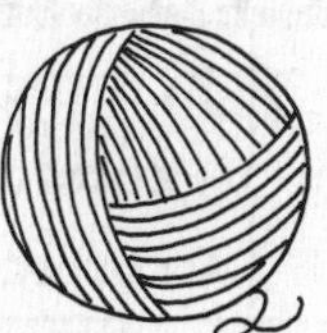

# Review

## PREPARING THE REVIEW

- Make one copy of **Practice Reproducible PA33** for each child.
- Write the child's name and today's date at the top of the review.

## ADMINISTERING THE REVIEW

- Administer the review to one child at a time.
- Follow these instructions for each item. Each phonemic awareness skill was taught in the lesson indicated in parentheses.

1. Identify the picture: **elephant.** Then ask children to write the number of syllables they hear in the word *elephant.* (Answer: 3; Lessons 23–24)
2. Identify each picture: **mouse, foot, roof,** and **boat.** Then ask children to circle the two pictures that have the same ending sound. (Answer: *foot, boat;* Lessons 25–27)
3. Identify each picture: **horn, hang, yarn,** and **yawn.** Then ask children to circle the two pictures that have the same ending sounds. (Answer: *horn, yarn;* Lessons 25–27)
4. Identify the picture: **tag.** Then ask children to write the letter that stands for the ending sound they hear in the word *tag.* (Answer: *G;* Lessons 28–29)
5. Identify the picture: **map.** Then ask children to write the letter that stands for the ending sound they hear in the word *map.* (Answer: *P;* Lesson 28–29)

## SCORING THE REVIEW

- Total the number of items answered correctly.
- Use the Percentage Table below to identify a percentage. Children should get at least 80 percent correct.
- Analyze each child's errors, using the lesson numbers provided above.
- Reteach those skills for which the child did not answer an item correctly.

**Percentage Table**

| | | | |
|---|---|---|---|
| **5 correct** | 100% | **2 correct** | 40% |
| **4 correct** | 80% | **1 correct** | 20% |
| **3 correct** | 60% | **0 correct** | 0% |

# Phonemic Awareness Review

| | |
|---|---|
| 1.  | |
| 2.     | |
| 3. 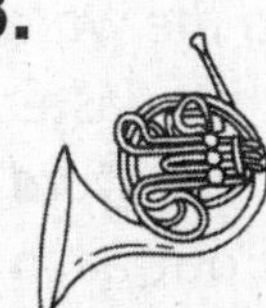    | |
| 4.  | |
| 5. 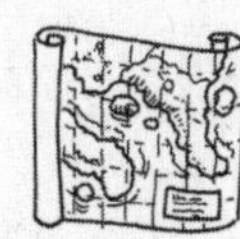 | |

# Blend Syllables

## TEACH/MODEL

**Introduce** Tell children that a syllable is a word part with one vowel sound. Words can be made up of one, two, or more syllables. Say: *The word* swim *has one syllable.* [Clap once as you say *swim.* Have children repeat.] *I hear one vowel sound, so it has one syllable. The word* swimming *has two syllables.* [Clap twice as you say the word *swimming.* Have children repeat.] *I hear two vowel sounds, so it has two syllables.* Tell children that today they will listen to the syllables of a word. Then you will help them put the syllables together to say the whole word.

Model blending syllables to form the word *apple.* Begin by saying the word, syllable by syllable. Clap once for each syllable and stretch out the sounds. Then slowly blend the syllables to say the whole word.

> **Think Aloud** *I am going to say a word syllable by syllable. I will clap to help me hear each syllable in the word.* [Clap the syllables as you say the word apple.] *Listen: /ap/ /pəl/. I heard two vowel sounds, which means there are two syllables. Now I will stretch each syllable, and then I will blend them together: /aaap/ /pəlll/.* [Stretch out or emphasize each sound. Pause between syllables but not between sounds.] *Now let's blend the syllables together. We'll clap each syllable slowly, and then we'll clap faster as we blend the word. Listen:* [Model blending syllables by clapping slowly at first and then faster as you blend the word] */aaap/ /pəlll/, /aap/ /pəll/, /ap/ /pəl/,* apple. *The word is* apple. *Now you try it with me.* [Have children repeat, stretching out each syllable. Ask them to hold two fingers under their chins so they can feel their chins drop as they say each syllable.]

## GUIDED PRACTICE

Guide children to blend the following syllables to make words. Continue to use the clapping technique to help children hear and blend the syllables. All the sample words begin with continuous sounds for ease in blending. Use these and other word sets. Provide corrective feedback.

| | | |
|---|---|---|
| in\|sect, insect | les\|son, lesson | num\|ber, number |
| sil\|ly, silly | un\|der, under | mar\|ket, market |

## APPLY

**Practice Reproducible** Have children complete **Practice Reproducible PA34.** Say the syllables of the words below. Have children blend the syllables. Then have children write the item number of the word they hear next to the correct picture. Provide corrective feedback and modeling, as needed.

**Answer Key: 1.** ze|bra **2.** el|bow **3.** lad|der **4.** wag|on

Name ____________________ Date __________



# Find the Picture

**Listen to the syllables. Put the syllables together. Find the picture that matches the word you hear. Write the number of the word in the circle.**

| ○ | ○ |
|---|---|
| ○ | ○ |

# Blend Syllables

## TEACH/MODEL

**Introduce** Tell children that learning to put syllables together to make words will help them as they read. Explain that a syllable is a word part with one vowel sound. Words can be made up of one, two, or more syllables. Say: *The word* sun *has one syllable.* [Clap once as you say *sun*. Have children repeat.] *I hear one vowel sound, so it has one syllable. The word* sunshine *has two syllables.* [Clap twice as you say the word *sunshine*. Have children repeat.] *I hear two vowel sounds, so it has two syllables.* Tell children that today they will listen to the syllables of a word. Then you will help them put the syllables together to say the whole word.

Model blending syllables to form the word *music*. Begin by saying the word, syllable by syllable. Clap once for each syllable and stretch out the sounds. Then slowly blend the syllables to say the whole word.

**Think Aloud** *I am going to say a word syllable by syllable. I will clap to help me hear each syllable in the word.* [Clap the syllables as you say *music*.] *Listen: /mū/ /zik/. I heard two vowel sounds, which means there are two syllables. Now listen as I string together, or blend, the syllables. I will stretch each syllable, and then I will blend them together: /mmmū/ /zzziiik/.* [Stretch or emphasize each sound. Pause between syllables but not between sounds.] *Now let's blend the syllables together. First we'll clap each syllable slowly, and then we'll clap faster as we blend the word.* [Model blending syllables by clapping slowly at first and then faster.] *Watch and listen as I clap and blend the syllables: /mmmū/ /zzziiik/, /mmū/ /zziik/, /mū/ /zik/,* music. *Now you try with me.* [Have children repeat, stretching each syllable. Ask them to hold two fingers under their chins so they can feel their chins drop as they say each syllable.]

## GUIDED PRACTICE

Guide children to blend the following syllables to make words. Continue to use the clapping technique to help children hear the syllables. Use these and other word sets. Provide corrective feedback.

| | | |
|---|---|---|
| zip\|per, zipper | fur\|ry, furry | or\|ange, orange |
| ro\|bot, robot | mus\|tache, mustache | stick\|er, sticker |

## APPLY

**Practice Reproducible** Have children complete **Practice Reproducible PA35.** Say the following syllables: **1.** mon|ster **2.** li|on **3.** flow|er **4.** sand|wich.

Have children blend the syllables and then draw a picture of the word created in the appropriate box. Provide corrective feedback and modeling, as needed.

Name ____________________ Date __________



## Draw It

**Listen to the syllables. Put the syllables together. Draw a picture of the word you made.**

| 1. | 2. |
| --- | --- |
| 3. | 4. |

# Blend Syllables

## TEACH/MODEL

**Introduce** Tell children a syllable is a word part with one vowel sound. Words can be made up of one, two, or more syllables. Say: *The word* happy *has two syllables.* [Clap twice as you say *happy.* Have children repeat.] *I hear two vowel sounds, so it has two syllables. The word* happiest *has three syllables.* [Clap three times as you say *happiest.* Have children repeat.] *I hear three vowel sounds, so it has three syllables.* Tell children that they will listen to the syllables of a word. Then you will help them put the syllables together to say the whole word.

Model blending syllables to form the word *alphabet.* Begin by saying the word, syllable by syllable. Clap once for each syllable and stretch out the sounds. Then slowly blend the syllables to say the whole word.

> **Think Aloud** *I am going to say a word syllable by syllable. I will clap to help me hear each syllable.* [Clap the syllables as you say *alphabet.*] *Listen: /al/ /fə/ /bet/. I heard three vowel sounds, which means there are three syllables. Now listen as I string together, or blend, the syllables. I will stretch each syllable and then blend them together: /aaalll/ /fffə/ /beeet/.* [Stretch or emphasize each sound. Pause between syllables but not between sounds.] *Now let's blend the syllables together. First we'll clap each syllable slowly, and then we'll clap faster as we blend the word.* [Model blending syllables by clapping slowly at first and then faster as you blend.] *Watch and listen as I clap and blend the syllables: /aaalll/ /fffə/ /beeet, /aall/ /ffə/ /beet/, /al/ /fə/ /bet/,* alphabet. *Now you try.* [Have children repeat. Ask them to hold two fingers under their chins so they can feel their chins drop as they say each syllable.]

## GUIDED PRACTICE

Guide children to blend the following syllables to make words. Continue to use the clapping technique to help children hear the syllables. Use these and other word sets. Provide corrective feedback.

| | | |
|---|---|---|
| help\|er, helper | e\|qual, equal | pho\|to\|graph, photograph |
| su\|gar, sugar | li\|brar\|y, library | news\|pa\|per, newspaper |

## APPLY

**Practice Reproducible** Have children complete **Practice Reproducible PA36.** Say the following syllables: **1.** moun|tain **2.** air|plane **3.** el|e|phant **4.** wa|ter|fall.

Have children blend the syllables and then draw a picture of the word created in the appropriate box. Provide corrective feedback and modeling as needed.

## Draw It

**Listen to the syllables. Put the syllables together. Draw a picture of the word you made.**

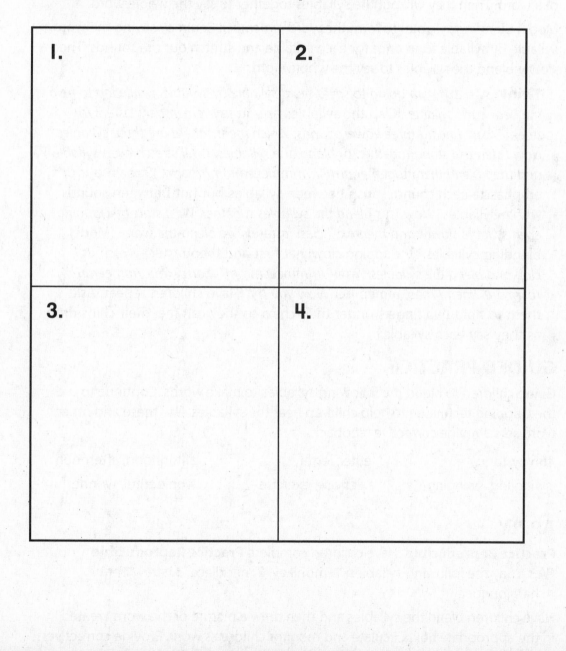

| I. | 2. |
|---|---|
| 3. | 4. |

# Blend Syllables

## TEACH/MODEL

**Introduce** Tell children a syllable is a word part with one vowel sound. Words can be made up of one, two, or more syllables. Say: Apartment *has three syllables.* [Clap three times as you say *apartment.* Have children repeat.] *I hear three vowel sounds, so it has three syllables.* Tell children they will listen to the syllables of a word. Then they will put the syllables together to say the whole word.

Model blending syllables to form the word *remember.* Begin by saying the word, syllable by syllable. Clap once for each syllable and stretch out the sounds. Then slowly blend the syllables to say the whole word.

**Think Aloud** *I am going to say a word syllable by syllable. I will clap to help me hear each syllable.* [Clap the syllables as you say *remember.*] *Listen: /ri/ /mem/ /bər/. I heard three vowel sounds, which means there are three syllables. Now listen as I string together, or blend, the syllables. I will stretch each syllable and then blend them together: /rrriii/ /mmmeeemmm/ /bərrr/.* [Stretch out or emphasize each sound. Pause between syllables but not between sounds within syllables.] *Now let's blend the syllables together. We'll start by clapping each syllable slowly, and then we'll clap faster as we blend the word.* [Model blending syllables by clapping slowly at first and then faster.] *Watch as I clap and blend the syllables: /rrriii/ /mmmeeemmm/ /bərrr/, /rrii/ /mmeemm/ /bərr/, /ri/ /mem/ /bər/,* remember. *Now you try.* [Have children repeat. Ask them to hold two fingers under their chins so they can feel their chins drop as they say each syllable.]

## GUIDED PRACTICE

Guide children to blend the following syllables to make words. Continue to use the clapping technique to help children hear the syllables. Use these and other word sets. Provide corrective feedback.

| | | |
|---|---|---|
| fun\|ny, funny | let\|ter, letter | af\|ter\|noon, afternoon |
| swing\|ing, swinging | ex\|er\|cise, exercise | won\|der\|ful, wonderful |

## APPLY

**Practice Reproducible** Have children complete **Practice Reproducible PA37.** Say the following syllables: **1.** mon|key **2.** neck|lace **3.** straw|ber|ry **4.** ham|bur|ger.

Have children blend the syllables and then draw a picture of the word created in the appropriate box. Circulate and monitor children's work. Provide corrective feedback and modeling as needed.

Name ______________________ Date __________



## Draw It

**Listen to the syllables. Put the syllables together. Draw a picture of the word you made.**

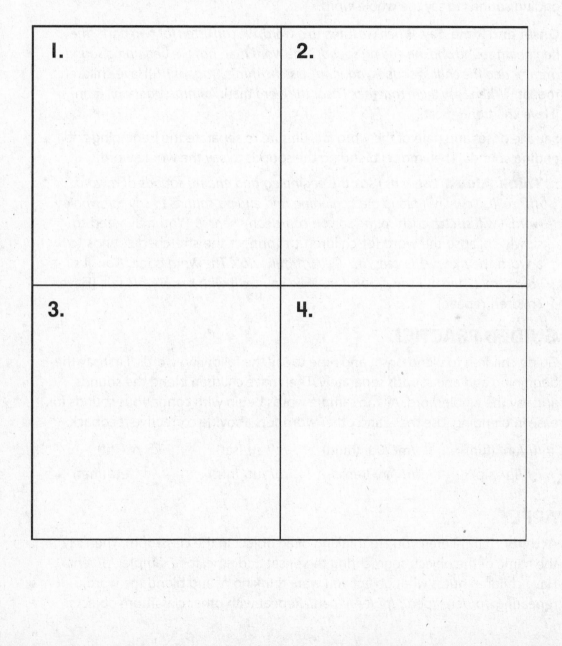

| **1.** | **2.** |
| --- | --- |
| **3.** | **4.** |

LESSON 38
Phonemic Awareness

# Blend Onset and Rime

## TEACH/MODEL

**Introduce** Tell children that part of learning to read is learning to be a careful listener. Explain that today they will learn to listen carefully to the beginning and ending sounds in words. Tell them that you will say the beginning and ending sounds of a word. Then they will string together, or blend, the beginning and ending sounds to say the whole word.

**Onset and Rime** Say: *When we listen to a word, we can listen for two parts, the beginning sound and the ending sounds. The word* man *has the beginning sound /mmm/ and the ending sounds /aaannn/. Listen: /mmm/ /aaannn/.* [Have children repeat.] *When I say them together, I hear the word* man: */mmm/ /aaannn/,* man. [Have children repeat.]

Say the onset and rime of the word *fall*. Be sure to separate the beginning and ending sounds. Then model blending the sounds to say the whole word.

> **Think Aloud** *Listen as I say the beginning and ending sounds of a word: /fff/ /ôlll/. Now I will blend the beginning and ending sounds to say the whole word. I will stretch each sound so you can clearly hear it.* [You may need to slowly collapse the word for children to connect the stretched sounds to a word they know.] *Listen: /fff/ /ôlll/, /ff/ /ôll/, /fôl/. The word is* fall. *Now it's your turn. Listen as I say /f/ /ôl/,* fall. *Now you try it with me: /f/ /ôl/,* fall. [Have children repeat.]

## GUIDED PRACTICE

Guide children to blend onset and rime to say the following words. First say the beginning and end sounds separately. Then have children blend the sounds and say the whole word. All the sample words begin with continuous sounds for ease in blending. Use these and other word sets. Provide corrective feedback.

| | | | |
|---|---|---|---|
| /f/ /un/ (fun) | /m/ /ud/ (mud) | /s/ /at/ (sat) | /f/ /it/ (fit) |
| /s/ /ip/ (sip) | /r/ /an/ (ran) | /n/ /ut/ (nut) | /m/ /et/ (met) |

## APPLY

**Activity** Tell children you are thinking of an object in the classroom. Then say the name of the object, segmenting the onset and rime, for example: /p/ /en/. Have children guess what object you were thinking of and blend the word, repeating: /p/ /en/, /pen/; /p/ /en/, /pen/. Repeat with other classroom objects.

# Blend Onset and Rime

## TEACH/MODEL

**Introduce** Tell children that part of learning to read is learning to be a careful listener. Explain that today they will learn to listen carefully to the sounds in words. Tell them that today they will listen for the beginning and ending sounds of a word. Then they will string together, or blend, the beginning and ending sounds to say the whole word.

**Onset and Rime** Say: *When we listen to a word, we can listen for two parts, the beginning sound and the ending sounds. The word* feet *has the beginning sound /fff/ and the ending sounds /ēt/. Listen: /fff/ /ēt/.* [Have children repeat.] *When I say them together, I hear the word* feet: */fff/ /ēt/,* feet. [Have children repeat.]

Say the onset and rime of the word *name*. Be sure to separate the beginning and ending sounds. Then model blending the sounds to say the whole word.

**Think Aloud** *Listen as I say the beginning and ending sounds of a word: /nnn/ /āmmm/. Now I will blend the beginning and ending sounds to say the whole word. I will stretch each sound so you can clearly hear it.* [You may need to slowly collapse the word for children to connect the stretched sounds to a word they know.] *Listen: /nnn/ /āmmm/, /nnāmm/, /nām/. The word is* name. *Now it's your turn. Listen as I say /nnn/ /āmmm/,* name. *Now you try it with me: /nnn/ /āmmm/,* name. [Have children repeat.]

## GUIDED PRACTICE

Guide children to blend onset and rime to say the following words. First say the beginning and ending sounds separately. Then have children blend the sounds and say the whole word. All the sample words begin with continuous sounds for ease in blending. Use these and other word sets. Provide corrective feedback.

| | | |
|---|---|---|
| /r/ /ān/ (rain) | /f/ /un/ (fun) | /s/ /ēt/ (seat) |
| /z/ /o͞o/ (zoo) | /l/ /īk/ (like) | /s/ /ām/ (same) |

## APPLY

**Activity** Tell children you will say the name of someone in the room. Then say the name, segmenting onset and rime, for example: /M/ /īk/. Have children guess whose name you were thinking of and blend it together: /M/ /īk/, /Mīk/, *Mike*. Repeat with other names.

# Blend Onset and Rime

## TEACH/MODEL

**Introduce** Tell children that part of learning to read is learning to be a careful listener. Explain that today they will learn to listen carefully to the sounds in words. Tell them that today they will listen for the beginning and ending sounds of a word. Then they will string together, or blend, the beginning and ending sounds to say the whole word.

**Onset and Rime** Say: *When we listen to a word, we can listen for two parts, the beginning sound, and the ending sounds. The word* sheep *has the beginning sound /sh/ and the ending sounds /ēp/. Listen: /sh/ /ēp/.* [Have children repeat.] *When I say them together, I hear the word* sheep*: /sh/ /ēp/,* sheep. [Have children repeat.]

Model saying the onset and rime of the word *spoon*. Then blend the sounds, stretching them so children can hear each sound. Say the whole word.

> **Think Aloud** *Listen as I say the beginning and ending sounds of a word: /sp/ /ünnn/. Now I will blend the beginning and ending sounds to say the whole word. I will stretch each sound so you can clearly hear it.* [You may need to slowly collapse the word for children to connect the stretched sounds to a word they know.] *Listen: /sssp/ /ünnn/, /sspünn/, /sp/ /ün/,* /spün/. *The word is* spoon. *Now it's your turn. Listen as I say /sp/ /ünnn/,* spoon. *Now you try it with me: /sp/* /ünnn/, spoon. [Have children repeat.]

## GUIDED PRACTICE

Guide children to blend onset and rime to say the following words. First say the beginning and ending sounds separately. Then have children blend the sounds and say the whole word. Use these and other word sets. Provide corrective feedback.

| | | |
|---|---|---|
| /sh/ /ip/ (ship) | /g/ /ift/ (gift) | /st/ /uff/ (stuff) |
| /fl/ /ip/ (flip) | /l/ /ast/ (last) | /f/ /ûrst/ (first) |

## APPLY

**Activity** Hold open a picture book so children can see a page. Tell them you are thinking of something in the picture. Then say the name of the image in the picture that you are thinking of, segmenting onset and rime. For example: /g/ /ûrl/. Have children guess what you were thinking of and blend the word as you point to the picture of it. Have them blend /g/ /ûrl/, /gûrl/; /g/ /ûrl/, /gûrl/. Repeat with other pictures.

# Segment Onset and Rime

## TEACH/MODEL

**Introduce** Tell children that you will help them to break apart a word into beginning and ending sounds. This will help them to read and write words.

**Onset and Rime** Say: *When we listen to a word, we can listen for two parts, the beginning sound and the ending sounds. The word* man *has the beginning sound /mmm/ and the ending sounds /aaannn/. Listen:* man, */mmm/ /aaannn/.* [Have children repeat.] *When I break apart the word* man, *I hear /mmm/ /aaannn/,* man. [Have children repeat.]

Model segmenting a word into its onset and rime using the word *run*. Stretch the beginning sound and then the ending sounds to break the word into parts.

**Think Aloud** *Listen as I say the word* run, */rrruuunnn/.* [Hold each sound for three seconds so children can hear the individual sounds. Do not pause between sounds.] *I hear /rrr/ at the beginning of* run, *so /rrr/ must be the beginning sound. I hear /uuunnn/ at the end of* run. *Those must be the ending sounds, /uuunnn/. Listen carefully as I divide* run *into beginning and ending sounds: /rrruuunnn/, /rrr/ /uuunnn/, /rr/ /uunn/, /r/ /un/. Now you try it with me:* run, */rrruuunnn/, /rrr/ /uuunnn/, /rr/ /uunn/, /r/ /un/.* [Have children repeat.]

## GUIDED PRACTICE

Guide children to segment familiar words into their beginning and ending sounds. Use these and other word sets. Provide corrective feedback.

| | | |
|---|---|---|
| ride, /r/ /īd/ | pet, /p/ /et/ | cup, /k/ /up/ |
| big, /b/ /ig/ | fun, /f/ /un/ | meet, /m/ /ēt/ |

## APPLY

**Activity** Set up a mini store in your classroom using school supplies, small objects, or pictures from magazines. Have children come to the store to "buy" one item. In order to buy an item, they must segment the item's name. For example, a child might say, "I would like to buy a /p/ /en/." If the child correctly segments the word, he or she can purchase the item.

# Segment Onset and Rime

## TEACH/MODEL

**Introduce** Tell children that you will help them to break apart a word into beginning and ending sounds. This will help them to read and write words. Explain that sometimes you can find a new word in the ending sounds of a longer word. Say: *When we listen to a word, we can listen for two parts, the beginning sound and the ending sounds. The word* cough *has the beginning sound /k/ and the ending sounds /ooofff/. Listen: /k/ /ooofff/.* [Have children repeat.] *When I say the end part, I hear the word* off.

Model saying a word, segmenting the ending sounds, and identifying the familiar word. Begin by saying the word *farm.* Divide the word into its beginning and ending sounds. Then identify the new word created in the ending sounds.

> **Think Aloud** *Listen as I say the word* farm, */fffärrrmmm/.* [Hold each sound for three seconds so children can hear the individual sounds. Do not pause between sounds.] *I hear /fff/ at the beginning of* farm, *so /fff/ must be the beginning sound. I hear /ärrrmmm/ at the end of* farm, *so those must be the ending sounds, /ärrrmmm/. Now listen carefully as I divide* farm *into beginning and ending sounds: /fffärrrmmm/, /fff/ /ärrrmmm/, /ff/ /ärrmm/, /f/ /ärm/. When we take off the beginning sound, /fff/, we can hear the familiar word* arm *at the end of the word* farm. *Listen again:* farm, */fff/ /ärrrmmm/,* arm. *Now you try it with me:* farm, */fff/ /ärrrmmm/,* arm. [Have children repeat.]

## GUIDED PRACTICE

Guide children to practice saying a word, segmenting the ending sounds, and identifying the familiar word. Use these and other word sets. Provide corrective feedback.

| | | |
|---|---|---|
| land, /l/ /and/ (and) | weight, /w/ /āt/ (eight) | seat, /s/ /ēt/ (eat) |
| mask, /m/ /ask/, (ask) | fold, /f/ /ōld/ (old) | more, /m/ /ōr/ (oar) |

## APPLY

**Activity** Say aloud some words. Ask children to segment each word and identify the familiar word they hear in the ending sounds. Provide clues as in the following examples: *Find something you see with in the word* pie [/p/ /ī/, eye]; *Find something cold in the word* rice [/r/ /īs/, ice]; *Find a bird that hoots in the word* towel [/t/ /oul/, owl].

# Segment Onset and Rime

## TEACH/MODEL

**Introduce** Tell children that you will help them to break apart a word into beginning and ending sounds. This will help them to read and write words. Explain that sometimes you can find a new word in the ending sounds of a longer word. Say: *When we listen to a word, we can listen for two parts. Today we will listen for the beginning sounds and the ending sounds. The word* trace *has the beginning sounds /tr/ and the ending sounds /ās/. Listen: trace, /tr/ / ās/.* [Have children repeat.] *When I say the ending part, I hear the word* ace.

Model saying a word, segmenting the ending sounds, and identifying the familiar word. Begin by saying the word *steal.* Divide the word into its beginning sounds and ending sounds. Then identify the new word created in the ending sounds.

> **Think Aloud** *Listen as I say the word* steal, */ssstēl/.* [Stretch out or emphasize each sound so children can hear the individual sounds. Do not pause between sounds.] *What sounds do I hear at the beginning? I hear /st/. What sounds do I hear at the ending? I hear /ēl/. Now listen carefully as I divide* steal *into its beginning sounds and ending sounds: /st/ /ēl/, /st/ /ēl/. I can hear the familiar word* eel *at the ending of the word* steal *when I take off the beginning sounds, /st/. Listen again:* steal, */st/ /ēl/,* eel. *Now you try it with me:* steal, */st/ /ēl/,* eel. [Have children repeat.]

## GUIDED PRACTICE

Guide children to practice saying a word, segmenting the ending sounds, and identifying the familiar word. Use these and other word sets. Provide corrective feedback.

| | | |
|---|---|---|
| chin, /ch/ /in/, in | share, /sh/ /âr/, air | price, /pr/ /īs/, ice |
| chart, /ch/ /ärt/, art | shout, /sh/ /out/, out | fly, /fl/ /ī/, eye |

## APPLY

**Activity** Say aloud some words. Ask children to segment each word and identify the familiar word they hear at the end of it. Provide clues as in the following examples: *Find a jungle animal in the word* grape [/gr/ /āp/, ape]; *Find the last part of a book in the word* friend [/fr/ /end/, end]; *Find what you might say if you fell down in the word* groups [/gr/ /üps/, oops]; *Find something a pen needs in order to do its job in the word* think [/th/ /ink/, ink].

# Review

## PREPARING THE REVIEW

- Make one copy of **Practice Reproducible PA44** for each child.
- Write the child's name and today's date at the top of the review.

## ADMINISTERING THE REVIEW

- Administer the review to one child at a time.
- Follow these instructions for each item. Each phonemic awareness skill was taught in the lessons indicated in parentheses.

1. Tell children to listen as you say a word in syllables. They will blend the syllables to form a word and then draw a picture of the word. Then say: *rain|bow.* (Answer: *rainbow;* Lessons 34–37)
2. Tell children to listen as you say a word in syllables. They will blend the syllables to form a word and then draw a picture of the word. Then say: *um|brel|la.* (Answer: *umbrella;* Lessons 34–37)
3. Tell children to listen as you say the beginning and ending sounds of a word. They will put the sounds together to form a word and draw a picture of the word. Then say: /s/ /un/. (Answer: *sun;* Lessons 38–40)
4. Identify each picture: **bat, pan,** and **ice.** Then ask children to circle the picture that matches the *ending* sounds of the word *mice.* (Answer: *ice*; Lessons 41–43)
5. Identify each picture: **ant, egg,** and **leaf.** Then ask children to circle the picture that matches the *ending* sounds of the word *plant.* (Answer: *ant*; Lessons 41–43)

## SCORING THE REVIEW

- Total the number of items answered correctly.
- Use the Percentage Table below to identify a percentage. Children should get at least 80 percent correct.
- Analyze each child's errors, using the lesson numbers provided above.
- Reteach those skills for which the child did not answer an item correctly.

| Percentage Table | | | |
|---|---|---|---|
| **5 correct** | 100% | **2 correct** | 40% |
| **4 correct** | 80% | **1 correct** | 20% |
| **3 correct** | 60% | **0 correct** | 0% |

Name ______________________ Date __________



# Phonemic Awareness Review

| |
|---|
| I. |
| 2. |
| 3. |
| 4.    |
| 5.    |

# Phoneme Identity: Medial Sounds (Long Vowels)

## TEACH/MODEL

**Introduce** Explain that you will help children listen for and compare the middle sound in words. Say: *The words* side *and* time *have the same middle sound: /ī/. Listen:* [Stretch out the middle sound] */s/ /ī/ /d/,* side*; /t/ /ī/ /m/,* time. [Have children repeat.] *The words* side *and* make *do not have the same middle sound. Listen:* [Stretch out the middle sound] */s/ /ī / /d/,* side; */m/ /ā/ /k/,* make. [Have children repeat.] Side *and* make *have different middle sounds: /ī/ and /ā/.* Distribute **Sound Boxes** to each child. Then model identifying the middle sound in three words and identifying the two words that have the same middle sound.

> **Think Aloud** *Listen as I say a word sound by sound. For each sound I say I will put down one counter: /n/ /ā / /m/. Now it's your turn. Say* name *with me and put down one counter for each sound you hear: /n/ /ā/ /m/.* [Check that each child has put down three counters.] *This time, listen for the sound you hear in the middle of the word* name: */n/ /ā/ /m/.* [Stretch out the middle sound.] *The middle sound is /ā/. Now I am going to say three words: /n/ /ā/ /m/,* name; */s/ /ā/ /l/,* sale; *and /r/ /ō/ /z/,* rose. [Have children repeat.] *Which of these words have the same middle sound?* Name *and* sale *do.* Rose *has a different middle sound, /ō/.*

## GUIDED PRACTICE

Have children practice identifying which word pairs have the same middle sound. Say the following words, one set at a time. Stretch out each middle sound. Have children use counters to represent individual sounds. Provide corrective feedback.

| | | |
|---|---|---|
| cube, vase, page | huge, reach, cute | white, same, life |
| home, need, phone | vote, team, week | bone, joke, dime |

## APPLY

**Practice Reproducible** Have children complete **Practice Reproducible PA45.** Say the name of each picture, clearly pronouncing each sound: (1. moon, lake, whale 2. soap, tube, coat 3. jeep, read, cube 4. bike, leash, vine). Have children repeat. Tell children to stretch the middle sound in each word when deciding which two words have the same middle sound, for example /m/ /ü/ /n/, *moon.* Then have them circle the two pictures in each row whose names have the same middle sound.

**Answer Key: 1.** *lake, whale* **2.** *soap, coat* **3.** *jeep, read* **4.** *bike, vine*

# Middle Sounds

**Say the name of each picture. Circle the two pictures in each row whose names have the same middle sound.**

**1.**

**2.**

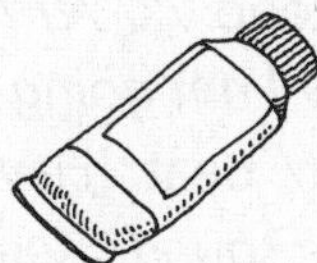

**3.**

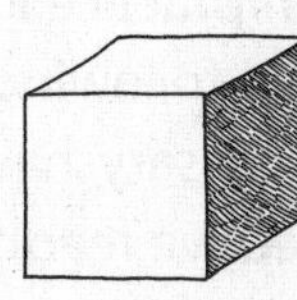

**4.**

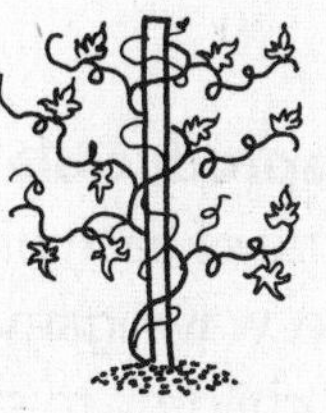

# Phoneme Identity: Medial Sounds (Long Vowels)

## TEACH/MODEL

**Introduce** Explain that you will help children listen for and compare the middle sound in words. Say: *The words* hope *and* joke *have the same middle sound, /ō/. Listen:* [Stretch out the middle sound] */h/ /ō / /p/,* hope; */j/ /ō/ /k/,* joke. [Have children repeat.] *The words* hope *and* rule *do not have the same middle sound. Listen:* [Stretch out the middle sound] */h/ /ō/ /p/,* hope; */r/ /ü/ /l/,* rule. [Have children repeat.] *The words* hope *and* rule *have different middle sounds: /ō/ and /ü/.*

Distribute **Sound Boxes** to each child. Then model identifying the middle sound in three words and identifying the two words that have the same middle sound.

> **Think Aloud** *Listen as I say a word sound by sound. For each sound I say, I will put down one counter: /k/ /ē/ /p/. Now it's your turn. Say the word* keep *with me and put down one counter for each sound you hear: /k/ /ē/ /p/.* [Check that each child has put down three counters.] *This time, listen for the sound you hear in the middle of the word* keep*: /k/ /ē/ /p/.* [Stretch out the middle sound.] *The middle sound is /ē/. Now I am going to say three words: /k/ /ē/ /p/,* keep; */sh/ /ī/ /n/,* shine; *and /b/ /ē/ /t/,* beat. [Have children repeat.] *Which of these words have the same middle sound?* Keep *and* beat *do.* Shine *has a different middle sound, /ī/.*

## GUIDED PRACTICE

Have children practice identifying which word pairs have the same middle sound. Say the following words, one set at a time. Stretch out each middle sound. As necessary, have children use counters to represent individual sounds. Provide corrective feedback.

| | | |
|---|---|---|
| teach, fade, mean | size, wait, cave | beak, nice, teeth |
| fuse, cute, weed | mice, line, rude | code, loaf, tame |

## APPLY

**Practice Reproducible** Have children complete **Practice Reproducible PA46.** Say the name of each picture, clearly pronouncing each sound: (1. hose, rope, bike 2. cone, wave, game 3. face, leaf, feet 4. mule, boat, cube). Have children repeat. Tell children to stretch the middle sound in each word when deciding which two words have the same middle sound, for example /h/ /ō/ /z/, *hose.* Then have them circle the two pictures in each row whose names have the same middle sound.

**Answer Key: 1.** *hose, rope* **2.** *wave, game* **3.** *leaf, feet* **4.** *mule, cube*

Name ______________________ Date ________

Practice Reproducible PA46

# Middle Sounds

**Say the name of each picture. Circle the two pictures in each row whose names have the same middle sound.**

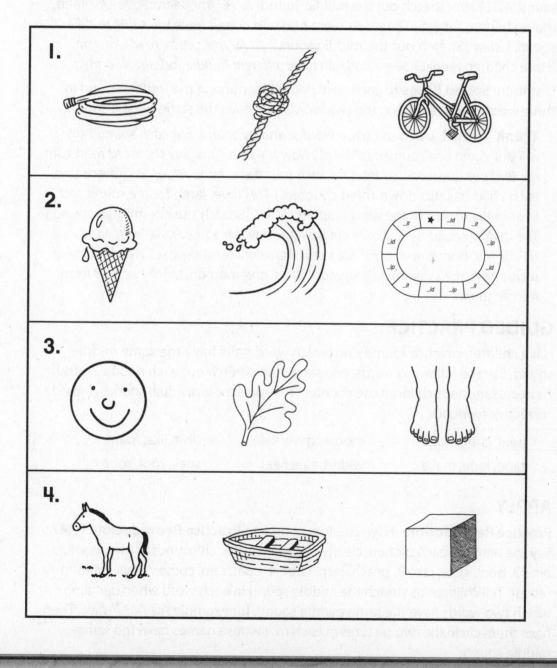

**1.**

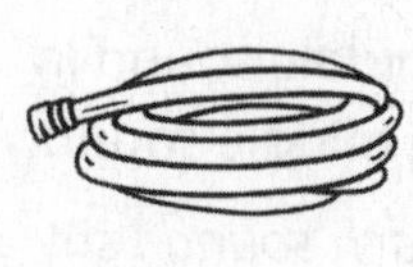  

**2.**

  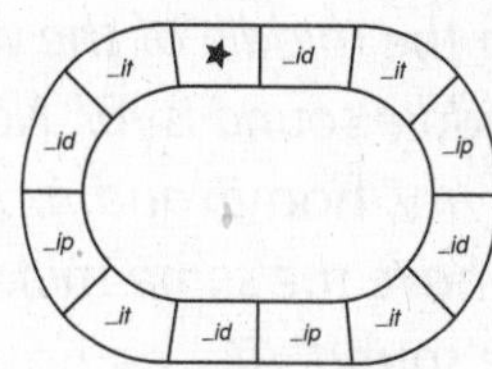


**3.**

 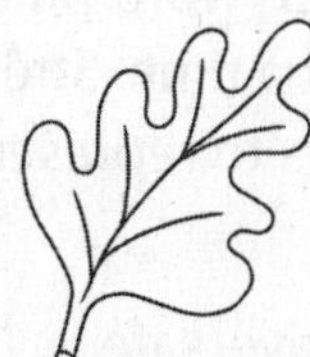 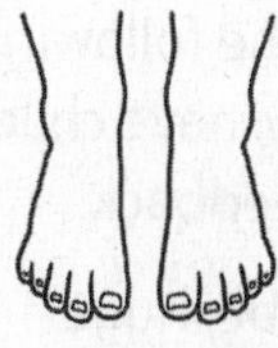

**4.**

  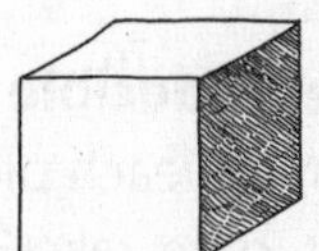

# Phoneme Identity: Medial Sounds (Long Vowels)

## TEACH/MODEL

**Introduce** Explain that you will help children listen for and compare the middle sound in words. Say: *The words* seem *and* feed *have the same middle sound, /ē/. Listen:* [Stretch out the middle sound] */s/ /ē/ /m/,* seem; */f/ /ē / /d/,* feed. [Have children repeat.] *The words* seem *and* rain *do not have the same middle sound. Listen:* [Stretch out the middle sound] */s/ /ē/ /m/,* seem; */r/ /ā/ /n/,* rain. [Have children repeat.] *Seem and* rain *have different middle sounds: /ē/ and /ā/.*

Distribute **Sound Boxes** to each child. Model identifying the middle sound in three words and identifying the two words that have the same middle sound.

> **Think Aloud** *Listen as I say a word sound by sound. For each sound I say, I will put down one counter: /r/ /ō/ /d/. Now it's your turn. Say the word* road *with me and put down one counter for each sound you hear: /r/ /ō/ /d/.* [Check that each child has put down three counters.] *This time, listen for the sound you hear in the middle of the word road: /r/ /ō/ /d/.* [Stretch out the middle sound.] *The middle sound is /ō/. Now I am going to say three words: /l/ /ī/ /t/,* light; */h/ /ō/ /m/,* home*; and /r/ /ō/ /d/,* road. [Have children repeat.] *Which of these words have the same middle sound?* Home *and* road *do.* Light *has a different middle sound, /ī/.*

## GUIDED PRACTICE

Have children practice identifying which word pairs have the same middle sound. Say the following words, one set a time. Stretch out each middle sound. As necessary, have children use counters to represent individual sounds. Provide corrective feedback.

| | | |
|---|---|---|
| peel, cube, huge | moose, gave, safe | dive, like, foam |
| tape, hide, make | wide, bean, heel | soak, root, robe |

## APPLY

**Practice Reproducible** Have children complete **Practice Reproducible PA47.** Say the name of each picture, clearly pronouncing each sound: (1. hive, hook, nine 2. boot, gate, rake 3. peach, jeep, cube 4. boat, rain, comb). Have children repeat. Tell children to stretch the middle sound in each word when deciding which two words have the same middle sound, for example /h/ /ī/ /v/, *hive*. Then have them circle the two pictures in each row whose names have the same middle sound.

**Answer Key: 1.** *hive, nine* **2.** *gate, rake* **3.** *peach, jeep* **4.** *boat, comb*

Name ______________________ Date __________

Practice Reproducible PA47

# Middle Sounds

**Say the name of each picture. Circle the two pictures in each row whose names have the same middle sound.**

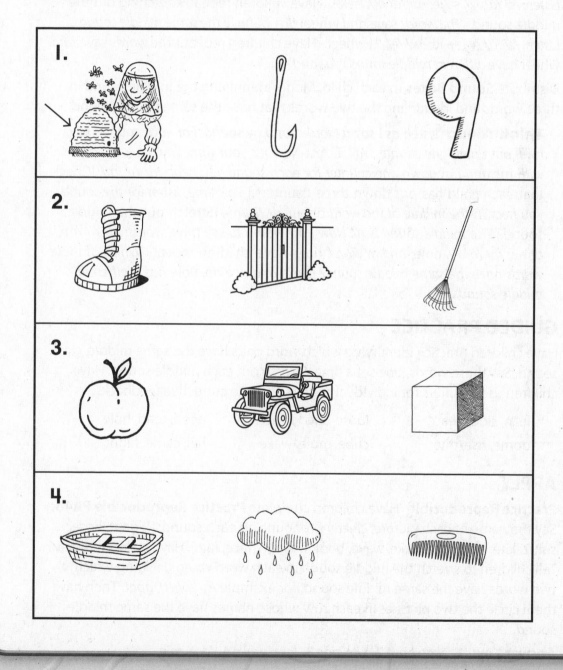

**1.**

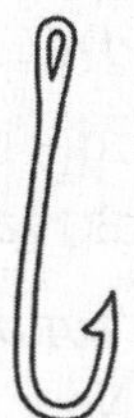

**2.**

**3.**

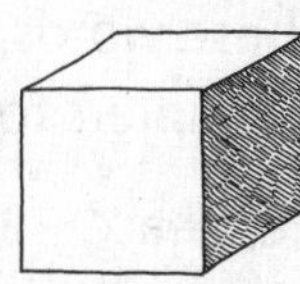

**4.**

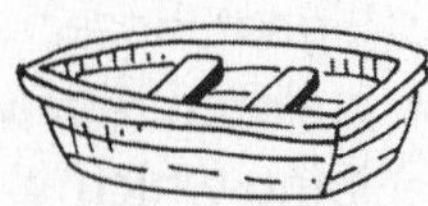

LESSON
48
Phonemic Awareness

# Phoneme Identity: Medial Sounds (Long Vowels)

## TEACH/MODEL

**Introduce** Explain that you will help children listen for and compare the middle sound in words. Say: *The words* save *and* bake *have the same middle sound, /ā/. Listen: /s/ /ā/ /v/,* save; */b/ /ā/ /k/,* bake. [Have children repeat, stretching out the middle sound.] *The words* save *and* wheel *do not have the same middle sound. Listen: /s/ /ā/ /v/,* save; */w/ /ē/ /l/,* wheel. [Have children repeat.] *The words* save *and* wheel *have different middle sounds: /ā/ and /ē/.*

Distribute **Sound Boxes** to each child. Model identifying the middle sound in three words and identifying the two words that have the same middle sound.

> **Think Aloud** *Listen as I say a word sound by sound. For each sound I say, I will put down one counter: /d/ /ī/ /m/. Now it's your turn. Say the word* dime *with me and put down one counter for each sound you hear: /d/ /ī/ /m/.* [Check that each child has put down three counters.] *This time, listen for the sound you hear in the middle of the word* dime: */d/ /ī/ /m/.* [Stretch out the middle sound.] *The middle sound is /ī/. Now I am going to say three words: /d/ /ī/ /m/,* dime; */p/ /ō/ /l/,* pole; *and /r/ /ī/ /s/,* rice. [Have children repeat.] *Which of these words have the same middle sound?* Dime *and* rice *do.* Pole *has a different middle sound, /ō/.*

## GUIDED PRACTICE

Have children practice identifying which word pairs have the same middle sound. Say these words, one set a time. Stretch out each middle sound. Have children use counters for individual sounds. Provide corrective feedback.

| | | |
|---|---|---|
| lean, side, peace | loose, shade, face | need, toad, hole |
| dome, rise, bite | cube, mule, wake | rail, came, night |

## APPLY

**Practice Reproducible** Have children complete **Practice Reproducible PA48.** Say the name of each picture, clearly pronouncing each sound: (1. goat, hose, suit 2. kite, leaf, ride 3. lake, wave, boot 4. moon, face, rain). Have children repeat. Tell children to stretch the middle sound in each word when deciding which two words have the same middle sound, for example /g/ /ō/ /t/, *goat*. Then have them circle the two pictures in each row whose names have the same middle sound.

**Answer Key: 1.** *goat, hose* **2.** *kite, ride* **3.** *lake, wave* **4.** *face, rain*

Name ______________________ Date __________

Practice Reproducible PA48

## Middle Sounds

**Say the name of each picture. Circle the two pictures in each row whose names have the same middle sound.**

1.

 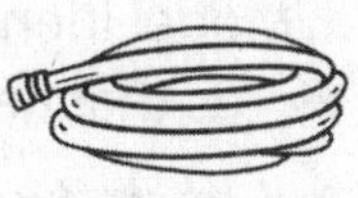 

2.

 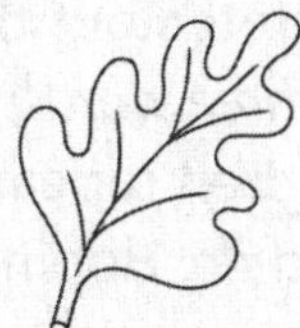 

3.

4.

# Phoneme Identity: Medial Sounds (Short Vowels)

## TEACH/MODEL

**Introduce** Explain that you will help children listen for and compare the middle sound in words. Say: *The words* not *and* job *have the same middle sound, /o/. Listen:* [Stretch out the middle sound] */n/ /ooo/ /t/, not; /j/ /ooo/ /b/,* job. [Have children repeat.] *The words* not *and* cap *do not have the same middle sound. Listen*: [Stretch out the middle sound] */n/ /ooo/ /t/,* not; */k/ /aaa/ /p/,* cap. [Have children repeat.] *The words* not *and* cap *have different middle sounds: /o/ and /a/.*

Distribute **Sound Boxes** to each child. Model identifying the middle sound in three words and identifying the two words that have the same middle sound.

> **Think Aloud** *Listen as I say a word sound by sound. For each sound I say, I will put down one counter: /w/ /e/ /t/. Now it's your turn. Say* wet *with me and put down one counter for each sound you hear: /w/ /e/ /t/.* [Check that each child has put down three counters.] *This time, listen for the sound you hear in the middle of* wet*: /w/ /eee/ /t/.* [Stretch out the middle sound.] *The middle sound is /e/. Now I am going to say three words: /h/ /ooo/ /p/,* hop; */w/ /eee/ /t/,* wet; *and /r/ /eee/ /d/,* red. [Have children repeat.] *Which of these words have the same middle sound?* Wet *and* red *do.* Hop *has a different middle sound, /o/.*

## GUIDED PRACTICE

Have children practice identifying which word pairs have the same middle sound. Say the following words, one set at a time. Stretch out each middle sound. As necessary, have children use counters to represent individual sounds. Provide corrective feedback.

| | | |
|---|---|---|
| dig, pan, mitt | hat, jam, lip | fun, will, bus |
| gum, cut, win | leg, cot, shop | sell, yet, knock |

## APPLY

**Practice Reproducible** Have children complete **Practice Reproducible PA49.** Say the name of each picture, clearly pronouncing each sound: (1. man, cup, bag 2. sock, web, ten 3. sun, bat, rug 4. wig, mop, lock). Have children repeat. Tell children to stretch the middle sound in each word when deciding which two words have the same middle sound, for example /m/ /aaa/ /n/, *man*. Have them circle the two pictures in each row whose names have the same middle sound.

**Answer Key: 1.** *man, bag* **2.** *web, ten* **3.** *sun, rug* **4.** *mop, lock*

Name ______________________ Date ________

Practice Reproducible PA49

# Middle Sounds

**Say the name of each picture. Circle the two pictures in each row whose names have the same middle sound.**

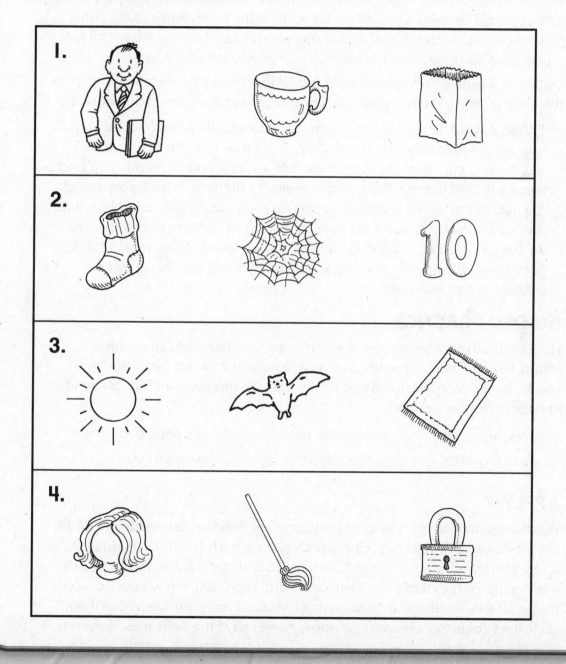

**1.**

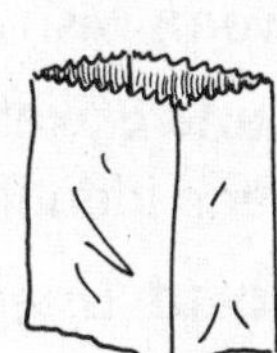

**2.**

**3.**

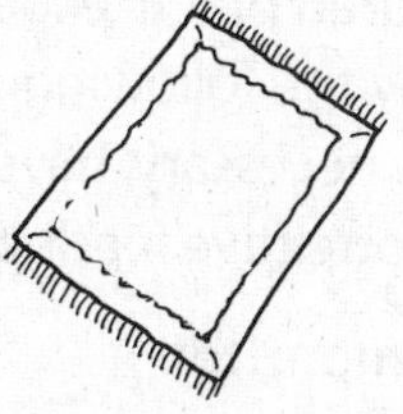

**4.**

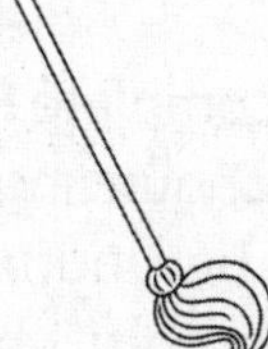

# Phoneme Identity: Medial Sounds (Short Vowels)

## TEACH/MODEL

**Introduce** Explain that you will help children listen for and compare the middle sound in words. Say: *The words* wish *and* dip *have the same middle sound, /i/. Listen:* [Stretch out the middle sound] */w/ /iii/ /sh/,* wish; */d/ /iii/ /p/,* dip. [Have children repeat.] *The words* wish *and* run *do not have the same middle sound. Listen:* [Stretch out the middle sound] */w/ /iii/ /sh/,* wish; */r/ /uuu/ /n/,* run. [Have children repeat.] *The words* wish *and* run *have different middle sounds: /i/ and /u/.*

Distribute **Sound Boxes** to each child. Model identifying the middle sound in three words, and identifying the two words that have the same middle sound.

> **Think Aloud** *Listen as I say a word sound by sound. For each sound I say, I will put down one counter: /b/ /a/ /k/. Now it's your turn. Say the word* back *with me and put down one counter for each sound you hear: /b/ /a/ /k/.* [Check that each child has put down three counters.] *This time, listen for the sound you hear in the middle of the word* back: */b/ /aaa/ /k/.* [Stretch out the middle sound.] *The middle sound is /a/. Now I am going to say three words: /b/ /aaa/ /k/,* back; */l/ /eee/ /t/,* let; *and /g/ /aaa/ /s/,* gas. [Have children repeat.] *Which of these words have the same middle sound?* Back *and* gas *do.* Let *has a different middle sound, /e/.*

## GUIDED PRACTICE

Have children practice identifying which word pairs have the same middle sound. Say the following words, one set at a time. Stretch out each middle sound. As necessary, have children use counters to represent individual sounds. Provide corrective feedback.

| | | |
|---|---|---|
| met, mom, top | cap, hug, mud | vet, dock, bed |
| fuzz, big, dish | tack, fan, miss | hum, sit, cub |

## APPLY

**Practice Reproducible** Have children complete **Practice Reproducible PA50.** Say the name of each picture, clearly pronouncing each sound: (1. ham, fish, bib 2. leg, van, map 3. duck, tub, pot 4. pen, bed, nut). Have children repeat. Tell children to stretch the middle sound in each word when deciding which two words have the same middle sound, for example /h/ /aaa/ /m/, *ham*. Then have them circle the two pictures in each row whose names have the same middle sound.

**Answer Key:** **1.** *fish, bib* **2.** *van, map* **3.** *duck, tub* **4.** *pen, bed*

Name ______________________ Date __________



# Middle Sounds

**Say the name of each picture. Circle the two pictures in each row whose names have the same middle sound.**

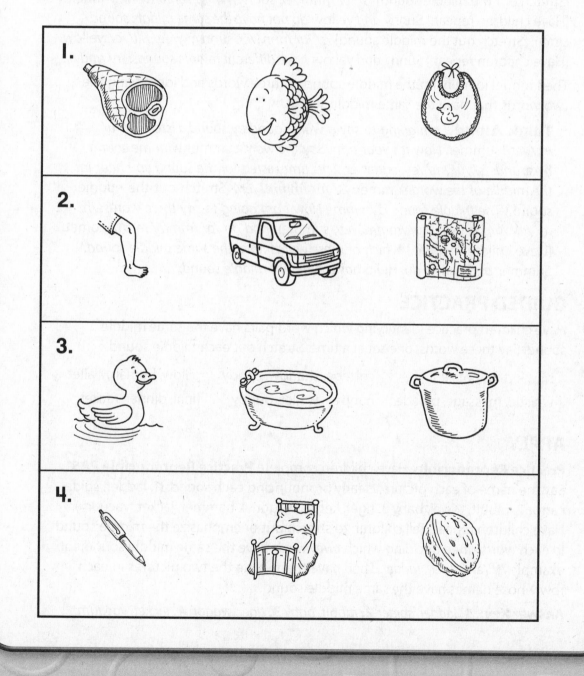

**1.**

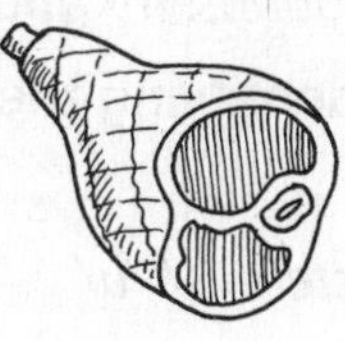

**2.**

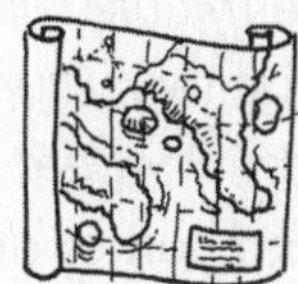

**3.**

**4.**

# Phoneme Identity: Medial Sounds (Consonants)

## TEACH/MODEL

**Introduce** Explain that you will help children listen for and compare the middle sound in words. Say: Sunny *and* winner *have the same middle sound, /n/. Listen:* [Stretch out the middle sound] */s/ /u/ /nnn/ /ē/,* sunny; */w/ /i/ /nnn/ /ə/ /r/,* winner. [Have children repeat.] Sunny *and* yellow *do not have the same middle sound. Listen:* [Stretch out the middle sound] */s/ /u/ /nnn/ /ē/,* sunny; */y/ /e/ /lll/ /ō/,* yellow. [Have children repeat.] *Sunny and* yellow *have different middle sounds: /n/ and /l/.*

Then model identifying the middle sound in three words and identifying the two words that have the same middle sound.

> **Think Aloud** *I am going to say a word sound by sound. Listen: /s/ /u/ /m/ /er/,* summer. *Now it's your turn. Say the word* summer *with me sound by sound: /s/ /u/ /m/ /er/,* summer. *This time, listen for the sound you hear in the middle of the word* summer: */s/ /u/ /mmm/ /er/.* [Stretch out the middle sound.] *The middle sound is /mmm/. Now I am going to say three words: /h/ /e/ /lll/ /ō/,* hello; */s/ /u/ /mmm/ /er/,* summer; *and /k/ /o/ /mmm/ /e/ /t/,* comet. [Have children repeat.] *Which of these words have the same middle sound?* Summer *and* comet *do.* Hello *has a different middle sound, /l/.*

## GUIDED PRACTICE

Have children practice identifying which word pairs have the same middle sound. Say these words, one set at a time. Stretch out each middle sound.

| | | |
|---|---|---|
| silly, kitten, notice | cottage, shadow, daddy | pillow, human, ballet |
| whistle, message, parade | happen, wallet, guppy | final, dinner, racket |

## APPLY

**Practice Reproducible** Have children complete **Practice Reproducible PA51.** Say the name of each picture, clearly pronouncing each sound: (1. ladder, spider, carrot 2. rabbit, towel, baby 3. tiger, kettle, wagon 4. hammer, jacket, vacuum). Have children repeat. Tell children to stretch out or emphasize the middle sound in each word when deciding which two words have the same middle sound, for example /l/ /a/ /d/ /er/, *ladder.* Then have them circle the two pictures in each row whose names have the same middle sound.

**Answer Key: 1.** *ladder, spider* **2.** *rabbit, baby* **3.** *tiger, wagon* **4.** *jacket, vacuum*

# Middle Sounds

**Say the name of each picture. Circle the two pictures in each row whose names have the same middle sound.**

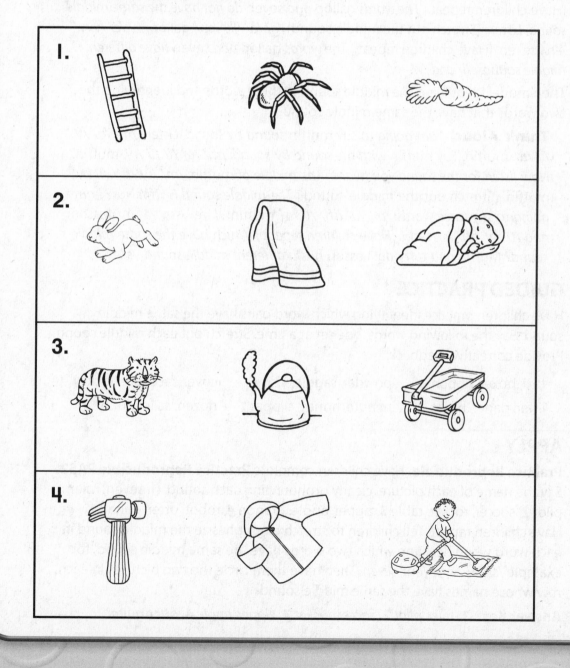

| | | | |
|---|---|---|---|
| **1.** | 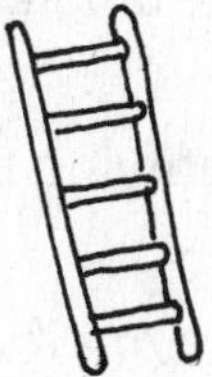 |  |  |
| **2.** |  | 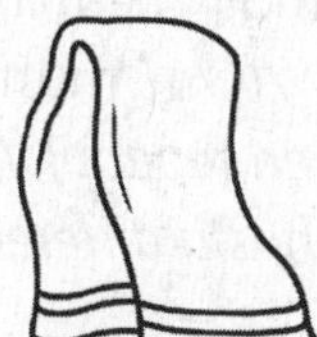 | 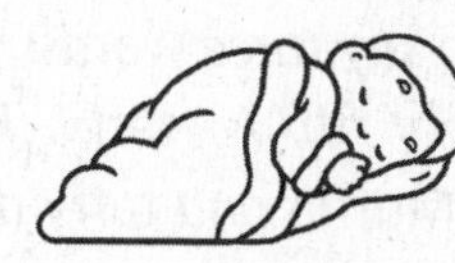 |
| **3.** |  |  |  |
| **4.** |  | 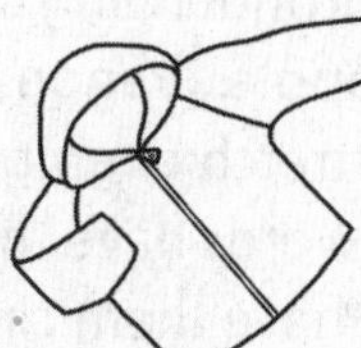 |  |

# Phoneme Identity: Medial Sounds (Consonants)

## TEACH/MODEL

**Introduce** Explain that you will help children listen for and compare the middle sound in words. Say: *The words* gallop *and* jolly *have the same middle sound, /lll/. Listen:* [Stretch out the middle sound] */g/ /a/ /lll/ /ep/,* gallop; */j/ /o/ /lll/ /ē/,* jolly. [Have children repeat.] *The words* gallop *and* seven *do not have the same middle sound. Listen:* [Stretch out the middle sound] */g/ /a/ /lll/ /ep/,* gallop; */s/ /e/ /vvv/ /en/,* seven. [Have children repeat.] *The words* gallop *and* seven *have different middle sounds: /l/ and /v/.*

Then model identifying the middle sound in three words and identifying the two words that have the same middle sound.

> **Think Aloud** *I am going to say* muffin *sound by sound. Listen: /m/ /u/ /f/ /i/ /n/,* muffin. *Say* muffin *with me sound by sound: /m/ /u/ /f/ /i/ /n/,* muffin. *Now listen for the sound you hear in the middle of* muffin*: /m/ /u/ /fff/ /i/ /n/,* muffin. [Stretch out the middle sound.] *The middle sound is /fff/. Now I am going to say three words: /m/ /u/ /fff/ /i/ /n/,* muffin; */l/ /e/ /sss/ /ə/ /n/,* lesson; *and /t/ /a/ /fff/ /ē/,* taffy. *[Have children repeat.] Which have the same middle sound?* Muffin *and* taffy *do.* Lesson *has a different middle sound, /s/.*

## GUIDED PRACTICE

Have children practice identifying which word pairs have the same middle sound. Say the following words, one set at a time. Stretch out each middle sound. Provide corrective feedback.

| | | |
|---|---|---|
| taxi, boxer, ribbon | powder, saddle, visit | cover, raccoon, hockey |
| litter, paper, hippo | minute, honey, slipper | dozen, sailor, fuzzy |

## APPLY

**Practice Reproducible** Have children complete **Practice Reproducible PA52.** Say the name of each picture, clearly pronouncing each sound: (1. seven, ruler, pilot 2. soccer, rocket, table 3. zipper, apple, dragon 4. robot, otter, guitar). Have children repeat. Tell children to stretch or emphasize the middle sound in each word when deciding which two words have the same middle sound, for example /s/ /e/ /vvv/ /en/, *seven*. Then have them circle the two pictures in each row whose names have the same middle sound.

**Answer Key: 1.** *ruler, pilot* **2.** *soccer, rocket* **3.** *zipper, apple* **4.** *otter, guitar*

Name ______________________ Date __________



## Middle Sounds

**Look at each picture. Circle the two pictures in each row whose names have the same middle sound.**

**1.**

**2.**

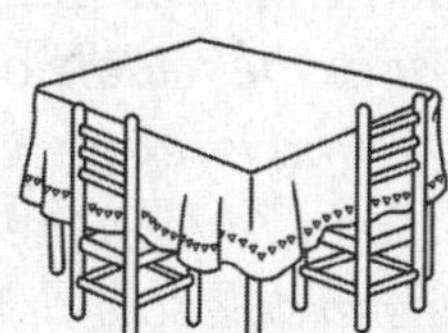

**3.**

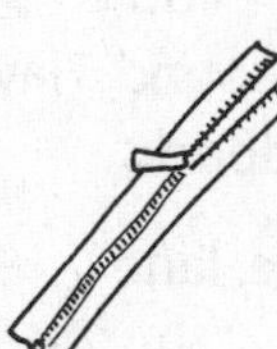

**4.**

LESSON
53
Phonemic Awareness

# Phoneme Categorization: Medial Sounds (Oddity Task)

## TEACH/MODEL

**Introduce** Explain that you will help children listen for and compare the middle sound in words. Say: *The words* late *and* cake *have the same middle sound, /ā /. Listen:* [Emphasize the middle sound] */l/ /ā / /t/,* late*; /k/ /ā/ /k/,* cake. [Have children repeat, stretching out the middle sound.] *The words* late *and* mice *do not have the same middle sound. Listen:* [Emphasize the middle sound] */l/ /ā/ /t/, late; /m/ /ī/ /s/,* mice. [Have children repeat.] *The words* late *and* mice *have different middle sounds: /ā/ and /ī/.*

Distribute **Sound Boxes.** Model identifying the middle sound in three words and identifying the word that does not have the same middle sound.

> **Think Aloud** *Listen as I say a word sound by sound. For each sound I say, I will put down one counter: /f/ /ē/ /t/. Now it's your turn. Say the word* feet *with me and put down one counter for each sound you hear. /f/ /ē/ /t/.* [Check that each child has put down three counters.] *This time, listen for the sound you hear in the middle of* feet*: /f/ /ē/ /t/.* [Stretch out the middle sound.] *The middle sound is /ē/. Now I am going to say three words: /g/ /ō/ /l/,* goal*; /f/ /ē/ /t/,* feet*; and /r/ /ē/ /l/,* real. [Have children repeat.] *Which of these words have the same middle sound?* Feet *and* real *do.* Goal *has a different middle sound, /ō/.*

## GUIDED PRACTICE

Have children practice identifying which word pairs have the same middle sound. Say these words, one set at a time. Stretch out each middle sound. Have children use counters for individual sounds. Provide corrective feedback.

| | | |
|---|---|---|
| wise, nine, mail | beach, fine, need | chase, rude, lane |
| queen, soak, toad | name, page, goat | mule, pile, cute |

## APPLY

**Practice Reproducible** Have children complete **Practice Reproducible PA53.** Say the name of each picture, clearly pronouncing each sound: (1. coat, bike, soap 2. cube, whale, face 3. vine, kite, read 4. queen, peach, comb). Have children repeat. Tell children to stretch the middle sound in each word when deciding which word does not have the same middle sound, for example /k/ /ō/ /t/, *coat.* Then have them circle the picture in each row whose name does **not** have the same middle sound as the others.

**Answer Key: 1.** *bike* **2.** *cube* **3.** *read* **4.** *comb*

# Middle Sounds

**Say the name of each picture. Circle the picture in each row whose name does NOT have the same middle sound as the others.**

1.

2.

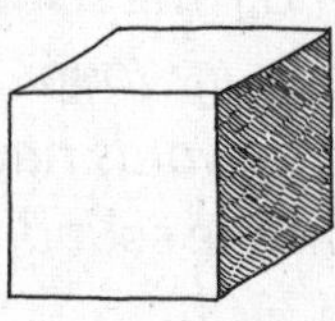

3.

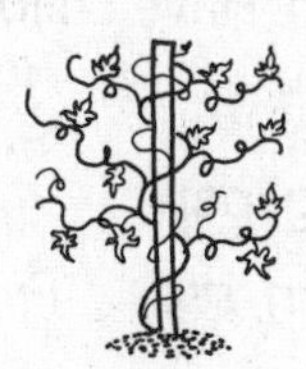

4.

# Phoneme Categorization: Medial Sounds (Oddity Task)

## TEACH/MODEL

**Introduce** Explain that you will help children listen for and compare the middle sound in words. Say: *The words* hum *and* sub *have the same middle sound, /u/. Listen:* [Stretch out the middle sound] */h/ /uuu/ /m/,* hum; */s/ /uuu/ /b/,* sub. [Have children repeat.] *The words* hum *and* fix *do not have the same middle sound. Listen: /h/ /uuu/ /m/,* hum; */f/ /iii/ /ks/,* fix. [Have children repeat.] *The words* hum *and* fix *have different middle sounds: /u/ and /i/.*

Distribute **Sound Boxes.** Model identifying the middle sound in three words and identifying the word that does not have the same middle sound.

> **Think Aloud** *Listen as I say a word sound by sound. For each sound I say, I will put down one counter: /r/ /o/ /k/. Now it's your turn. Say* rock *with me and put down one counter for each sound you hear. /r/ /o/ /k/.* [Check that each child has put down three counters.] *This time, listen for the sound you hear in the middle of* rock*: /r/ /ooo/ /k/.* [Stretch out the middle sound.] *The middle sound is /o/. Now I am going to say three words: /r/ /ooo/ /k/,* rock*; /g/ /ooo/ /t/,* got*; and /h/ /eee/ /n/,* hen. [Have children repeat.] *Which of these words have the same middle sound?* Rock *and* got *do.* Hen *has a different middle sound, /e/.*

## GUIDED PRACTICE

Have children practice identifying which word pairs have the same middle sound. Say these, one set at a time. Stretch out each middle sound. Have children use counters for individual sounds. Provide corrective feedback.

| | | |
|---|---|---|
| buzz, tell, mug | hop, nod, quack | laugh, jug, pan |
| win, sad, dig | jet, pen, kick | chop, men, set |

## APPLY

**Practice Reproducible** Have children complete **Practice Reproducible PA54.** Say the name of each picture, clearly pronouncing each sound: (1. log, net, bed 2. bug, hat, duck 3. fish, cat, pan 4. mitt, pig, bus). Have children repeat. Tell children to stretch the middle sound in each word when deciding which word does not have the same middle sound, for example /l/ /ooo/ /g/, *log*. Then have them circle the picture in each row whose name does **not** have the same middle sound as the others.

**Answer Key: 1.** *log* **2.** *hat* **3.** *fish* **4.** *bus*

Name ______________________ Date __________



# Middle Sounds

**Say the name of each picture. Circle the picture in each row whose name does NOT have the same middle sound as the others.**

**1.**

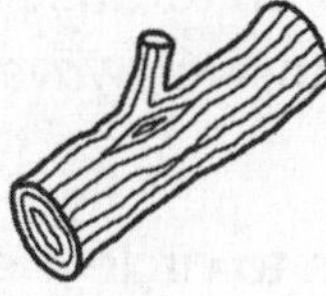

**2.**

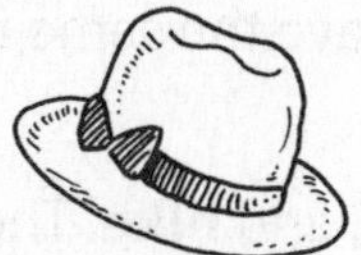

**3.**

**4.**

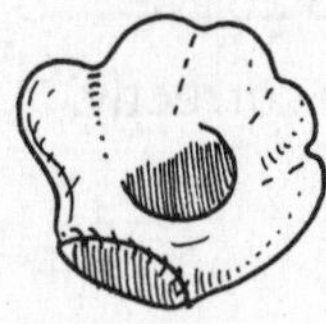

# Review

## PREPARING THE REVIEW

- Make one copy of **Practice Reproducible PA55** for each child.
- Write the child's name and today's date at the top of the review.

## ADMINISTERING THE REVIEW

- Administer the review to one child at a time.
- Follow these instructions for each item. Each phonemic awareness skill was taught in the lesson or lessons indicated in parentheses.

1. Identify each picture: **rope, wave,** and **gate.** Then ask children to circle the two pictures whose names have the same middle sound. (Answer: *wave, gate;* Lessons 45–48)
2. Identify each picture: **dog, fan,** and **mop.** Then ask children to circle the two pictures whose names have the same middle sound. (Answer: *dog, mop;* Lessons 49–50)
3. Identify each picture: **dragon, seven,** and **tiger.** Then ask children to circle the two pictures whose names have the same middle sound. (Answer: *dragon, tiger;* Lessons 51–52)
4. Identify each picture: **nine, goat,** and **bike.** Then ask children to circle the picture whose name does **not** have the same middle sound. (Answer: *goat;* Lesson 53)
5. Identify each picture: **pen, web,** and **van.** Then ask children to circle the picture whose name does **not** have the same middle sound. (Answer: *van;* Lesson 54)

## SCORING THE REVIEW

- Total the number of items answered correctly.
- Use the Percentage Table below to identify a percentage. Children should get at least 80 percent correct.
- Analyze each child's errors, using the lesson numbers provided above.
- Reteach those skills for which the child did not answer an item correctly.

| Percentage Table | | | |
|---|---|---|---|
| **5 correct** | 100% | **2 correct** | 40% |
| **4 correct** | 80% | **1 correct** | 20% |
| **3 correct** | 60% | **0 correct** | 0% |

# Phonemic Awareness Review

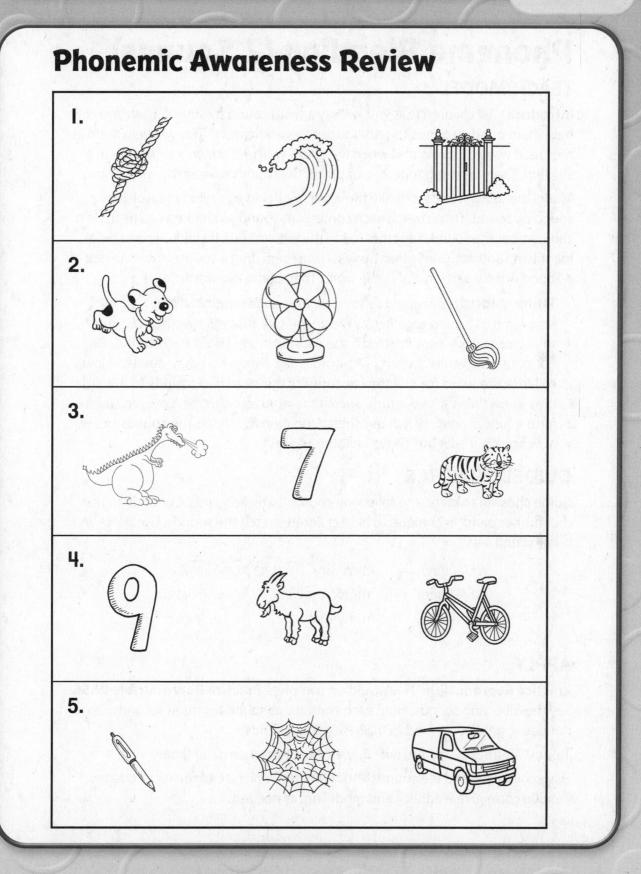

| | | | |
|---|---|---|---|
| 1. | 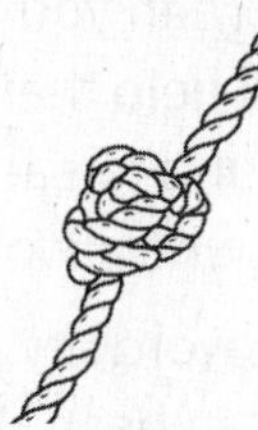 | 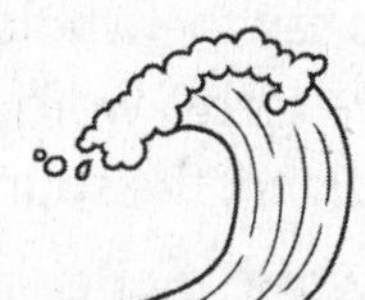 | 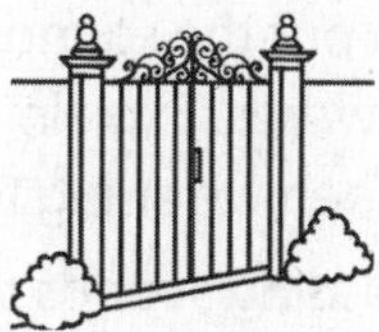 |
| 2. | 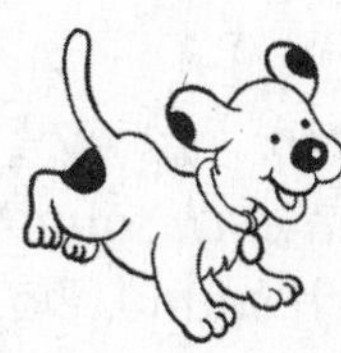 | 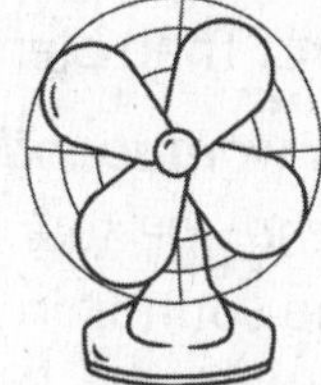 | 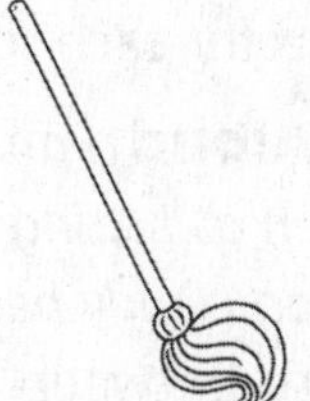 |
| 3. | 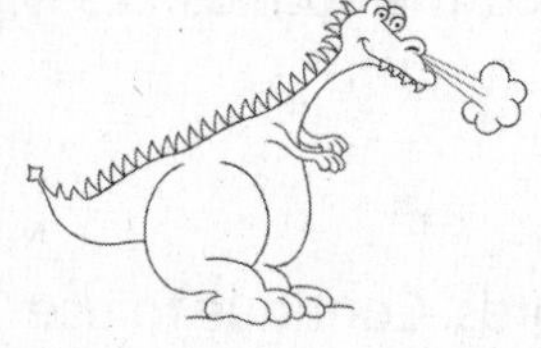 | 7 | 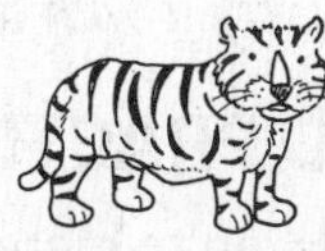 |
| 4. | 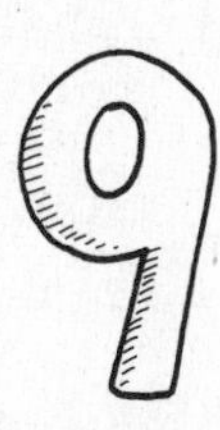 | 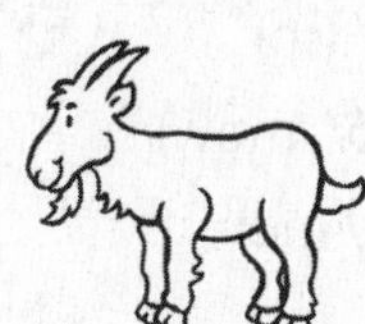 | 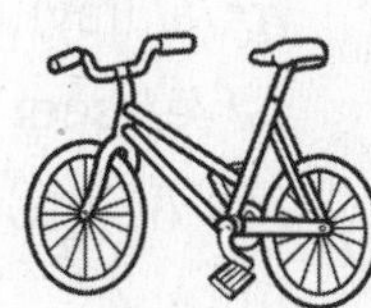 |
| 5. | 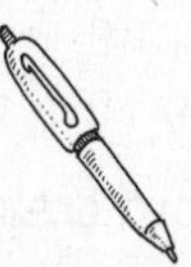 | 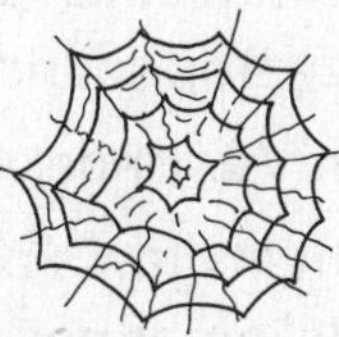 | 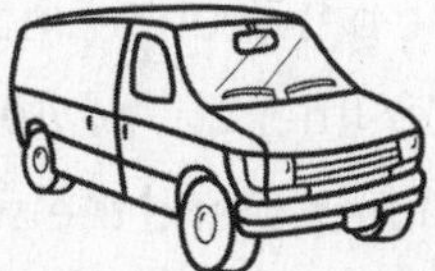 |

# Phoneme Blending (2 Sounds)

## TEACH/MODEL

**Introduce** Tell children that you will say a word sound by sound. Then you will help them put the sounds together to say the whole word. This will help them as they read words. Explain that when we read a word we attach a sound to each spelling. Then we string together, or blend, the sounds to read the whole word.

Model blending sounds to make the word *say.* Begin by saying the word *say* sound by sound. Then stretch each continuous sound so children can hear. Help children put the sounds together to say the whole word. If children need help identifying sounds, use **Sound Boxes.** Have them drag a counter into one box of a Sound Box for each sound in the word. Then blend the word.

**Think Aloud** *I am going to say a word sound by sound. Listen: /sss/ /ā/. Now listen as I string together, or blend, the sounds. I will stretch each sound so you can clearly hear it.* Stretch the sounds in *say.* [Hold each sound. Do not pause between sounds.] *The word is* say. [Note: You may need to slowly collapse the word for children to connect the stretched sounds to a word they know.] *Now it's your turn. Stretch the word* say *with me. Let's pretend we have a rubber band. Watch as I stretch the sounds.* Stretch the sounds in *say. Now you try it with me.* [Have children repeat.]

## GUIDED PRACTICE

Guide children to blend the following sounds to make words. Continue to use the "rubber band" technique to help children stretch the sounds. Use these and other sound sets.

| | | |
|---|---|---|
| /r/ /ā/ (ray) | /s/ /ō/ (so) | /r/ /ō/ (row) |
| /s/ /ē/ (see) | /m/ /ō/ (mow) | /s/ / ü/ (Sue) |
| /m/ /ī/ (my) | /n/ /ō/ (no) | /n/ / ü/ (new) |

## APPLY

**Practice Reproducible** Have children complete **Practice Reproducible PA56.** Say the following sounds. Hold each continuous sound for three seconds. Do not pause between sounds. Emphasize stop sounds.

**1.** /m/ /ē/ (me) **2.** /w/ / ē/ (we) **3.** /sh/ / ü/ (shoe) **4.** /n/ / ē/ (knee)

Have children blend the sounds and then draw a picture of the word created. Provide corrective feedback and modeling, as needed.

# Draw It

**Listen to the sounds. Put the sounds together. Draw a picture of the word you made.**

| **1.** | **2.** |
| --- | --- |
| **3.** | **4.** |

# Phoneme Blending (2 Sounds)

## TEACH/MODEL

**Introduce** Tell children that you will say a word sound by sound. Then you will help them put the sounds together to say the whole word. This will help them as they read words. Explain that when we read a word we attach a sound to each spelling. Then we string together, or blend, the sounds to read the whole word.

Model blending sounds to make the word *low.* Begin by saying the word *low* sound by sound. Then stretch each continuous sound so children can hear. Help children put the sounds together to say the whole word *low.* If children need help identifying sounds, use **Sound Boxes.** Have them drag a counter into one box of a Sound Box for each sound in the word. Then blend the word.

> **Think Aloud** *I am going to say a word sound by sound. Listen: /lll/ /ō/. Now listen as I string together, or blend, the sounds. I will stretch each sound so you can clearly hear it.* Stretch the sounds in *low. The word is* low. [Note: You may need to slowly collapse the word for children to connect the stretched sounds to a word they know.] *Now it's your turn. Stretch* low *with me. Let's pretend we have a rubber band. Watch as I stretch the sounds.* Stretch the sounds in *low. Now you try it with me.* [Have children repeat.]

## GUIDED PRACTICE

Guide children to blend the following sounds to make words. Continue to use the "rubber band" technique to help children stretch the sounds. Use these and other sound sets.

| | | |
|---|---|---|
| /l/ /ī/ (lie) | /sh/ /ē/ (she) | /s/ /ō/ (so) |
| /l/ /ē/ (Lee) | /sh/ /ō/ (show) | /z/ /ü/ (zoo) |

## APPLY

**Activity** Read aloud the following sentences, reading each word as shown in sound segments. Have children orally blend each word and then say it.

- On the farm, I hear /m/ /ü/. What did I hear? (moo)
- She has a /n/ /ü/ dress. What kind of dress does she have? (new)
- His birthday is in /m/ /ā/. When is his birthday? (in May)
- The class will go to the /z/ /ü/. Where will the class go? (to the zoo)
- I will eat lunch /n/ /ou/. When will I eat lunch? (now)

# Phoneme Blending (3 Sounds)

## TEACH/MODEL

**Introduce** Tell children that you will say a word sound by sound. Then you will help them put the sounds together to say the whole word. This will help them as they read words.

Model blending sounds to make the word *fan*. Begin by saying the word *fan* sound by sound. Then stretch each sound so children can hear. Help children put the sounds together to say the whole word. If children need help identifying sounds, use **Sound Boxes.** Have them drag a counter into one box of a Sound Box for each sound in the word. Then blend the word.

> **Think Aloud** *I am going to say a word sound by sound. Listen: /fff/ /aaa/ /nnn/. Now listen as I string together, or blend, the sounds. I will stretch each sound so you can clearly hear it: /fffaaannn/.* [Hold each sound for three seconds. Do not pause between sounds.] *The word is* fan. [Note: You may need to slowly collapse the word for children to connect the stretched sounds to a word they know.] *Now it's your turn. Stretch the word* fan *with me. Let's pretend we have a rubber band. Watch as I stretch the sounds: /fffaaannn/. Now you try it with me.* [Have children repeat.]

## GUIDED PRACTICE

Guide children to blend the following sounds to make words. Continue to use the "rubber band" technique to help children stretch the sounds. Use these and other sound sets.

| | | |
|---|---|---|
| /f/ /a/ /t/ (fat) | /m/ /ā/ /k/ (make) | /s/ /a/ /t/ (sat) |
| /f/ /i/ /n/ (fin) | /m/ /u/ /d/ (mud) | /s/ /ā/ /m/ (same) |
| /f/ /ī/ /n/ (fine) | /n/ /o/ /t/ (not) | /s/ /ī/ /d/ (side) |
| /l/ /e/ /t/ (let) | /n/ /a/ /p/ (nap) | /v/ /e/ /t/ (vet) |
| /l/ /ī/ /k/ (like) | /r/ u/ /g/ (rug) | /z/ /i/ /p/ (zip) |

## APPLY

**Activity** Ask children to blend the sounds of the following words one at a time. Then have them point to the body part they have just named.

- /n/ /ō/ /z/ (nose)
- /f/ /u̇/ /t/ (foot)
- /n/ /e/ /k/ (neck)
- /f/ /ā/ /s/ (face)
- /l/ /e/ /g/ (leg)
- /l/ /i/ /p/ (lip)

LESSON
59
Phonemic Awareness

# Phoneme Blending (3 Sounds)

## TEACH/MODEL

**Introduce** Tell children that you will say a word sound by sound. Then you will help them put the sounds together to say the whole word. This will help them as they read words. Explain that when we read a word we attach a sound to each spelling. Then we string together, or blend, the sounds to read the whole word.

Model blending sounds to make the word *sat.* Begin by saying the word *sat* sound by sound. Then stretch each continuous sound so children can hear. Help children put the sounds together to say the whole word. If children need help identifying sounds, use **Sound Boxes.** Have them drag a counter into one box of a Sound Box for each sound in the word. Then blend the word.

**Think Aloud** *I am going to say a word sound by sound. Listen: /sss/ /aaa/ /t/. Now listen as I string together, or blend, the sounds. I will stretch each sound so you can clearly hear it: /sssaaat/.* [Hold each sound for three seconds. Do not pause between sounds.] *The word is* sat. [Note: You may need to slowly collapse the word for children to connect the stretched sounds to a word they know. For example, /sssaaat/, /ssaat/, /sat/. The word is *sat.*] *Now it's your turn. Stretch the word* sat *with me. Let's pretend we have a rubber band.* [Hold your hands in front of you as if you are holding a rubber band.] *Watch as I stretch the sounds: /sssaaat/.* [Model pulling the rubber band apart as you stretch the sounds.] *Now you try it with me.* [Have children repeat.]

## GUIDED PRACTICE

Guide children to blend the following sounds to make words. Continue to use the "rubber band" technique to help children stretch the sounds. Use these and other sound sets:

| | | |
|---|---|---|
| /f/ /i/ /sh/ (fish) | /m/ /a/ /n/ (man) | /r/ /u/ /n/ (run) |
| /f/ /u/ /n/ (fun) | /m/ /o/ /p/ (mop) | /r/ /a/ /t/ (rat) |
| /l/ /o/ /k/ (lock) | m/ /e/ /s/ (mess) | /v/ /a/ /n/ (van) |

## APPLY

**Practice Reproducible** Have children complete **Practice Reproducible PA59.** Say the following sounds. Hold each continuous sound for three seconds. Do not pause between sounds. Emphasize stop sounds.

**1.** /f/ /a/ /n/ (fan) **2.** /m/ /o/ /p/ (mop) **3.** /n/ /e/ /t/ (net) **4.** /r/ /o/ /k/ (rock)

Have children blend the sounds, then draw a picture of the word created. Provide corrective feedback.

## Draw It

**Listen to the sounds. Put the sounds together. Draw a picture of the word you made.**

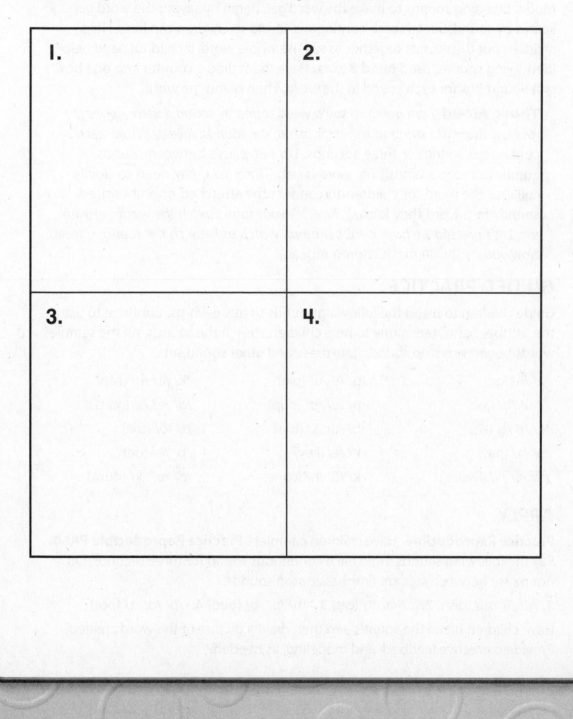

| 1. | 2. |
|---|---|
| 3. | 4. |

# Phoneme Blending (2 and 3 Sounds)

## TEACH/MODEL

**Introduce** Tell children that you will say a word sound by sound. Then you will help them put the sounds together to say the whole word. This will help them as they read words.

Model blending sounds to make the word *get*. Begin by saying the word *get* sound by sound. Stretch each continuous sound so children can hear. Help children put the sounds together to say the whole word. If children need help identifying sounds, use **Sound Boxes.** Have them drag a counter into one box of a Sound Box for each sound in the word. Then blend the word.

> **Think Aloud** *I am going to say a word sound by sound. Listen: /g/ /eee/ /t/. Now listen as I string together, or blend, the sounds: /geeet/.* [Hold each continuous sound for three seconds. Do not pause between sounds. Emphasize stop sounds.] *The word is* get. [Note: You may need to slowly collapse the word for children to connect the stretched or emphasized sounds to a word they know.] *Now it's your turn. Stretch the word* get *with me. Let's pretend we have a rubber band. Watch as I stretch the sounds: /geeet/. Now you try it with me.* [Children repeat.]

## GUIDED PRACTICE

Guide children to blend the following sounds to make words. Continue to use the "rubber band" technique to help children stretch the sounds. All the sample words begin with stop sounds. Use these and other sound sets.

| | | |
|---|---|---|
| /g/ /ō/ (go) | /p/ /i/ /n/ (pin) | /k/ /a/ /p/ (cap) |
| /j/ o/ /b/ (job) | /p/ /u/ /p/ (pup) | /g/ /e/ /s/ (guess) |
| /k/ /i/ /t/ (kit) | /b/ /u/ /s/ (bus) | /t/ /ō/ (toe) |
| /p/ /ā/ (pay) | /k/ /ē/ (key) | /b/ /ē/ (be) |
| /D/ /ā/ /v/ (Dave) | /k/ /ō/ /n/ (cone) | /d/ /u/ /k/ (duck) |

## APPLY

**Practice Reproducible** Have children complete **Practice Reproducible PA60.** Say the following sounds. Hold each continuous sound for three seconds. Do not pause between sounds. Emphasize stop sounds.

**1.** /d/ /i/ /sh/ (dish) **2.** /c/ /a/ /t/ (cat) **3.** /b/ /u/ /g/ (bug) **4.** /p/ /o/ /t/ (pot)

Have children blend the sounds and then draw a picture of the word created. Provide corrective feedback and modeling, as needed.

## Draw It

**Listen to the sounds. Put the sounds together.**
**Draw a picture of the word you made.**

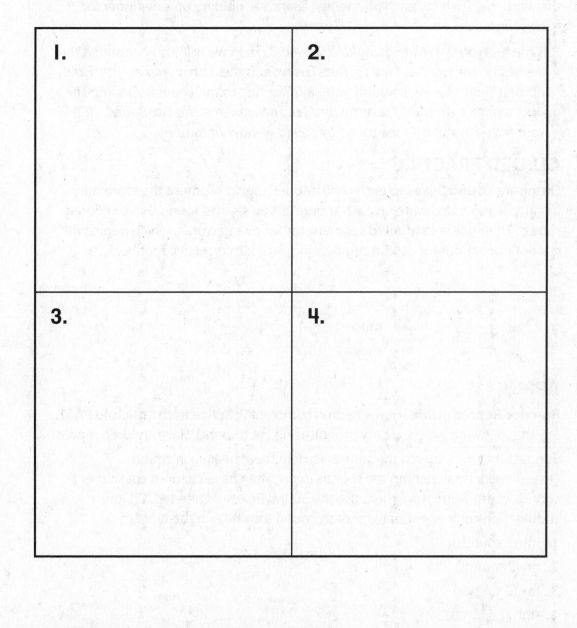

| 1. | 2. |
| --- | --- |
| 3. | 4. |

# Phoneme Segmenting (2 Sounds)

## TEACH/MODEL

**Introduce** Tell children that you will help them break apart a word sound by sound. This will help them as they write words. Explain that when we write a word we think about each sound and attach a spelling to it.

Model segmenting a word into phonemes using the word *me*. Begin by saying the word *me*. Then say each phoneme separately, holding up one finger for each sound.

**Think Aloud** *We are going to say a word. Then we will say each sound that we hear in the word. Let me try first. The word is* me. *Listen: /mmm/ /ē/.* [Hold up one finger for each sound you say.] *The first sound I hear is /mmm/. The next sound I hear is /ē/. I hear /mmm/ /ē/. The word* me *has two sounds. It's your turn. Say* me *with me sound by sound. Ready? /mmm/ /ē/.*

## GUIDED PRACTICE

Distribute **Sound Boxes** to each child. Model how to segment the word *me* again, placing one counter in each square as you say the sound. Have children repeat. Then guide children to segment the following words, which begin with continuous sounds for ease in segmenting. Provide corrective feedback.

| | |
|---|---|
| low | ray |
| lie | so |
| moo | see |
| may | say |

## APPLY

**Practice Reproducible** Have children complete **Practice Reproducible PA61.** Say the following words, clearly pronouncing each sound. Have children repeat.

Suggest that they stretch the sounds to help them hear each sound. Demonstrate by stretching the sounds in *my*. Then have children count the sounds in the word. Have them use the Sound Boxes, as needed. Children should then color one square for each sound they hear in the word.

1. my (2 sounds)
2. no (2 sounds)
3. ray (2 sounds)
4. sigh (2 sounds)

# Sound Boxes

**Listen to each word. Count the sounds. Then color in one box for each sound.**

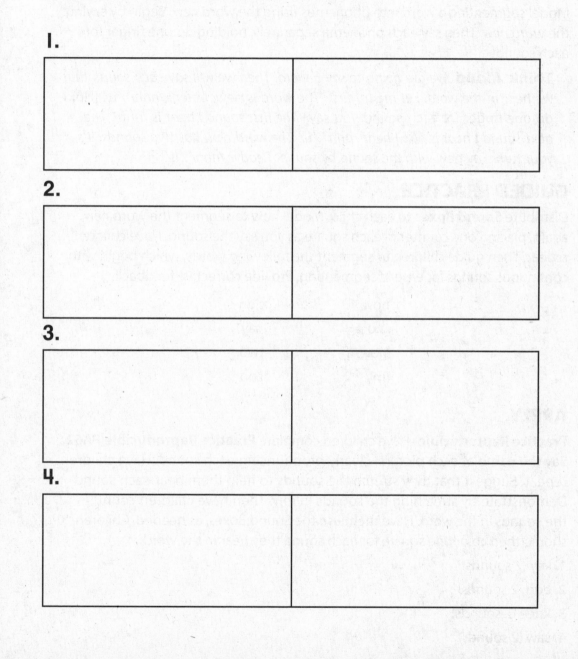

1.

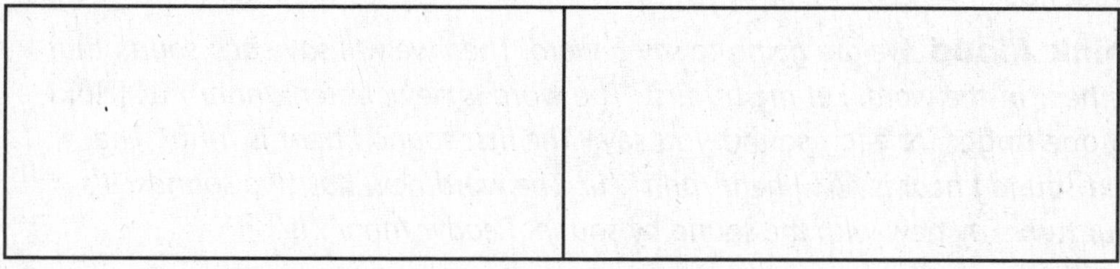

2.

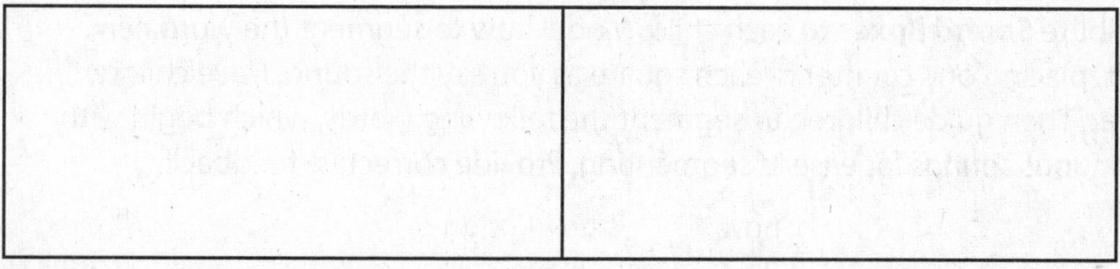

3.

| | |
|---|---|
| | |

4.

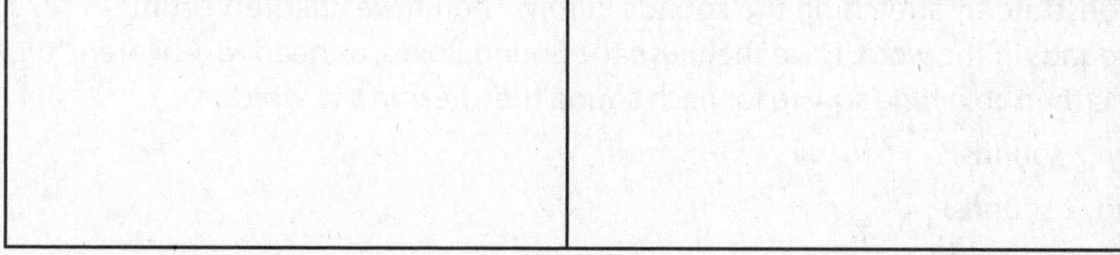

LESSON
62
Phonemic Awareness

# Phoneme Segmenting (2 Sounds)

## TEACH/MODEL

**Introduce** Tell children that you will help them break apart a word sound by sound. This will help them as they write words. Explain that when we write a word we think about each sound and attach a spelling to it.

Model segmenting a word into phonemes using the word *new*. Begin by saying the word *new*. Then say each phoneme separately, holding up one finger for each sound.

> **Think Aloud** *We are going to say a word. Then we will say each sound that we hear in the word. Let me try first. The word is* new. *Listen: /nnn/ / ü/.* [Hold up one finger for each sound you say.] *The first sound I hear is /nnn/. The next sound I hear is / ü/. I hear /nnn/ / ü/. The word* new *has two sounds. It's your turn. Say* new *with me sound by sound. Ready? /nnn/ / ü/.*

## GUIDED PRACTICE

Distribute **Sound Boxes** to each child. Model how to segment the word *new* again, placing one counter in each square as you say the sound. Have children repeat. Then guide children to segment the following words, which begin with continuous sounds for ease in segmenting. Provide corrective feedback.

| | |
|---|---|
| now | sigh |
| no | say |
| mow | two |
| my | zoo |

## APPLY

**Practice Reproducible** Have children complete **Practice Reproducible PA62.** Say the name of each picture, clearly pronouncing each sound. Have children repeat. Suggest that they stretch the sounds to help them hear each sound. Demonstrate by stretching the sounds in *row*. Then have children count the sounds in the word. Have them use the Sound Boxes, as needed. Children should then color one square for each sound they hear in the word.

**1.** key (2 sounds)

**2.** egg (2 sounds)

**3.** knee (2 sounds)

**4.** saw (2 sounds)

Name ______________________ Date ________

Practice Reproducible PA62

# Sound Boxes

**Say the name of each picture. Count the sounds. Then color in one box for each sound.**

| | | |
|---|---|---|
| 1.  | | |
| 2. 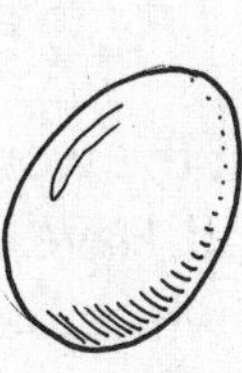 | | |
| 3. 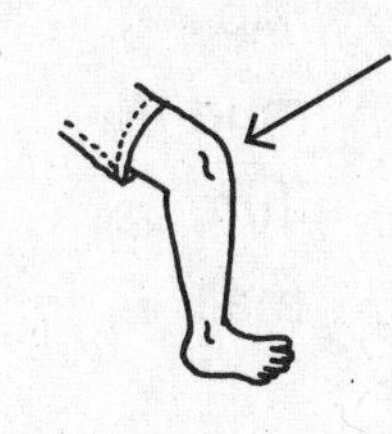 | | |
| 4.  | | |

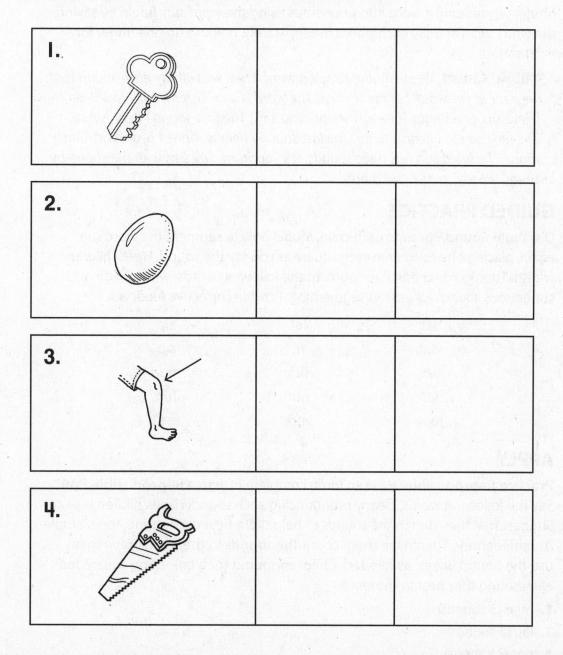

# Phoneme Segmenting (3 Sounds)

## TEACH/MODEL

**Introduce** Tell children that you will help them break apart a word sound by sound. This will help them as they write words. Explain that when we write a word we think about each sound and attach a spelling to it.

Model segmenting a word into phonemes using the word *sun*. Begin by saying the word *sun*. Then say each phoneme separately, holding up one finger for each sound.

**Think Aloud** *We are going to say a word. Then we will say each sound that we hear in the word. Let me try first. The word is* sun. *Listen: /sss/ /uuu/ /nnn/.* [Hold up one finger for each sound you say.] *The first sound I hear is /sss/. The next sound I hear is /uuu/. The last sound I hear is /nnn/. I hear /sss/ /uuu/ /nnn/. The word* sun *has three sounds. It's your turn. Say* sun *with me sound by sound. Ready? /sss/ /uuu/ /nnn/.*

## GUIDED PRACTICE

Distribute **Sound Boxes** to each child. Model how to segment the word *sun* again, placing one counter in each square as you say the sound. Have children repeat. Then guide children to segment the following words, which begin with continuous sounds for ease in segmenting. Provide corrective feedback.

| | | |
|---|---|---|
| sat | let | zip |
| net | fit | rip |
| late | sick | mud |
| fell | nut | fun |
| rope | vote | mail |

## APPLY

**Practice Reproducible** Have children complete **Practice Reproducible PA63.** Say the following words, clearly pronouncing each sound. Have children repeat. Suggest that they stretch the sounds to help them hear each sound, for example /mmmeeennn/. Then have them count the sounds in the word. Have them use the Sound Boxes, as needed. Children should then color one square for each sound they hear in the word.

1. men (3 sounds)
2. lap (3 sounds)
3. not (3 sounds)
4. rain (3 sounds

Name ______________________ Date __________



# Sound Boxes

**Listen to each word. Count the sounds. Then color in one box for each sound.**

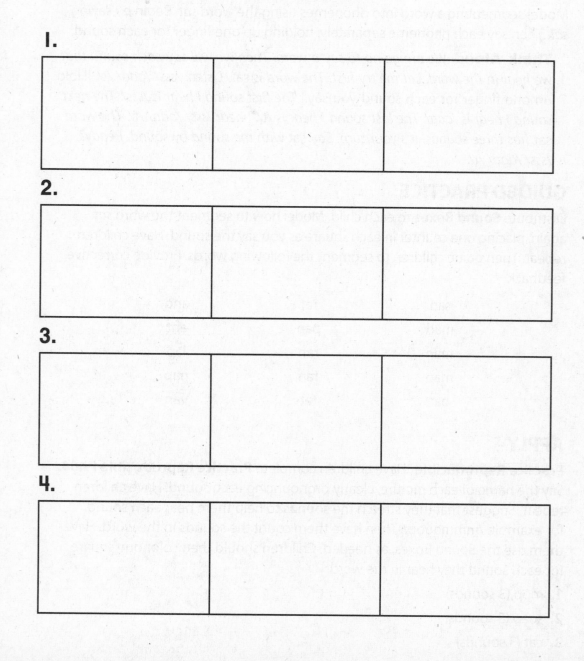

**1.**

| | | |
|---|---|---|
| | | |

**2.**

| | | |
|---|---|---|
| | | |

**3.**

| | | |
|---|---|---|
| | | |

**4.**

LESSON 64
Phonemic Awareness

# Phoneme Segmenting (3 Sounds)

## TEACH/MODEL

**Introduce** Tell children that you will help them break apart a word sound by sound. This will help them as they write words. Explain that when we write a word we think about each sound and attach a spelling to it.

Model segmenting a word into phonemes using the word *sat*. Begin by saying *sat*. Then say each phoneme separately, holding up one finger for each sound.

> **Think Aloud** *We are going to say a word. Then we will say each sound that we hear in the word. Let me try first. The word is* sat. *Listen: /sss/ /aaa/ /t/.* [Hold up one finger for each sound you say.] *The first sound I hear is /sss/. The next sound I hear is /aaa/. The last sound I hear is /t/. I hear /sss/ /aaa/ /t/. The word* sat *has three sounds. It's your turn. Say* sat *with me sound by sound. Ready? /sss/ /aaa/ /t/.*

## GUIDED PRACTICE

Distribute **Sound Boxes** to each child. Model how to segment the word *sat* again, placing one counter in each square as you say the sound. Have children repeat. Then guide children to segment the following words. Provide corrective feedback.

| | | |
|---|---|---|
| sad | rat | and |
| mad | pan | ant |
| man | ran | lap |
| map | fan | nap |
| bat | fat | van |

## APPLY

**Practice Reproducible** Have children complete **Practice Reproducible PA64.** Say the name of each picture, clearly pronouncing each sound. Have children repeat. Suggest that they stretch the sounds to help them hear each sound, for example /mmmooop/. Then have them count the sounds in the word. Have them use the Sound Boxes, as needed. Children should then color one square for each sound they hear in the word.

1. mop (3 sounds)
2. soap (3 sounds)
3. cat (3 sounds)
4. fan (3 sounds)

Name ______________________ Date __________

Practice Reproducible PA64

# Sound Boxes

**Say the name of each picture. Count the sounds. Then color in one box for each sound.**

| | | | |
|---|---|---|---|
| **1.** 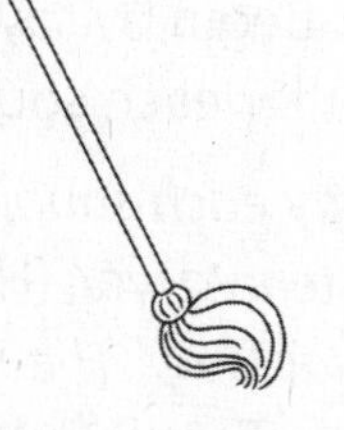 | | | |
| **2.**  | | | |
| **3.**  | | | |
| **4.**  | | | |

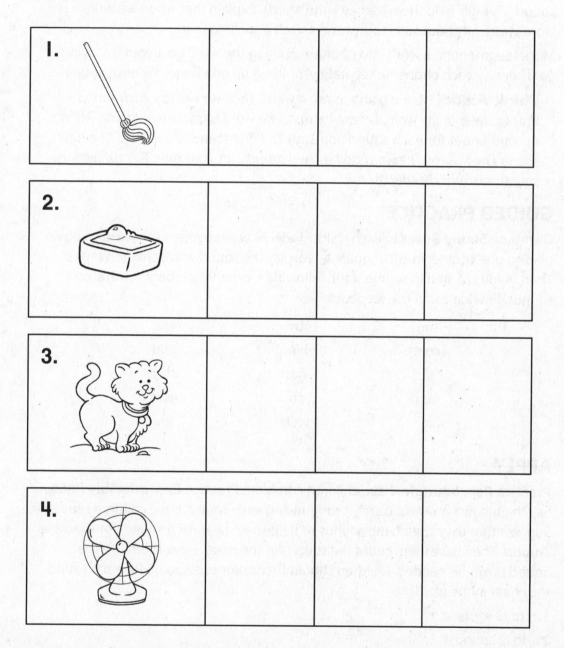

# Phoneme Segmenting (2 and 3 Sounds)

## TEACH/MODEL

**Introduce** Tell children that you will help them break apart a word sound by sound. This will help them as they write words. Explain that when we write a word we think about each sound and attach a spelling to it.

Model segmenting a word into phonemes using the word *go*. Begin by saying *go*. Then say each phoneme separately, holding up one finger for each sound.

> **Think Aloud** *We are going to say a word. Then we will say each sound that we hear in the word. Let me try first. The word is* go. *Listen: /g/ /ō/.* [Hold up one finger for each sound you say.] *The first sound I hear is /g/. The next sound I hear is /ō/. The word* go *has two sounds. It's your turn. Say* go *with me sound by sound. Ready? /g/ /ō/.*

## GUIDED PRACTICE

Distribute **Sound Boxes** to each child. Model how to segment the word *go* again, placing one counter in each square as you say the sound. Have children repeat. Then guide children to segment the following words, which begin with stop sounds. Provide corrective feedback.

| | | |
|---|---|---|
| tug | by | kite |
| coat | him | you |
| we | gas | day |
| jam | to | gum |
| high | web | pie |

## APPLY

**Practice Reproducible** Have children complete **Practice Reproducible PA65.** Say the following words, clearly pronouncing each sound. Have children repeat. Suggest that they stretch the sounds to help them hear each sound, for example /kuuut/. Then have them count the sounds in the word. Have them use the Sound Boxes, as needed. Children should then color one square for each sound they hear in the word.

1. cut (3 sounds)
2. do (2 sounds)
3. hay (2 sounds)
4. bean (3 sounds)

# Sound Boxes

**Listen to each word. Count the sounds. Then color in one box for each sound.**

**1.**

**2.**

**3.**

**4.**

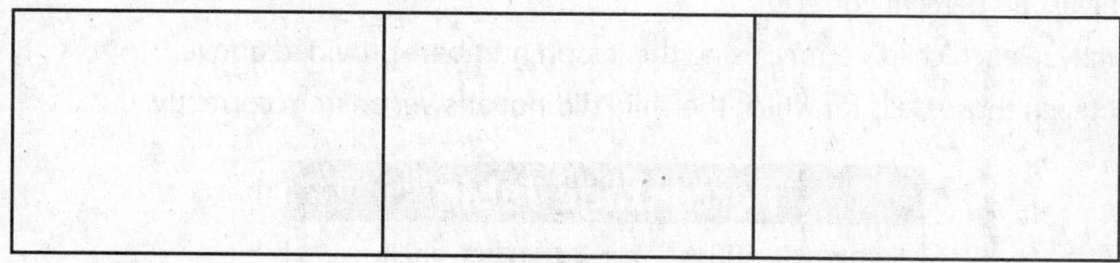

# Review

## PREPARING THE REVIEW

- Make one copy of **Practice Reproducible PA66** for each child.
- Write the child's name and today's date at the top of the review.

## ADMINISTERING THE REVIEW

- Administer the review to one child at a time.
- Follow these instructions for each item. Each phonemic awareness skill was taught in the lessons indicated in parentheses.

1. Identify each picture: **ice, zoo,** and **ax.** Then ask students to listen to the following sounds, blend the sounds, and circle the picture: /z/ /$\overline{oo}$/. (Answer: *zoo*; Lessons 56–57)
2. Identify each picture: **rug, mop,** and **feet.** Then ask children to listen to the following sounds, blend the sounds, and circle the picture: /f/ /ē/ /t/. (Answer: *feet*; Lessons 58–60)
3. Identify the picture: **log.** Then ask children to repeat the picture name, count the sounds, and color in one box for each sound: *log*. (Answer: 3 sounds; Lessons 61–65)
4. Identify the picture: **key.** Then ask children to repeat the picture name, count the sounds, and color in one box for each sound: *key.* (Answer: 2 sounds; Lessons 61–65)
5. Identify the picture: **nut.** Then ask children to listen to the following word, count the sounds, and color in one box for each sound: *nut.* (Answer: 3 sounds; Lessons 61–65)

## SCORING THE REVIEW

- Total the number of items answered correctly.
- Use the Percentage Table below to identify a percentage. Children should get at least 80 percent correct.
- Analyze each child's errors, using the lesson numbers provided above.
- Reteach those skills for which the child did not answer an item correctly.

| Percentage Table | | | |
|---|---|---|---|
| **5 correct** | 100% | **2 correct** | 40% |
| **4 correct** | 80% | **1 correct** | 20% |
| **3 correct** | 60% | **0 correct** | 0% |

Name ______________________ Date __________



# Phonemic Awareness Review

1.

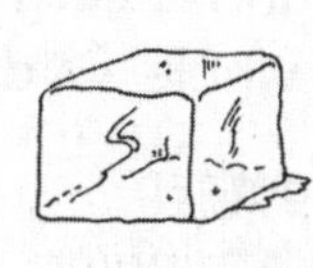

2.

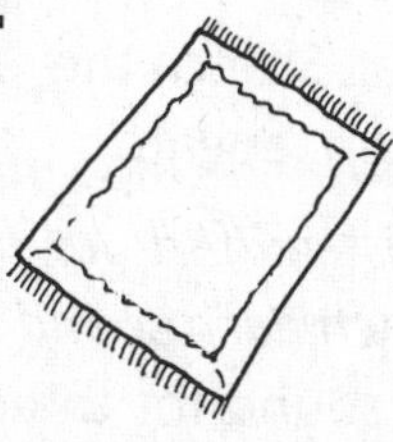
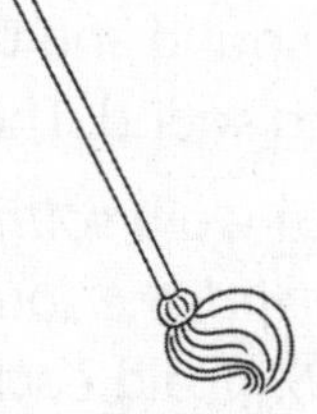
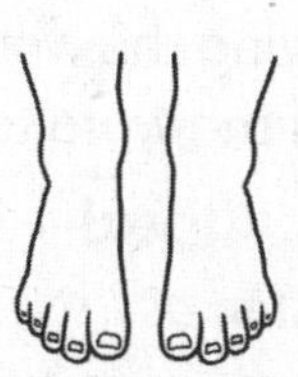

| | | | |
|---|---|---|---|
| 3. 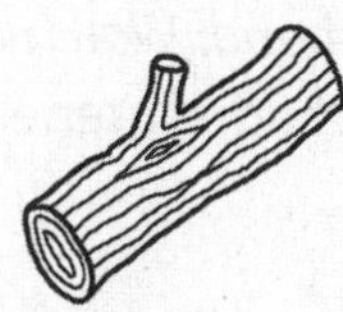 | | | |
| 4.  | | | |
| 5.  | | | |

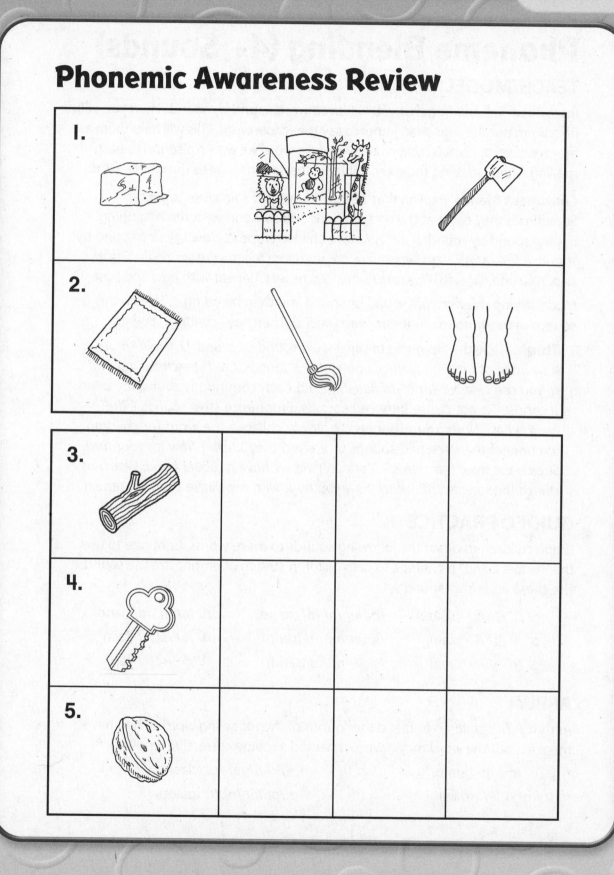

LESSON
67
Phonemic Awareness

# Phoneme Blending (4+ Sounds)

## TEACH/MODEL

**Introduce** Tell children that you will say a word sound by sound. Then you will help them put the sounds together to say the whole word. This will help them as they read words. Explain that when we read a word we attach a sound to each spelling. Then we string together, or blend, the sounds to read the whole word.

**Consonant Blends** Explain that certain sounds are said close together. Sometimes they come at the end of words and sometimes at the beginning. Say *lap* sound by sound: /l/ /a/ /p/. Have children repeat. Now say *slap* sound by sound: /s/ /l/ /a/ /p/. Say: *Two sounds are said close together at the beginning of* slap, */sss/ and /lll/, /ssssslllap/.* Have children repeat. Repeat with *pass* and *past*.

Model saying the word *flat* sound by sound and then blending it. Stretch the sounds of the word to emphasize each sound. Then have children repeat.

**Think Aloud** *I am going to say a word sound by sound. Listen: /f/ /l/ /a/ /t/. Now listen as I string together, or blend, the sounds. I will stretch each sound so you can clearly hear it: /ffflllaaat/.* [Hold each continuous sound for three seconds. Do not pause between sounds. Emphasize stop sounds.] *The word is* flat. [Note: You may need to slowly collapse the word for children to connect the stretched sounds to a word they know.] *Now it's your turn. Stretch the word* flat *with me. Let's pretend we have a rubber band. Watch as I stretch the sounds: /ffflllaaat/. Now you try it with me.* [Have children repeat.]

## GUIDED PRACTICE

Guide children to blend the following sounds to make words. Continue to use the "rubber band" technique to help children stretch or emphasize the sounds. Use these and other sound sets.

| | | |
|---|---|---|
| /p/ /l/ /ē/ /z/ (please) | /b/ /e/ /n/ /d/ (bend) | /l/ /a/ /n/ /d/ (land) |
| /p/ /l/ /ā/ /t/ (plate) | /s/ /e/ /n/ /d/ (send) | /f/ /a/ /s/ /t/ (fast) |
| /g/ /r/ /ā/ /t/ (great) | /s/ /a/ n/ /d/ (sand) | /l/ /a/ /s/ /t/ (last) |

## APPLY

**Activity** Ask children to blend the sounds of the following words. Then have them act out the word they have just named. Provide corrective feedback.

- /j/ /u/ /m/ /p/ (jump)
- /s/ /m/ /ī/ /l/ (smile)
- /k/ /l/ /a/ /p/ (clap)
- /p/ /ā/ /n/ /t/ (paint)

# Phoneme Blending (4+ Sounds)

## TEACH/MODEL

**Introduce** Tell children that you will say a word sound by sound. Then you will help them put the sounds together to say the whole word. This will help them as they read words.

**Consonant Blends** Review that certain sounds are said very close together. Say *fall* sound by sound: /f/ /ô/ /l/. Have children repeat. Now say *fault* sound by sound: /f/ /ô/ /l/ /t/. Say: *Two sounds are said close together at the end of* fault, */lll/ and /t/, /fôlllt/.* Have children repeat. Repeat with *right* and *fright*.

Model saying the word *most* sound by sound and then blending it. Stretch the sounds of the word to emphasize each sound. Then have children repeat.

> **Think Aloud** *I am going to say a word sound by sound. Listen: /m/ /ō/ /s/ /t/. Now listen as I string together, or blend, the sounds. I will stretch each sound so you can clearly hear it.* Stretch the sounds in *most.* [Hold each continuous sound for three seconds. Do not pause between sounds. Emphasize stop sounds.] The word is *most. Now it's your turn. Stretch the word* most *with me. Let's pretend we have a rubber band. Watch as I stretch the sounds. Now you try it with me.* [Have children repeat.]

## GUIDED PRACTICE

Guide children to blend the following sounds to make words. Continue to use the "rubber band" technique to help children stretch the sounds. Use these and other sound sets.

| | | |
|---|---|---|
| /h/ /a/ /n/ /d/ (hand) | /s/ /p/ /ü/ /n/ (spoon) | /b/ /l/ /a/ /k/ (black) |
| /h/ /e/ /l/ /p/ (help) | /s/ /p/ /i/ /l/ (spill) | /s/ /n/ /a/ /k/ (snack) |
| /g/ /ō/ /l/ /d/ (gold) | /ch/ /ē/ /z/ (cheese) | /f/ /l/ /ō/ /t/ (float) |
| /g/ /i/ /f/ /t/ (gift) | /ch/ /a/ /m/ /p/ (champ) | /f/ /l/ /i/ /p/ flip) |

## APPLY

**Activity** Read aloud the following clues, reading each word as shown in sound segments. Have children orally blend each word and then say it. Provide corrective feedback.

- I'm thinking of a color. It's /b/ /r/ /ou/ /n/. What am I thinking of? (brown)
- I'm thinking of a direction. It's /w/ /e/ /s/ /t/. What am I thinking of? (west)
- I'm thinking of a fruit. It's a /g/ /r/ /ā/ /p/. What am I thinking of? (grape)

# Phoneme Blending (4+ Sounds)

## TEACH/MODEL

**Introduce** Tell children that you will say a word sound by sound. Then you will help them put the sounds together to say the whole word. This will help them as they read words.

**Consonant Blends** Review that certain sounds are said very close together. Say *rap* sound by sound: /r/ /a/ /p/. Have children repeat. Now say *trap* sound by sound: /t/ /r/ /a/ /p/. Say: *Two sounds are said close together at the beginning of* trap, */t/ and /rrr/, /trrrap/.* Have children repeat. Repeat with *love* and *glove.*

Model saying the word *slip* sound by sound and then blending it. Stretch the sounds of the word to emphasize each sound. Then have children repeat.

> **Think Aloud** *I am going to say a word sound by sound. Listen: /s/ /l/ /i/ /p/. Now listen as I string together, or blend, the sounds. I will stretch each sound so you can clearly hear it: /sssllliip/. The word is* slip. *Now it's your turn. Stretch the word* slip *with me. Let's pretend we have a rubber band. Watch as I stretch the sounds: /ssslllliiip/. Now you try it with me.* [Have children repeat.]

## GUIDED PRACTICE

Guide children to blend the following sounds to make words. Continue to use the "rubber band" technique to help children stretch the sounds. Use these and other sound sets

| | |
|---|---|
| /t/ /r/ /ā/ /n/ (train) | /s/ /t/ /a/ /m/ /p/ (stamp) |
| /f/ /r/ /ü/ /t/ (fruit) | /s/ /t/ /u/ /m/ /p/ (stump) |
| /k/ /a/ /m/ /p/ (camp) | /g/ /r/ /ou/ /n/ /d/ (ground) |
| /ch/ /a/ /n/ /s/ (chance) | /f/ /r/ /e/ /n/ /d/ (friend) |

## APPLY

**Practice Reproducible** Have children complete **Practice Reproducible PA69.** Say the following sounds. Do not pause between sounds.

**1.** /n/ /e/ /s/ /t/ (nest) **2.** /f/ /l/ /a/ /g/ (flag)
**3.** /s/ /n/ /ā/ /k/ (snake) **4.** /t/ /r/ /u/ /k/ (truck)

Have children blend the sounds and then draw a picture of the word created. Circulate and monitor children's work. Provide corrective feedback.

Name ______________________ Date __________

Practice Reproducible PA69

## Draw It

**Listen to the sounds. Put the sounds together. Draw a picture of the word you made.**

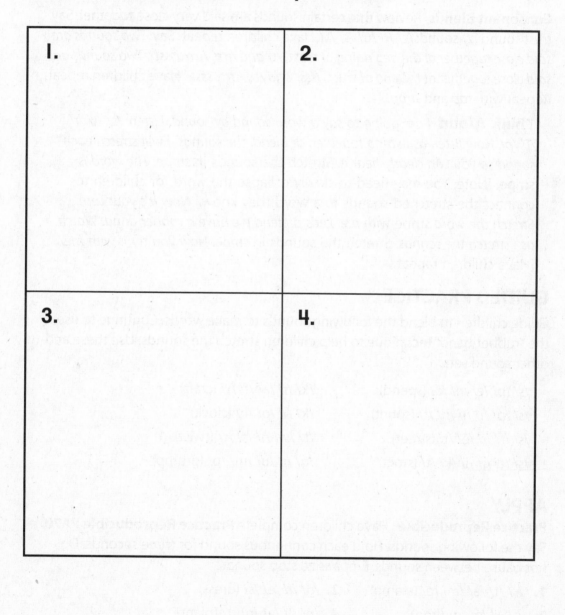

| 1. | 2. |
|---|---|
| 3. | 4. |

# Phoneme Blending (4+ Sounds)

## TEACH/MODEL

**Introduce** Tell children that you will say a word sound by sound. Then you will help them put the sounds together to say the whole word. This will help them as they read words.

**Consonant Blends** Review that certain sounds are said very close together. Say *trust* sound by sound: /t/ /r/ /u/ /s/ /t/. Have children repeat. Say: *Two sounds are said close together at the beginning of* trust, */t/ and /rrr/, /trrrussst/. Two sounds are said close together at the end of* trust, */sss/ and /t/, /trrrussst/.* Have children repeat. Repeat with *rap* and *strap*.

**Think Aloud** *I am going to say a word sound by sound. Listen: /s/ /t/ /r/ /ī/ /p/. Now listen as I string together, or blend, the sounds. I will stretch each sound so you can clearly hear it.* Stretch the sounds in *stripe. The word is* stripe. [Note: You may need to slowly collapse the word for children to connect the stretched sounds to a word they know.] *Now it's your turn. Stretch the word* stripe *with me. Let's pretend we have a rubber band. Watch as I stretch the sounds.* Stretch the sounds in *stripe. Now you try it with me.* [Have children repeat.]

## GUIDED PRACTICE

Guide children to blend the following sounds to make words. Continue to use the "rubber band" technique to help children stretch the sounds. Use these and other sound sets:

/s/ /p/ /e/ /n/ /d/ (spend)
/s/ /p/ /r/ /i/ /n/ /t/ (sprint)
/s/ /t/ /r/ /ē/ /t/ (street)
/s/ /t/ /r/ /i/ /k/ /t/ (strict)
/k/ /r/ /a/ /f/ /t/ (craft)
/k/ /l/ /o/ /k/ (clock)
/t/ /w/ /i/ /s/ /t/ (twist)
/g/ /r/ /u/ /m/ /p/ (grump)

## APPLY

**Practice Reproducible** Have children complete **Practice Reproducible PA70.** Say the following sounds. Hold each continuous sound for three seconds. Do not pause between sounds. Emphasize stop sounds.

**1.** /s/ /t/ /a/ /m/ /p/ (stamp)
**2.** /d/ /r/ /e/ /s/ (dress)
**3.** /f/ /r/ /o/ /g/ (frog)
**4.** /p/ /l/ /a/ /n/ /t/ (plant)

Have children blend the sounds and then draw a picture of the word created. Circulate and monitor children's work. Provide corrective feedback.

Name ______________________ Date ________

Practice Reproducible PA70

## Draw It

**Listen to the sounds. Put the sounds together. Draw a picture of the word you made.**

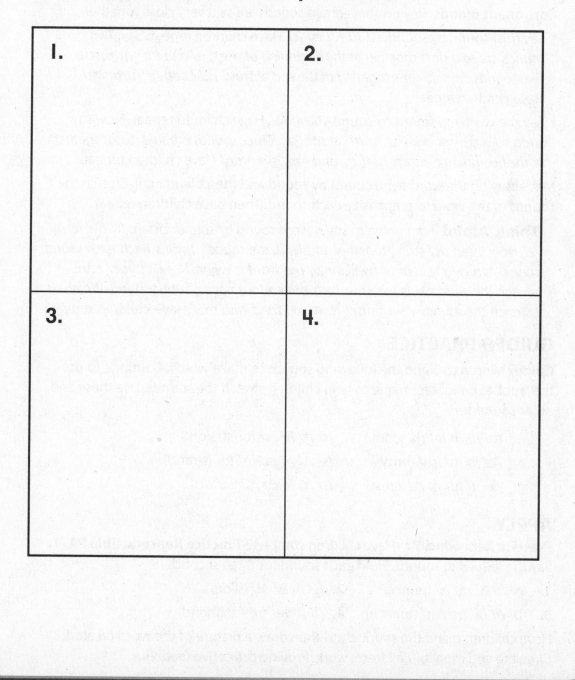

| I. | 2. |
|---|---|
| 3. | 4. |

# Phoneme Blending (4+ Sounds)

## TEACH/MODEL

**Introduce** Tell children that you will say a word sound by sound. Then you will help them put the sounds together to say the whole word. This will help them as they read words.

**Consonant Blends** Review that certain sounds are said very close together.

- Say *trust* sound by sound: /t/ /r/ /u/ /s/ /t/. Have children repeat. Say: *Two sounds are said close together at the beginning of* trust, */t/ and /rrr/, /trrrussst/. Two sounds are said close together at the end of* trust, */sss/ and /t/, /trrrussst/.* Have children repeat.
- Say the word *rap* sound by sound: /r/ /a/ /p/. Have children repeat. Now say *strap* sound by sound: /s/ /t/ /r/ /a/ /p/. Say: *Three sounds are said close together at the beginning of* strap, */sss/, /t/, and /rrr/, /ssstrrrap/.* Have children repeat.

Model saying the word *twins* sound by sound and then blending it. Stretch the sounds of the word to emphasize each sound. Then have children repeat.

> **Think Aloud** *I am going to say a word sound by sound. Listen: /t/ /w/ /i/ /n/ /z/. Now listen as I string together, or blend, the sounds. I will stretch each sound so you can clearly hear it: /twiiinnnz/. The word is* twins. *Now it's your turn. Stretch the word* twins *with me. Let's pretend we have a rubber band. Watch as I stretch the sounds: /twiiinnnz/. Now you try it with me.* [Have children repeat.]

## GUIDED PRACTICE

Guide children to blend the following sounds to make words. Continue to use the "rubber band" technique to help children stretch the sounds. Use these and other sound sets:

| | |
|---|---|
| /d/ /r/ /i/ /n/ /k/ (drink) | /s/ /t/ /r/ /ā/ /t/ (straight) |
| /b/ /r/ /u/ /sh/ (brush) | /s/ /t/ /r/ /a/ /n/ /d/ (strand) |
| /k/ /r/ /u/ /s/ /t/ (crust) | /s/ /t/ /r/ /i/ /p/ (strip) |

## APPLY

**Practice Reproducible** Have children complete **Practice Reproducible PA71.** Say the following sounds. Hold each sound for three seconds.

**1.** /p/ /r/ /i/ /n/ /s/ (prince) **2.** /s/ /l/ /ī/ /d/ (slide)

**3.** /b/ /r/ /a/ /n/ /ch/ (branch) **4.** /f/ /r/ /e/ /n/ /d/ (friend)

Have children blend the sounds and then draw a picture of the word created. Circulate and monitor children's work. Provide corrective feedback.

Name ______________________ Date __________ Practice Reproducible PA71

## Draw It

**Listen to the sounds. Put the sounds together. Draw a picture of the word you made.**

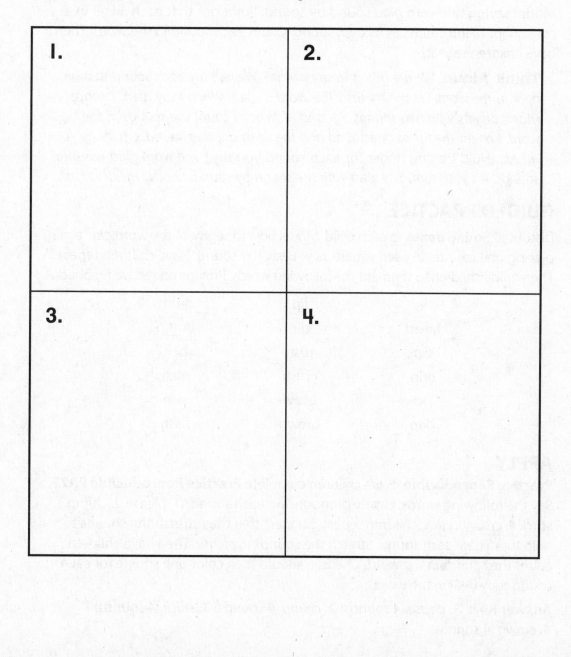

| 1. | 2. |
|---|---|
| 3. | 4. |

# Phoneme Segmenting (4+ Sounds)

## TEACH/MODEL

**Introduce** Tell children that you will help them break apart a word sound by sound. This will help them as they write words. Explain that when we write a word we think about each sound and attach a spelling to it.

Model saying the word *glad* sound by sound. Point out that each letter in a consonant blend counts as its own sound. Count each sound in the word. Then have children repeat.

**Think Aloud** *We are going to say a word. We will say each sound that we hear in the word. Let me try first. The word is* glad. *When I say* glad, *I notice that it begins with two sounds, /g/ and /l/. When I count the sounds in the word, I count the /g/ as one sound and the /l/ as another sound. Listen: /g/ /l/ /a/ /d/.* [Hold up one finger for each sound you say.] *The word* glad *has four sounds. It's your turn. Say* glad *with me sound by sound. Ready? /g/ /l/ /a/ /d/.*

## GUIDED PRACTICE

Distribute **Sound Boxes** to each child. Model how to segment the word *glad* again, placing one counter in each square as you say the sound. Have children repeat. Then guide children to segment the following words. Provide corrective feedback.

| | | |
|---|---|---|
| red | lip | drum |
| bread | clip | bump |
| dip | rush | belt |
| drip | crush | melt |
| lap | brow | skin |
| clap | brown | flash |

## APPLY

**Practice Reproducible** Have children complete **Practice Reproducible PA72.** Say the following words, clearly pronouncing each sound: (1. please 2. chimp 3. stuck 4. crown). Have children repeat. Suggest that they stretch the sounds to help them hear each sound. Stretch the sounds in *please*. Then have children count the sounds in the word. Children should then color one square for each sound they hear in the word.

**Answer Key: 1.** *please* (4 sounds) **2.** *chimp* (4 sounds) **3.** *stuck* (4 sounds) **4.** *crown* (4 sounds)

Name ______________________ Date __________

Practice Reproducible PA72

# Sound Boxes

**Listen to each word. Count the sounds. Then color in one box for each sound.**

**1.**

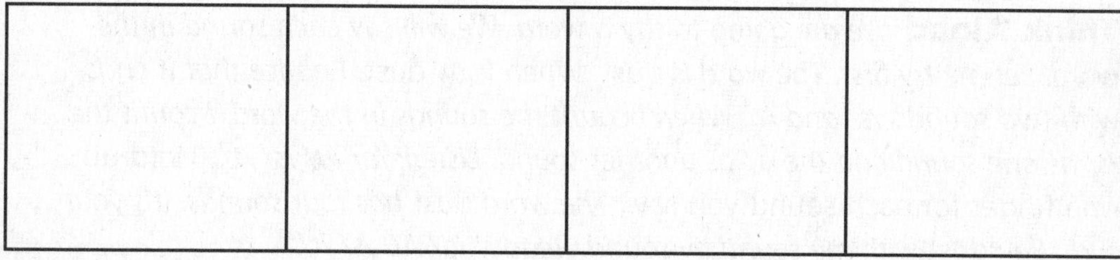

**2.**

**3.**

**4.**

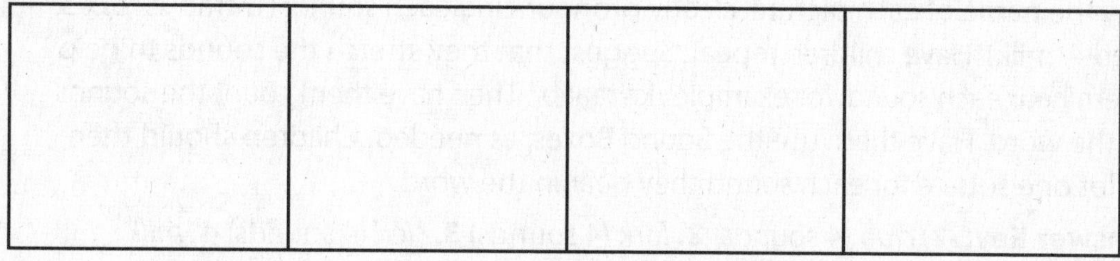

LESSON
73
Phonemic Awareness

# Phoneme Segmenting (4+ Sounds)

## TEACH/MODEL

**Introduce** Tell children that you will help them break apart a word sound by sound. This will help them as they write words. Explain that when we write a word we think about each sound and attach a spelling to it.

Model saying *dust* sound by sound. Point out that each letter in a consonant blend counts as its own sound. Count each sound. Then have children repeat.

**Think Aloud** *We are going to say a word. We will say each sound in the word. Let me try first. The word is* dust. *When I say* dust, *I notice that it ends with two sounds, /s/ and /t/. When I count the sounds in the word, I count the /s/ as one sound and the /t/ as another sound. Listen: /d/ /u/ /s/ /t/.* [Hold up one finger for each sound you say.] *The word* dust *has four sounds. It's your turn. Say* dust *with me sound by sound. Ready? /d/ /u/ /s/ /t/.*

## GUIDED PRACTICE

Distribute **Sound Boxes** to each child. Model how to segment the word *dust* again, placing one counter in each square as you say the sound. Have children repeat. Then guide children to segment the following words. Provide corrective feedback.

| | | |
|---|---|---|
| rust | west | cream |
| rest | raft | dream |
| last | sweet | step |
| fast | short | grand |
| feast | flame | bridge |

## APPLY

**Practice Reproducible** Have children complete **Practice Reproducible PA73.** Say the name of each picture, clearly pronouncing each sound: (1. crab 2. fork 3. sled 4. milk). Have children repeat. Suggest that they stretch the sounds to help them hear each sound, for example /krrraaab/. Then have them count the sounds in the word. Have them use the Sound Boxes, as needed. Children should then color one square for each sound they hear in the word.

**Answer Key: 1.** *crab* (4 sounds) **2.** *fork* (4 sounds) **3.** *sled* (4 sounds) **4.** *milk* (4 sounds)

Name ______________________ Date __________



# Sound Boxes

**Say the name of each picture. Count the sounds. Then color in one box for each sound.**

| | | | | |
|---|---|---|---|---|
| 1.  | | | | |
| 2. 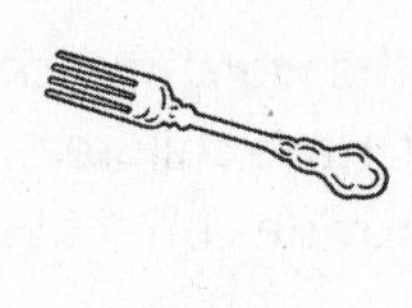 | | | | |
| 3. 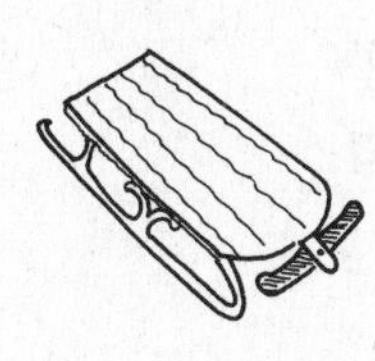 | | | | |
| 4.  | | | | |

LESSON
74
Phonemic Awareness

# Phoneme Segmenting (4+ Sounds)

## TEACH/MODEL

**Introduce** Tell children that you will help them break apart a word sound by sound. This will help them as they write words. Explain that when we write a word we think about each sound and attach a spelling to it.

Model saying the word *branch* sound by sound. Point out that each letter in a consonant blend counts as its own sound. Count each sound in the word. Then have children repeat.

**Think Aloud** *Now I am going to say a word. I want you to say each sound in the word. Let me try first. The word is* branch. *When I say* branch, *I notice that it begins with two sounds, /b/ and /r/. When I count the sounds in the word, I count /b/ as one sound and /r/ as another sound. Listen: /b/ /r/ /a/ /n/ /ch/.* [Hold up one finger for each sound you say.] *The word* branch *has five sounds. It's your turn. Say* branch *with me sound by sound. Ready? /b/ /r/ /a/ /n/ /ch/.*

## GUIDED PRACTICE

Distribute **Sound Boxes** to each child. Model how to segment the word *branch* again, placing one counter in each square as you say the sound. Have children repeat. Then guide children to segment the following words. Provide corrective feedback.

| | | |
|---|---|---|
| stork | trust | twist |
| planes | blend | sport |
| stump | bench | scrubs |
| plant | strange | string |
| price | cart | strong |

## APPLY

**Practice Reproducible** Have children complete **Practice Reproducible PA74.** Say the following words, clearly pronouncing each sound: (1. split 2. heart 3. strict 4. ground). Have children repeat. Suggest that they stretch the sounds to help them hear each sound, for example /sssplllliiit/. Then have them count the sounds. Children should color one square for each sound they hear.

**Answer Key: 1.** *split* (5 sounds) **2.** *heart* (4 sounds) **3.** *strict* (6 sounds) **4.** *ground* (5 sounds)

Name ______________________ Date __________

Practice Reproducible PA74

## Sound Boxes

**Listen to each word. Count the sounds. Then color in one box for each sound.**

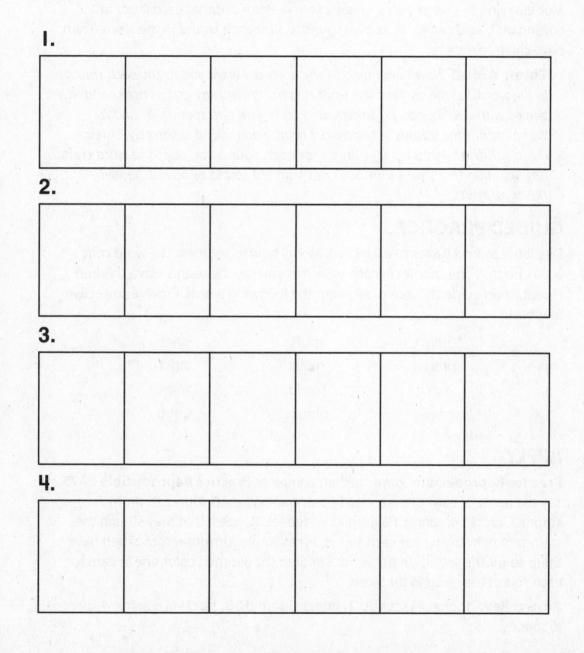

**1.**

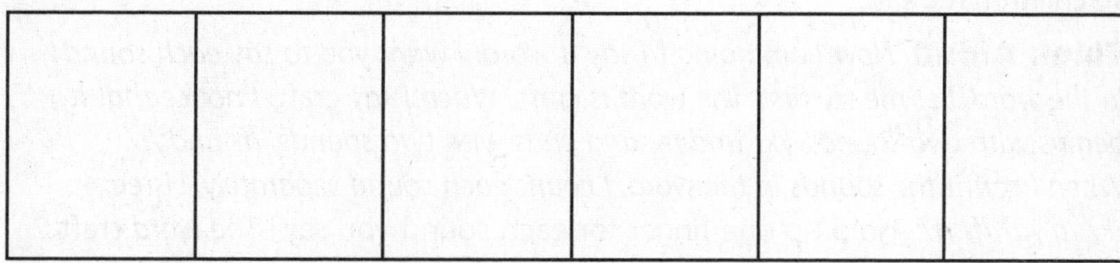

**2.**

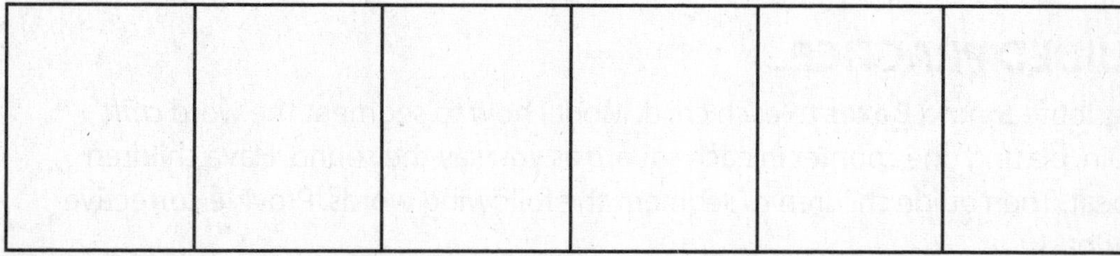

**3.**

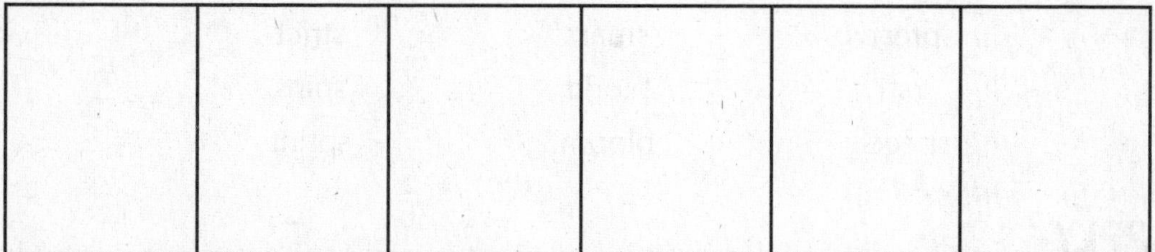

**4.**

# Phoneme Segmenting (4+ Sounds)

## TEACH/MODEL

**Introduce** Tell children that you will help them break apart a word sound by sound. This will help them as they write words. Explain that when we write a word we think about each sound and attach a spelling to it.

Model saying the word *craft* sound by sound. Point out that each letter in a consonant blend counts as its own sound. Count each sound in the word. Then have children repeat.

> **Think Aloud** *Now I am going to say a word. I want you to say each sound in the word. Let me try first. The word is* craft. *When I say* craft, *I notice that it begins with two sounds, /k/ and /r/, and ends with two sounds, /f/ and /t/. When I count the sounds in the word, I count each sound separately. Listen: /k/ /r/ /a/ /f/ /t/.* [Hold up one finger for each sound you say.] *The word* craft *has five sounds. It's your turn. Say* craft *with me sound by sound. Ready? /k/ /r/ /a/ /f/ /t/.*

## GUIDED PRACTICE

Distribute **Sound Boxes** to each child. Model how to segment the word *craft* again, placing one counter in each square as you say the sound. Have children repeat. Then guide children to segment the following words. Provide corrective feedback.

| | | |
|---|---|---|
| front | sport | print |
| spreads | smart | strict |
| raft | blond | spins |
| speech | bloom | sprint |

## APPLY

**Practice Reproducible** Have children complete **Practice Reproducible PA75.** Say the name of each picture, clearly pronouncing each sound: (1. drum 2. stripes 3. blocks 4. sprint). Have children repeat. Suggest that they stretch the sounds to help them hear each sound, for example /drrruuummm/. Then have them count the sounds in the word. Children should then color one square for each sound they hear in the word.

**Answer Key: 1.** *drum* (4 sounds) **2.** *stripes* (6 sounds) **3.** *blocks* (5 sounds) **4.***sprint* (6 sounds)

# Sound Boxes

**Say the name of each picture. Count the sounds. Then color in one box for each sound.**

| | | | | | | |
|---|---|---|---|---|---|---|
| 1.  | | | | | | |
| 2.  | | | | | | |
| 3.  | | | | | | |
| 4.  | | | | | | |

# Phoneme Segmenting (4+ Sounds)

## TEACH/MODEL

**Introduce** Tell children that you will help them break apart a word sound by sound. This will help them as they write words. Explain that when we write a word we think about each sound and attach a spelling to it.

Model saying the word *stamp* sound by sound. Point out that each letter in a consonant blend counts as its own sound. Count each sound in the word. Then have children repeat.

> **Think Aloud** *Now I am going to say a word. I want you to say each sound. Let me try first. The word is* stamp. *When I say* stamp, *I notice that it begins with two sounds, /s/ and /t/, and ends with two sounds, /m/ and /p/. When I count the sounds in the word, I count each one separately. Listen: /s/ /t/ /a/ /m/ /p/.* [Hold up one finger for each sound you say.] *Stamp has five sounds. It's your turn. Say* stamp *with me sound by sound. Ready? /s/ /t/ /a/ /m/ /p/.*

## GUIDED PRACTICE

Distribute **Sound Boxes** to each child. Model how to segment the word *stamp* again, placing one counter in each square as you say the sound. Have children repeat. Then guide children to segment the following words. Provide corrective feedback.

| | | |
|---|---|---|
| stand | spend | trunk |
| strand | draft | front |
| sprout | drink | frost |
| spray | blink | porch |

## APPLY

**Practice Reproducible** Have children complete **Practice Reproducible PA76.** Say the name of each picture, clearly pronouncing each sound: (1. stream 2. plant 3. slide 4. clouds). Have children repeat. Suggest that they stretch the sounds to help them hear each sound. Stretch the sounds in *stream*. Then have children count the sounds in the word. Children should then color one square for each sound they hear in the word.

**Answer Key: 1.** *stream* (5 sounds) **2.** *plant* (5 sounds) **3.** *slide* (4 sounds) **4.** *clouds* (5 sounds)

Name ____________________ Date __________



# Sound Boxes

**Listen to each word. Count the sounds. Then color in one box for each sound.**

| | | | | | |
|---|---|---|---|---|---|
| 1.  | | | | | |
| 2.  | | | | | |
| 3.  | | | | | |
| 4.  | | | | | |

# Review

## PREPARING THE REVIEW

- Make one copy of **Practice Reproducible PA77** for each child.
- Write the child's name and today's date at the top of the review.

## ADMINISTERING THE REVIEW

- Administer the review to one child at a time.
- Follow these instructions for each item. Each phonemic awareness skill was taught in the lessons indicated in parentheses.

1. Identify each picture: **swim, paint,** and **jump.** Then ask children to listen to the following sounds, blend the sounds, and circle the picture: */j/ /u/ /m/ /p/.* (Answer: *jump*; Lessons 69–71)
2. Identify each picture: **gifts, street,** and **nest.** Then ask children to listen to the following sounds, blend the sounds, and circle the picture: */g/ /i/ /f/ /t/ /s/.* (Answer: *gifts*; Lessons 69–71)
3. Identify the picture: **milk.** Then ask children to listen to the following word, count the sounds, and color in one box for each sound: *milk*. (Answer: 4 sounds; Lessons 72–76)
4. Identify the picture: **stripes.** Then ask children to listen to the following word, count the sounds, and color in one box for each sound: *stripes*. (Answer: 6 sounds; Lessons 72–76)
5. Identify the picture: **clouds.** Then ask children to listen to the following word, count the sounds, and color in one box for each sound: *clouds*. (Answer: 5 sounds; Lessons 72–76)

## SCORING THE REVIEW

- Total the number of items answered correctly.
- Use the Percentage Table below to identify a percentage. Children should get at least 80 percent correct.
- Analyze each child's errors, using the lesson numbers provided above.
- Reteach those skills for which the child did not answer an item correctly.

**Percentage Table**

| | | | |
|---|---|---|---|
| **5 correct** | 100% | **2 correct** | 40% |
| **4 correct** | 80% | **1 correct** | 20% |
| **3 correct** | 60% | **0 correct** | 0% |

# Phonemic Awareness Review

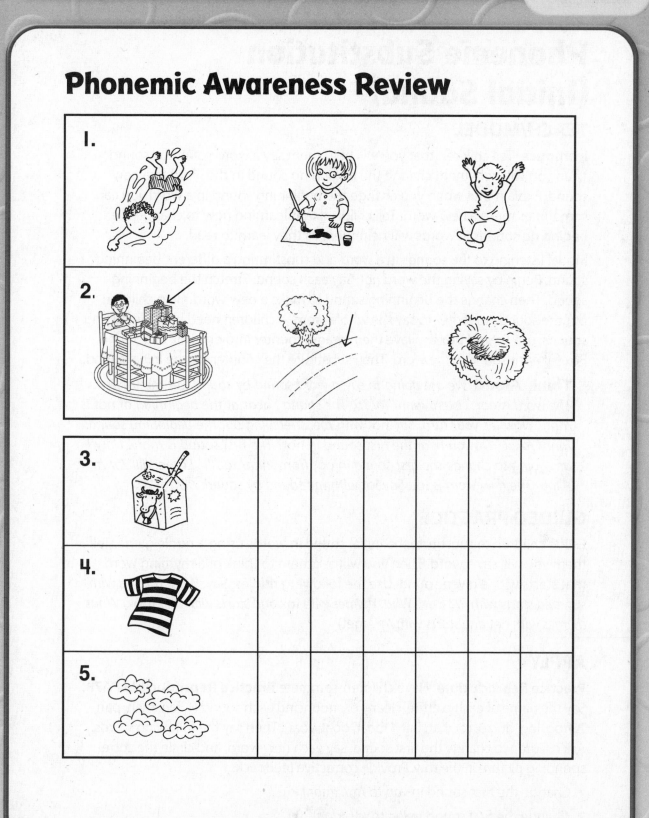

| | | |
|---|---|---|
| I.  |  |  |
| 2. 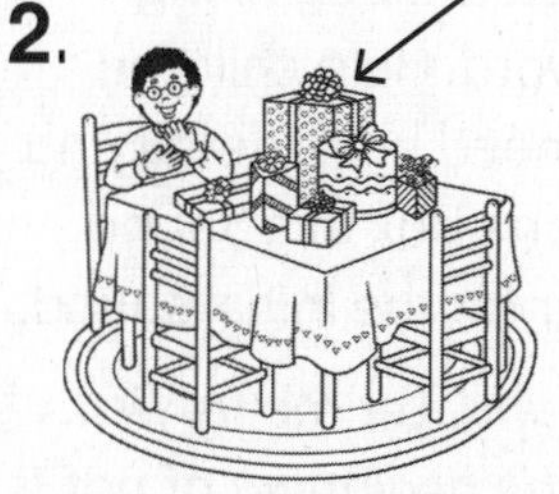 | 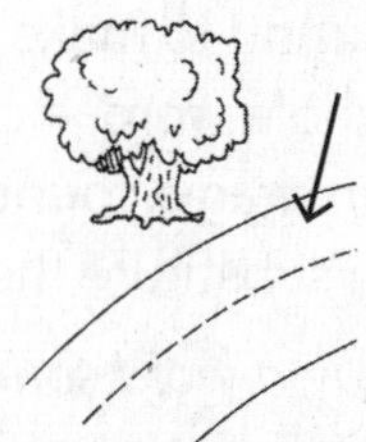 |  |

| | | | | | |
|---|---|---|---|---|---|
| 3.  | | | | | |
| 4.  | | | | | |
| 5.  | | | | | |

LESSON
78
Phonemic Awareness

# Phoneme Substitution (Initial Sound)

## TEACH/MODEL

**Introduce** Tell children that you will help them say a word sound by sound. Then you will help them change the beginning sound in the word to a new sound. Explain that when you change the beginning sound in a word you can sometimes make a new word. Tell children that learning how to change the beginning sounds in words will help them as they learn to read.

Model listening to the sounds in a word and substituting a different beginning sound. Begin by saying the word *not*. Say each sound. Stretch the beginning sound. Then change the beginning sound to make a new word. Help children put the sounds together to say the whole word. If children need help identifying sounds, use **Sound Boxes**. Have them drag a counter into one box of a Sound Box for each sound in the word. Then substitute the counter for the initial sound.

> **Think Aloud** *We are going to say a word sound by sound. Let me try first. The word is* not. *Listen: /nnn/ /o/ /t/. The sound I hear at the beginning of* not *is /nnn/. Now it's your turn. Say* not *with me, stretching out the beginning sound: /nnn/ /o/ /t/. Do you hear the first sound in* not*? The first sound is /nnn/. Now I am going to change the first sound in* not *from /nnn/ to /lll/. Listen: /lll/ /o/ /t/, /lllot/. The new word is* lot. *Say* lot *with me sound by sound: /lll/ /o/ /t/.*

## GUIDED PRACTICE

Guide children to substitute the initial sound in words using a riddle game. Tell them you will say a word. Then you will ask them to think of a rhyming word that starts with a given sound. Use the following riddles. Say: *What rhymes with* sun *and starts with /r/?* (run) *What rhymes with* fox *and starts with /b/?* (box) *What rhymes with* net *and starts with /g/?* (get)

## APPLY

**Practice Reproducible** Have children complete **Practice Reproducible PA78.** Say the name of each picture, clearly pronouncing each sound (1. fan, man, pan 2. frog, log, dog 3. cat, hat, bat 4. boat, goat, coat). Then say the following words. Ask children to change the first sound, say each new word, and circle the corresponding picture in the row. Provide corrective feedback.

**1.** Change the first sound in *van* to /m/. *(man)*

**2.** Change the first sound in *log* to /d/. *(dog)*

**3.** Change the first sound in *sat* to /b/. *(bat)*

**4.** Change the first sound in *note* to /b/. *(boat)*

# Sound Switch

**Listen to each word your teacher says. Change the first sound to the new sound you hear. Circle the picture of the word formed.**

1.

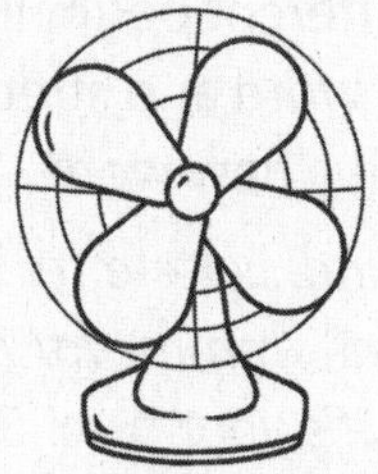

2.

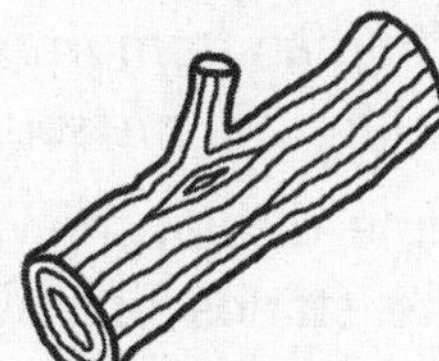

3.

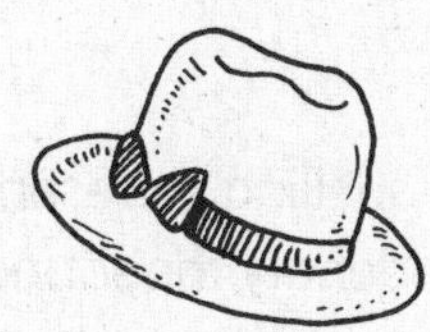

4.

LESSON
79
Phonemic Awareness

# Phoneme Substitution (Initial Sound)

## TEACH/MODEL

**Introduce** Tell children that you will help them say a word sound by sound. Then you will help them change the beginning sound in the word to a new sound. Explain that when you change the beginning sound in a word you can sometimes make a new word.

Model listening to the sounds in a word and substituting a different beginning sound. Begin by saying the word *man.* Say each sound in the word and stretch the beginning sound. Then change the beginning sound to make a new word.

> **Think Aloud** *We are going to say a word sound by sound. Let me try first. The word is* man. *Listen:* [Stretch out the beginning sound] */mmm/ /a/ /n/. The sound I hear at the beginning of* man *is /mmm/. Now it's your turn. Say* man *with me sound by sound, stretching out the beginning sound: /mmm/ /a/ /n/. Do you hear the first sound in* man*? The first sound is /mmm/. Now I am going to change the first sound in* man *from /mmm/ to /fff/. Listen: /fff/ /a/ /n/, /fffan/. The new word is* fan. *Say* fan *with me sound by sound: /fff/ /a/ /n/.*

**Word-Building Cards** One at a time, display the Word-Building Cards *m, a,* and *n.* Identify the sound that each letter stands for. Have children repeat the sounds. Then use the Word-Building Cards to spell *man.* Model how to blend *man.* Show the Word-Building Card *f,* and identify the sound it stands for. Replace the letter *m* in *man* with the letter *f,* and model how to blend the new word, *fan.*

## GUIDED PRACTICE

Guide children in identifying sound-spelling correspondences. One at a time, display the Word-Building Cards *h, o,* and *t.* Identify the sound that each letter stands for. Have children repeat the sounds. Then use Word-Building Cards to spell the word *hot.* Model how to blend *hot.* Replace the letter *h* in *hot* with the letter *p* and model how to blend the new word, *pot.* Continue using the Word-Building Cards to build the following words and substitute initial sounds. Help children read each word.

net, pet, met    mop, top, hop    tan, man, pan

## APPLY

**Practice Reproducible** Help children cut apart the letter cards on **Practice Reproducible PA79.** Have partners use the letter cards to build and read the following words, one at a time. Ask them to change the first letter in each word to make as many new words as they can. Provide corrective feedback.

**hen** (ten, men, pen) **map** (tap, nap) **top** (mop, hop) **pat** (hat, mat)

## Letter Cards

**Cut out the letter cards. Use them to build and read words.**

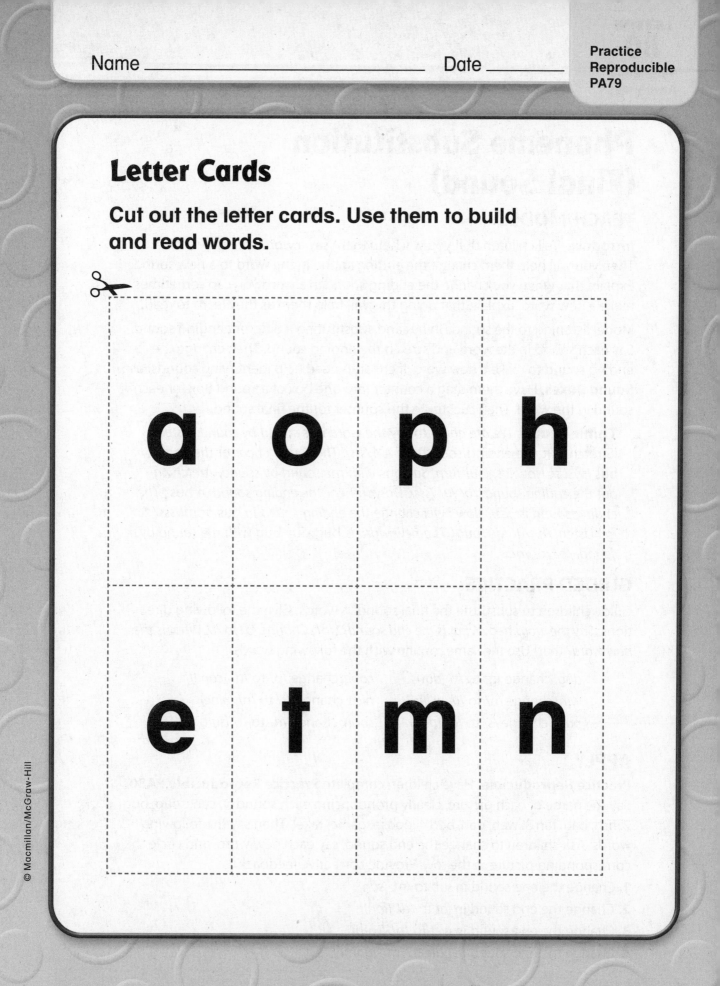

| a | o | p | h |
|---|---|---|---|
| e | t | m | n |

# Phoneme Substitution (Final Sound)

## TEACH/MODEL

**Introduce** Tell children that you will help them say a word sound by sound. Then you will help them change the ending sound in the word to a new sound. Explain that when you change the ending sound in a word you can sometimes make a new word. Explain that doing this will help them as they learn to read.

Model listening to the sounds in *bus* and substituting a different ending sound. Say each sound in the word and stretch the ending sound. Then change the ending sound to make a new word. If children need help identifying sounds, use **Sound Boxes.** Have them drag a counter into one box of a Sound Box for each sound in the word. Then substitute the counter for the final sound.

> **Think Aloud** *We are going to say the word* bus *sound by sound. Listen:* [Stretch out the ending sound] */b/ /u/ /sss/. The sound I hear at the end of* bus *is /sss/. Now it's your turn. Say* bus *with me sound by sound, stretching out the ending sound: /b/ /u/ /sss/. Do you hear the ending sound in* bus*? The ending sound is /sss/. Now I will change the ending sound in* bus *from /sss/ to /g/. Listen: /b/ /u/ /g/, /bug/. The new word is* bug. *Say* bug *with me sound by sound: /b/ /u/ /g/.*

## GUIDED PRACTICE

Guide children to substitute the final sound in words. Give the following directions: *Say the word* had. *What is the end sound?* (/d/) *Change /d/ to /t/. What is the new word?* (hat) Use the same routine with the following words.

*dog:* change /g/ to /t/ *(dot)*
*win:* change /n/ to /l/ *(will)*
*pass:* change /s/ to /d/ *(pad)*
*cape:* change /p/ to /n/ *(cane)*
*nice:* change /s/ to /n/ *(nine)*
*soon:* change /n/ to /t/ *(suit)*

## APPLY

**Practice Reproducible** Have children complete **Practice Reproducible PA80.** Say the name of each picture, clearly pronouncing each sound (1. sun, soap, bug 2. fish, bag, fan 3. web, pan, bed 4. goose, game, rake). Then say the following words. Ask children to change the end sound, say each new word, and circle the corresponding picture in the row. Provide corrective feedback.

**1.** Change the end sound in *sub* to /n/. *(sun)*
**2.** Change the end sound in *fat* to /n/. *(fan)*
**3.** Change the end sound in *wet* to /b/. *(web)*
**4.** Change the end sound in *gate* to /m/. *(game)*

Name ______________________ Date ____________ **Practice Reproducible PA80**

# Sound Switch

**Listen to each word your teacher says. Change the end sound to the new sound you hear. Circle the picture of the word formed.**

**1.**

**2.**

 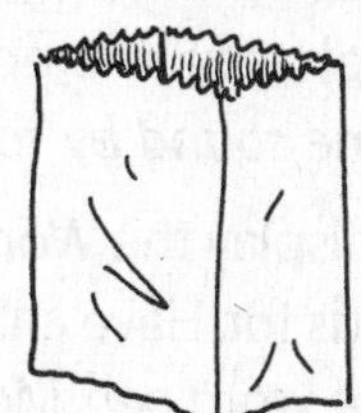 

**3.**

**4.**

 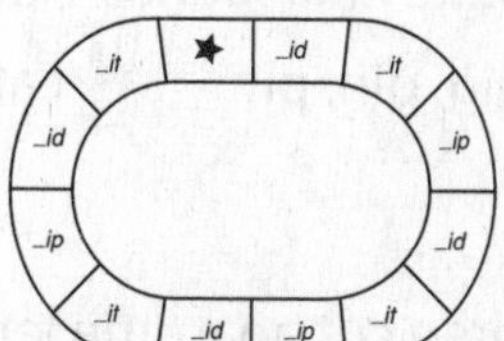 

# Phoneme Substitution (Final Sound)

## TEACH/MODEL

**Introduce** Tell children that you will help them say a word sound by sound. Then you will help them change the ending sound in the word to a new sound. Explain that when you change the ending sound in a word you can sometimes make a new word. Explain that learning how to change the ending sounds in words will help them as they learn to read.

Model listening to the sounds in a word and substituting a different ending sound. Begin by saying the word *pen*. Say each sound in the word and stretch the ending sound. Then change the ending sound to make a new word.

> **Think Aloud** *We are going to say* pen *sound by sound. Listen:* [Stretch out the ending sound] */p/ /e/ /nnn/. The sound I hear at the end of* pen *is /nnn/. Say* pen *with me sound by sound, stretching out the ending sound: /p/ /e/ /nnn/. The ending sound is /nnn/. Now I am going to change the ending sound in* pen *from /nnn/ to /t/. Listen:* [Emphasize the ending sound] */p/ /e/ /t/, /pet/. The new word is* pet. *Say* pet *with me sound by sound: /p/ /e/ /t/.*

**Word-Building Cards** One at a time, display the Word-Building Cards *p*, *e*, and *n*. Identify the sound that each letter stands for. Have children repeat the sounds. Then use the Word-Building Cards to spell the word *pen*. Model how to blend the word *pen*. Show the Word-Building Card *t*, and identify the sound it stands for. Replace the letter *n* in *pen* with the letter *t*, and model how to blend the new word, *pet*.

## GUIDED PRACTICE

Guide children in identifying sound-spelling correspondences. One at a time, display the Word-Building Cards *t*, *i*, and *p*. Identify the sound that each letter stands for. Have children repeat the sounds. Then use the Word-Building Cards to spell the word *tip*. Model how to blend the word *tip*. Replace the letter *p* in *tip* with the letter *n* and model how to blend the new word, *tin*. Continue using the Word-Building Cards to build the following words and substitute final sounds. Help children read each word.

tap, tan, tag    pig, pin, pit    cat, can, cap

## APPLY

**Practice Reproducible** Help children cut apart the letter cards on **Practice Reproducible PA81.** Have partners use the letter cards to build and read the following words, one at a time. Ask them to change the final letter in each word to make as many new words as they can. Provide corrective feedback.

**fit** (fig, fin) **can** (cap, cat) **pin** (pig, pit) **tag** (tan, tap)

# Letter Cards

**Cut out the letter cards. Use them to build and read words.**

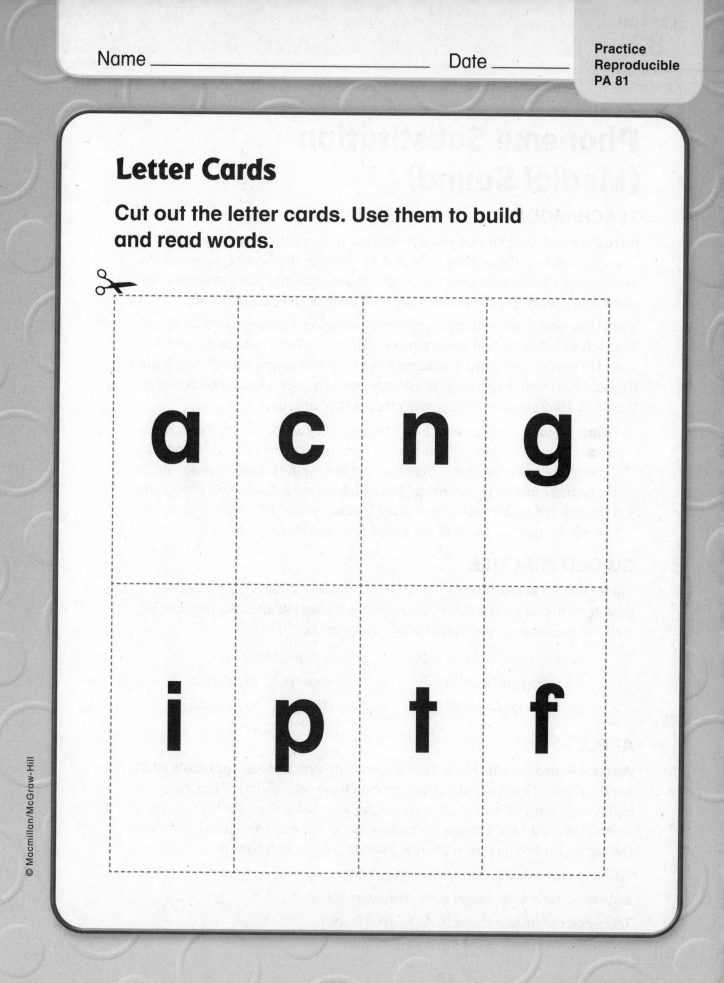

| a | c | n | g |
|---|---|---|---|
| i | p | t | f |

LESSON
82
Phonemic Awareness

# Phoneme Substitution (Medial Sound)

## TEACH/MODEL

**Introduce** Tell children that you will help them say a word sound by sound. Then you will help them change the middle sound in the word to a new sound. Explain that when you change the middle sound in a word you can sometimes make a new word. Explain that this will help them as they learn to read.

Model listening to the sounds in *top* and substituting a different middle sound. Say each sound in *top* and stretch the middle sound. Then change the middle sound to make a new word. If children need help identifying sounds, use **Sound Boxes.** Have them drag a counter into one box of a Sound Box for each sound in the word. Then substitute the counter for the medial sound.

> **Think Aloud** *We are going to say* top *sound by sound. Listen:* [Stretch the middle sound] */t/ /ooo/ /p/. The sound I hear in the middle of* top *is /ooo/. Say* top *with me sound by sound, stretching out the middle sound: /t/ /ooo/ /p/. Do you hear the middle sound in* top*? The middle sound is /ooo/. Now I am going to change the middle sound from /ooo/ to /aaa/. Listen: /t/ /aaa/ /p/, /tap/. The new word is* tap. *Say* tap *with me sound by sound: /t/ /aaa/ /p/.*

## GUIDED PRACTICE

Guide children to substitute the middle sound in words. Say: *Say the word* nut. *What is the middle sound? (/uuu/) Change /uuu/ to /eee/. What is the new word?* (net) Use the same routine with the following words.

*hum:* change /u/ to /a/ *(ham)*
*fell:* change /e/ to /i/ *(fill)*
*goat:* change /ō/ to /e/ *(get)*
*ride:* change /ī/ to /e/ *(red)*
*heap:* change /ē/ to /o/ *(hop)*
*tune:* change / ü/ to /a/ *(tan)*

## APPLY

**Practice Reproducible** Have children complete **Practice Reproducible PA82.** Say the name of each picture, clearly pronouncing each sound (1. log, bag, bed 2. map, pig, ball 3. dog, car, duck 4. king, wig, web). Then say the following words. Ask children to change the middle sound, say each new word, and circle the corresponding picture in the row. Provide corrective feedback.

**1.** Change the middle sound in *bug* to /a/. *(bag)*

**2.** Change the middle sound in *mop* to /a/. *(map)*

**3.** Change the middle sound in *deck* to /u/. *(duck)*

**4.** Change the middle sound in *wag* to /i/. *(wig)*

# Sound Switch

**Listen to each word your teacher says. Change the middle sound to the new sound you hear. Circle the picture of the word formed.**

1\.

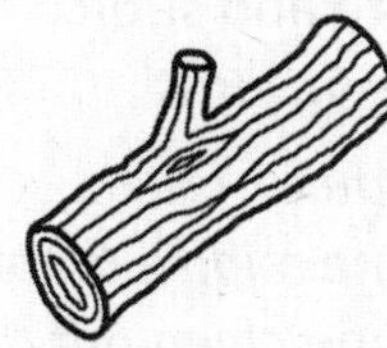 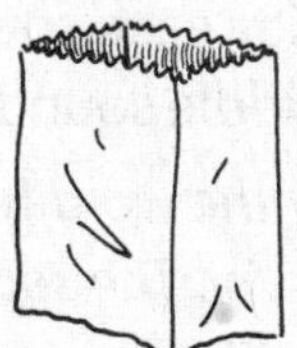 

2\.

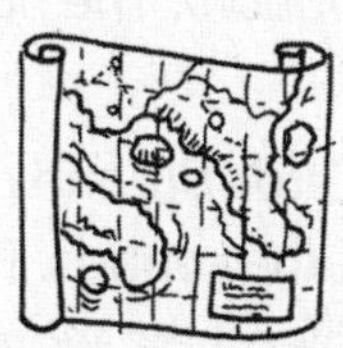  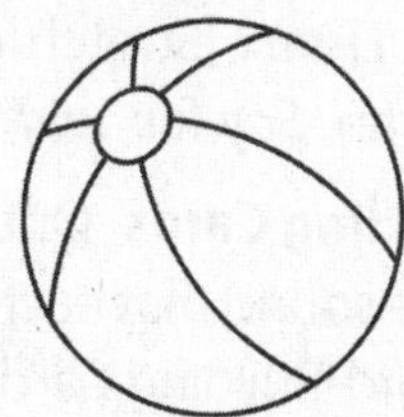

3\.

4\.

LESSON
83
Phonemic Awareness

# Phoneme Substitution (Medial Sound)

## TEACH/MODEL

**Introduce** Tell children that you will help them say a word sound by sound. Then you will help them change the middle sound in the word to a new sound. Explain that when you change the middle sound in a word you can sometimes make a new word. Explain that this will help them as they learn to read.

Model listening to the sounds in a word and substituting a different middle sound. Begin by saying the word *fun*. Say each sound in the word and stretch the middle sound. Then change the middle sound to make a new word.

> **Think Aloud** *We are going to say the word* fun *sound by sound. Listen:* [Stretch the middle sound] */f/ /uuu/ /n/. The sound I hear in the middle of* fun *is /uuu/. Now it's your turn. Say* fun *with me sound by sound, stretching out the middle sound: /f/ /uuu/ /n/. Do you hear the middle sound in* fun*? The middle sound is /uuu/. Now I am going to change the middle sound in* fun *from /uuu/ to /aaa/. Listen:* [Stretch out the middle sound] */f/ /aaa/ /n/, /faaan/. The new word is* fan. *Say* fan *with me sound by sound: /f/ /aaa/ /n/.*

**Word-Building Cards** One at a time, display the Word-Building Cards *f*, *u*, and *n*. Identify the sound that each letter stands for. Have children repeat the sounds. Then use the Word-Building Cards to spell the word *fun*. Model how to blend the word *fun*. Show the Word-Building Card *a*, and identify the sound it stands for. Replace the letter *u* in *fun* with the letter *a*, and model how to blend the new word, *fan*.

## GUIDED PRACTICE

Guide children in identifying sound-spelling correspondences. One at a time, display the Word-Building Cards *s*, *i*, and *p*. Identify the sound that each letter stands for. Have children repeat the sounds. Then use the Word-Building Cards to spell the word *sip*. Model how to blend the word *sip*. Replace the letter *i* in *sip* with the letter *a* and model how to blend the new word, *sap*. Continue using the Word-Building Cards to build the following words and substitute medial sounds. Help children read each word.

pan, pen, pin    top, tap, tip    sit, sat, set

## APPLY

**Practice Reproducible** Help children cut apart the letter cards on **Practice Reproducible PA83.** Have partners use the letter cards to build and read the following words, one at a time. Ask them to change the middle letter in each word to make new words. Provide corrective feedback.

**bat** (bet, bit) **ten** (tan, tin) **pet** (pot, pat, pit) **tap** (top, tip)

# Letter Cards

**Cut out the letter cards. Use them to build and read words.**

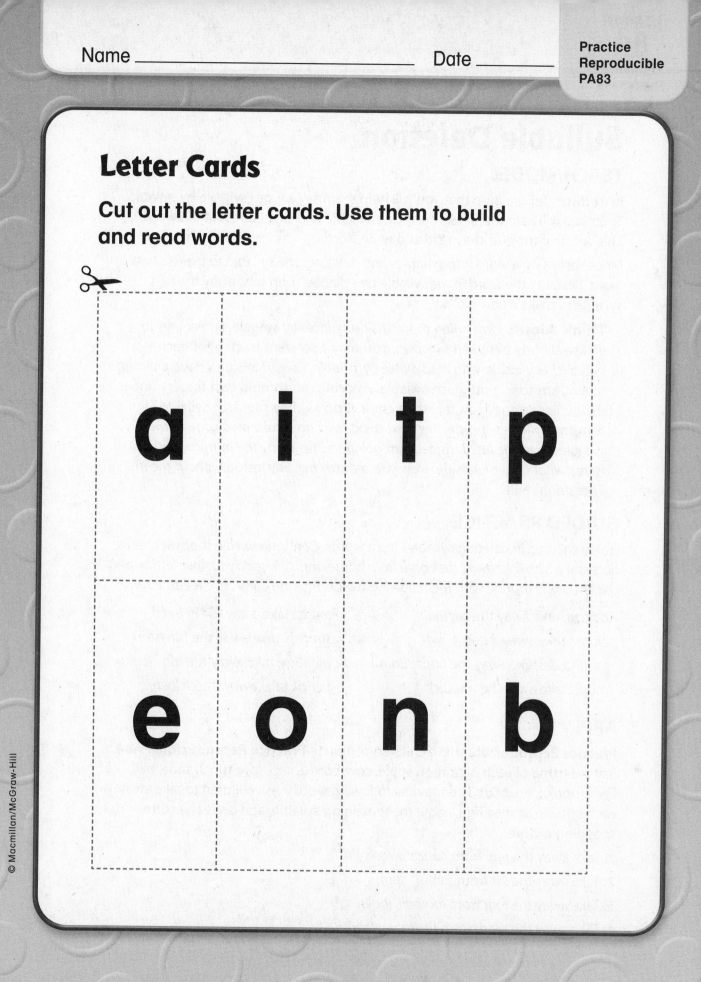

| | | | |
|---|---|---|---|
| a | i | t | p |
| e | o | n | b |

# Syllable Deletion

## TEACH/MODEL

**Introduce** Tell children that you will help them say a word syllable by syllable. Then you will help them take away one syllable and say the rest of the word. This will help them as they read and write words.

Model breaking a word into syllables and deleting one syllable to make a new word. First, say the word *inside* syllable by syllable. Then take away the first syllable to make a new word.

**Think Aloud** *I am going to say* inside *syllable by syllable. Listen:* in|side. [Pause slightly between syllables. You may also want to clap for each syllable.] *Say* inside *with me syllable by syllable. Ready?* in|side. [Have children repeat, stretching out each syllable. Ask children to hold two fingers under their chins so they can feel their chins drop as they say each syllable.] *I hear two syllables:* in|side. *The next thing I will do is take away one of the syllables from the word* inside. *I am going to take away the* in *from* inside. *Here's what I have left:* side. *Now you try with me. Say* inside *without the* in. *That's right,* side.

## GUIDED PRACTICE

Guide children in deleting syllables from words. Continue to clap the syllables as necessary. Say: *Take away the* home *from* homework. *What do you have left?* (work) Use the same routine with the following words. Provide corrective feedback.

*haircut:* take away the *cut (hair)*
*elbow:* take away the *el (bow)*
*farmhouse:* take away the *house (farm)*
*music:* take away the *mu (sic)*
*insect:* take away the *in (sect)*
*starfish:* take away the *fish (star)*
*mailbox:* take away the *mail (box)*
*pencil:* take away the *cil (pen)*

## APPLY

**Practice Reproducible** Have children complete **Practice Reproducible PA84.** Say the name of each picture (1. apple, cow, corn 2. sun, saw, tub 3. shoe, ball, fox 4. book, pen, bed). Then say the following words. Ask children to take away each syllable as specified, name the remaining syllable, and circle the corresponding picture.

**1.** Take away the *pop* from *popcorn. (corn)*
**2.** Take away the *set* from *sunset. (sun)*
**3.** Take away the *foot* from *football. (ball)*
**4.** Take away the *room* from *bedroom. (bed)*

# Syllables

**Listen to each word your teacher says. Take away one syllable. Circle the picture for the syllable that is left.**

| | | | |
|---|---|---|---|
| 1. |  |  | 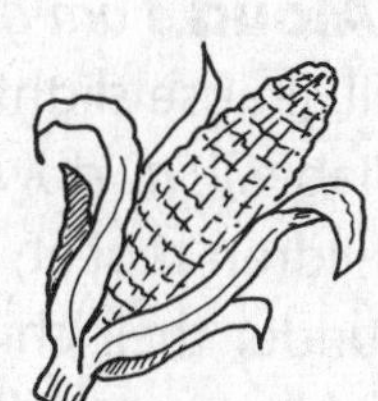 |
| 2 |  |  |  |
| 3. |  | 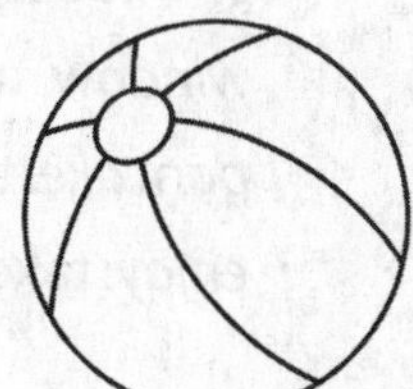 |  |
| 4. | 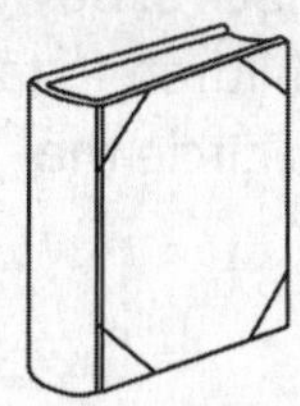 |  |  |

# Syllable Deletion

## TEACH/MODEL

**Introduce** Tell children that you will help them say a word syllable by syllable. Then you will help them take away one syllable and say the rest of the word. This will help them as they read and write words.

Model breaking a word into syllables and deleting one syllable to make a new word. First, say the word *downhill* syllable by syllable. Then take away the last syllable to make a new word.

**Think Aloud** *I am going to say* downhill *syllable by syllable. Listen:* down|hill. [Pause slightly between syllables. You may also want to clap for each syllable.] *Say* downhill *with me syllable by syllable. Ready?* down|hill. [Have children repeat, stretching out each syllable. Ask children to hold two fingers under their chins so they can feel their chins drop as they say each syllable.] *I hear two syllables:* down|hill. *The next thing I will do is take away one syllable from* downhill. *I will take away the* hill *from* downhill. *What's left?* Down. *Now you try with me. Say* downhill *without the* hill. *That's right,* down.

## GUIDED PRACTICE

Guide children in deleting syllables from words. Continue to clap the syllables as necessary. Say: *Take away the* bow *from* rainbow. *What do you have left?* (rain) Use the same routine with the following words. Provide corrective feedback.

*moonlight:* take away the *light (moon)*
*seashell:* take away the *shell (sea)*
*number:* take away the *num (ber)*
*morning:* take away the *morn (ing)*
*goldfish:* take away the *fish (gold)*
*tiger:* take away the *ger (ti)*
*bathrobe:* take away the *bath (robe)*
*window:* take away the *win (dow)*
*pancake:* take away the *cake (pan)*
*enjoy:* take away the *en (joy)*

## APPLY

**Practice Reproducible** Have children complete **Practice Reproducible PA85.** Say the name of each picture (1. bike, cup, hand 2. whale, watch, lock 3. boy, hook, bat 4. key, wave, ring). Then say the following words. Ask children to take away each syllable as specified, name the remaining syllable, and circle the corresponding picture.

1. Take away the *cake* from *cupcake. (cup)*
2. Take away the *dog* from *watchdog. (watch)*
3. Take away the *cow* from *cowboy. (boy)*
4. Take away the *ear* from *earring. (ring)*

Name ______________________ Date __________

# Syllables

**Listen to each word your teacher says. Take away one syllable. Circle the picture for the syllable that is left.**

**1.**

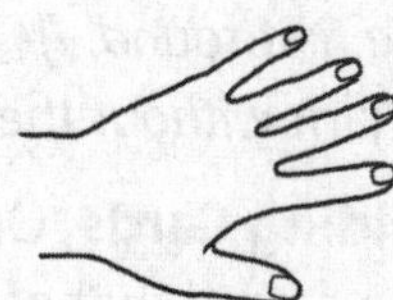

**2.**

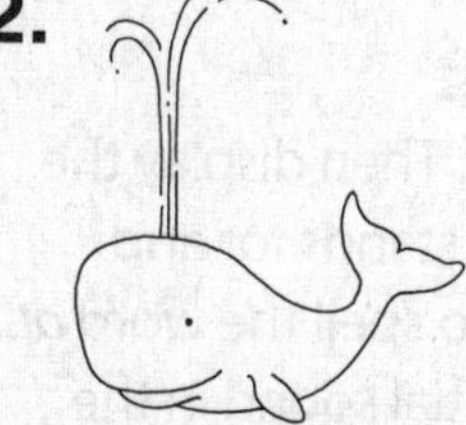

**3.**

**4.**

# Initial Sound Deletion

## TEACH/MODEL

**Introduce** Tell children that they will say a word sound by sound. Then you will help them take away the first sound and say the sounds that are left.

Model breaking a word into sounds and deleting the first sound. Then take away the first sound and say the sounds that are left.

> **Think Aloud** *We are going to say* jam *sound by sound. Listen: /j/ /a/ /m/.* [Pause slightly between each sound.] *Now you say* jam *with me sound by sound. Ready? /j/ /a/ /m/. I hear three sounds: /j/ /a/ /m/,* jam. *Next, we will take away the first sound, /j/, from* jam. *Here's what I have left:* am. *Now you try with me. Say* jam *without the /j/. That's right,* am. *That's a word, as in "I am going."*

**Word-Building Cards** One at a time, display the Word-Building Cards *a* and *m*. Identify the sound that each letter stands for. Have children repeat the sounds. Then use the Word-Building Cards to spell the word *am*. Model how to blend the word *am*.

## GUIDED PRACTICE

Model taking away the first sound /k/ in *cat* to form the word *at*. Then display the Word-Building Cards *a* and *t*. Identify the sound that each letter stands for and have children repeat the sounds. Use the Word-Building Cards to spell the word *at*. Have children read the word with you. Continue deleting the initial sound in the following words and using the Word-Building Cards to build the new words. Help children read each word. Point out that when you delete the first sound sometimes you get a real word, such as *an*, and sometimes you get a nonsense word, such as *ix*.

*man:* take away the /m/ *(an)*
*fix:* take away the /f/ *(ix)*
*top:* take away the /t/ *(op)*
*win:* take away the /w/ *(in)*
*box:* take away the /b/ *(ox)*
*sat:* take away the /s/ *(at)*

## APPLY

**Practice Reproducible** Help children cut apart the letter cards on **Practice Reproducible PA86.** Work through the following activity as a whole group or have children work in pairs. Say each of the following words. Ask children to take away the first sound, say the new word, and build it with the letter cards. Have children read the words to confirm their answers. Provide corrective feedback.

*fog:* take away the /f/ *(og)*
*map:* take away the /m/ *(ap)*
*chin:* take away the /ch/ *(in)*
*hug:* take away the /h/ *(ug)*
*Don:* take away the /d/ *(on)*
*lit:* take away the /l/ *(it)*

Name ________________________ Date __________



## Letter Cards

**Cut out the letter cards. Use them to build and read words.**

| | | | |
|---|---|---|---|
| a | o | g | n |
| i | u | t | p |

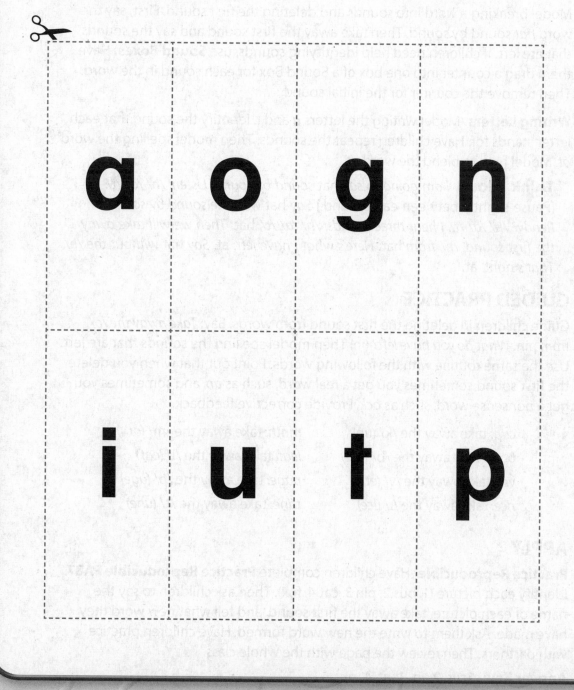

# Initial Sound Deletion

## TEACH/MODEL

**Introduce** Tell children that you will help them say a word sound by sound. Then you will help them take away the first sound and say the sounds that are left. This will help them as they read and write words.

Model breaking a word into sounds and deleting the first sound. First, say the word *hat* sound by sound. Then take away the first sound and say the sounds that are left. If children need help identifying sounds, use **Sound Boxes.** Have them drag a counter into one box of a Sound Box for each sound in the word. Then remove the counter for the initial sound.

**Writing Letters** Model writing the letters *a* and *t*. Identify the sound that each letter stands for. Have children repeat the sounds. Then model spelling the word *at*. Model how to blend the word *at*.

> **Think Aloud** *I am going to say* hat *sound by sound. Listen: /h/ /a/ /t/.* [Pause slightly between each sound.] *Say* hat *with me sound by sound. Ready? /h/ /a/ /t/. I hear three sounds: /h/ /a/ /t/,* hat. *Then we will take away the first sound, /h/, from* hat. *Here's what I have left:* at. *Say* hat *without the /h/. That's right,* at.

## GUIDED PRACTICE

Guide children in deleting the first sound from words. Say: *Take away the /p/ from* pin. *What do you have left?* (in) Then model spelling the sounds that are left. Use the same routine with the following words. Point out that when you delete the first sound sometimes you get a real word, such as *up*, and sometimes you get a nonsense word, such as *ock*. Provide corrective feedback.

*cup:* take away the /k/ *(up)*
*boat:* take away the /b/ *(oat)*
*vet:* take away the /v/ *(et)*
*rice:* take away the /r/ *(ice)*
*math:* take away the /m/ *(ath)*
*leaf:* take away the /l/ *(eaf)*
*page:* take away the /p/ *(age)*
*tune:* take away the /t/ *(une)*

## APPLY

**Practice Reproducible** Have children complete **Practice Reproducible PA87.** Identify each picture (1. bus 2. pin 3. cat 4. fox). Then ask children to say the name of each picture, take away the first sound, and tell what new word they have made. Ask them to write the new word formed. Have children practice with partners. Then review the page with the whole class.

**Answer Key: 1.** *us* **2.** *in* **3.** *at* **4.** *ox*

# Write Words

**Say the name of each picture. Then take away the first sound. Say the new word you have made. Write the new word.**

| | |
|---|---|
| 1. | |
| 2. | |
| 3. | |
| 4. | |

# Review

## PREPARING THE REVIEW

- Make one copy of **Practice Reproducible PA88** for each child.
- Write the child's name and today's date at the top of the review.

## ADMINISTERING THE REVIEW

- Administer the review to one child at a time.
- Follow these instructions for each item. Each phonemic awareness skill was taught in the lessons indicated in parentheses.

1. Identify the picture: **book, vine,** and **bike.** Then ask children to change the beginning sound in *like* to /b/, say the new word, and then circle the picture that shows the new word. (Answer: *bike*; Lessons 78–79)
2. Identify each picture: **kite, wave,** and **whale.** Then ask children to change the ending sound in *wait* to /v/, say the new word, and then circle the picture that shows the new word. (Answer: *wave*; Lessons 80–81)
3. Identify each picture: **net, knot** and **nut.** Then ask children to change the middle sound in *note* to /e/, say the new word, and then circle the picture that shows the new word. (Answer: *net*; Lessons 82–83)
4. Identify each picture: **duck, door,** and **draw.** Then ask children to take away the *bell* from *doorbell*, say the syllable that is left, and circle the picture that shows the remaining syllable. (Answer: *door*; Lessons 84–85)
5. Identify each picture: **egg, up,** and **ox.** Then ask children to take away the beginning sound /l/ in *locks*, say the new word, and circle the picture that shows the new word. (Answer: *ox*; Lessons 86–87)

## SCORING THE REVIEW

- Total the number of items answered correctly.
- Use the Percentage Table below to identify a percentage. Children should get at least 80 percent correct.
- Analyze each child's errors, using the lesson numbers provided above.
- Reteach those skills for which the child did not answer an item correctly.

| Percentage Table | | | |
|---|---|---|---|
| **5 correct** | 100% | **2 correct** | 40% |
| **4 correct** | 80% | **1 correct** | 20% |
| **3 correct** | 60% | **0 correct** | 0% |

Name ______________________ Date __________



# Phonemic Awareness Review

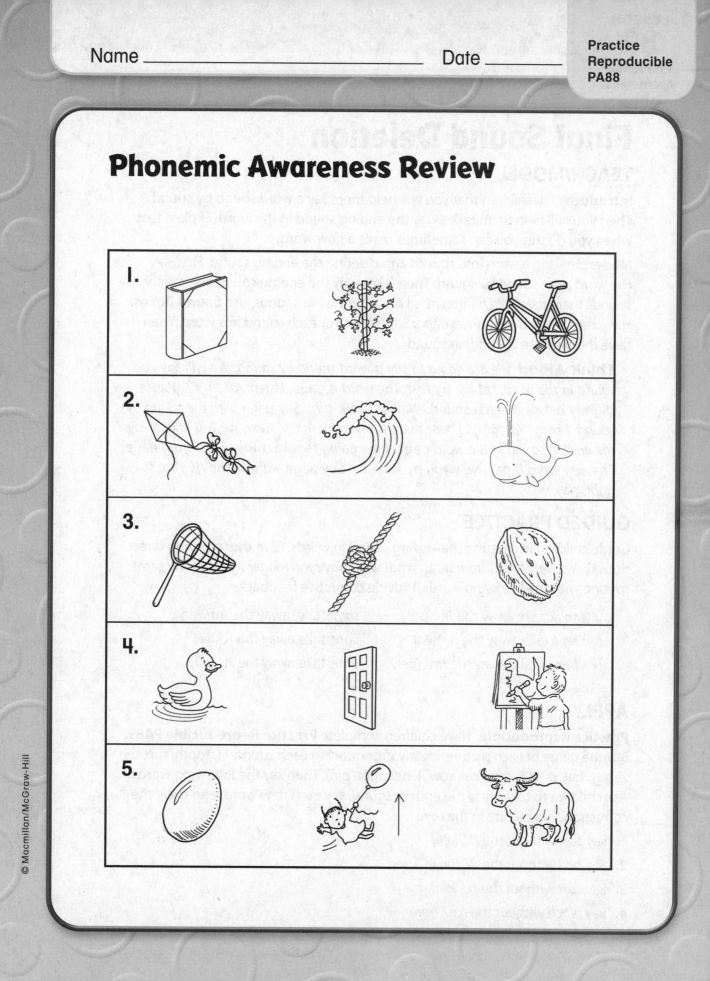

| | | | |
|---|---|---|---|
| 1. | 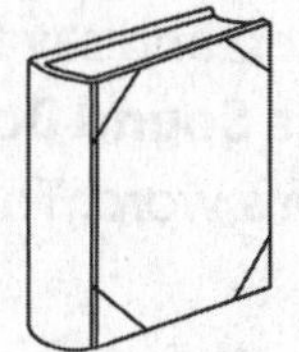 | 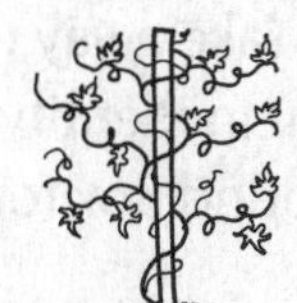 |  |
| 2. |  |  |  |
| 3. |  |  |  |
| 4. |  |  |  |
| 5. |  |  |  |

# Final Sound Deletion

## TEACH/MODEL

**Introduce** Tell children that you will help them say a word sound by sound. Then you will help them take away the ending sound in the word. Explain that when you do this you can sometimes make a new word.

Model breaking a word into sounds and deleting the ending sound. First, say the word *page* sound by sound. Then take away the ending sound and say the sounds that are left. If children need help identifying sounds, use **Sound Boxes.** Have them drag one counter into a Sound Box for each sound in a word. Then have them delete the ending sound.

**Think Aloud** *We are going to say a word sound by sound. We will say each sound in the word. Let me try first. The word is* page. *Listen: /p/ /ā/ /j/.* [Pause slightly between each sound.] *Now it's your turn. Say* page *with me sound by sound. Ready? /p/ /ā/ /j/. I hear three sounds: /p/ /ā/ /j/. Next, we will take away the ending sound in the word* page. *I am going to take away the /j/ from* page. *The new word is* pay. *Now you try with me. Say* page *without the /j/. That's right,* pay.

## GUIDED PRACTICE

Guide children in deleting the ending sound in words. Give the following directions: *Take away the /t/ from* goat. *What word have you made?* (go) Use the same routine with the following words. Provide corrective feedback.

*soak:* take away the /k/ *(so)*
*seal:* take away the /l/ *(sea)*
*beam:* take away the /m/ *(bee)*
*same:* take away the /m/ *(say)*
*light:* take away the /t/ *(lie)*
*date:* take away the /t/ *(day)*

## APPLY

**Practice Reproducible** Have children complete **Practice Reproducible PA89.** Say the name of each picture, clearly pronouncing each sound: (1. tooth, tub, ten 2. boy, bat, bike 3. crab, car, cow 4. pen, pot, pin). Then say the following words. Ask children to take away the ending sound, say each new word, and circle the corresponding picture in the row.

1. Say *tent* without the /t/. *(ten)*
2. Say *boil* without the /l/. *(boy)*
3. Say *cart* without the /t/. *(car)*
4. Say *pinch* without the /ch/. *(pin)*

Name ______________________ Date __________



## Take Away a Sound

**Listen to each word your teacher says. Take away the ending sound. Circle the picture of the word formed.**

**1.**

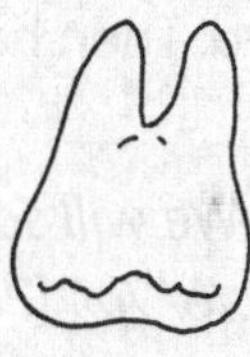

**2.**

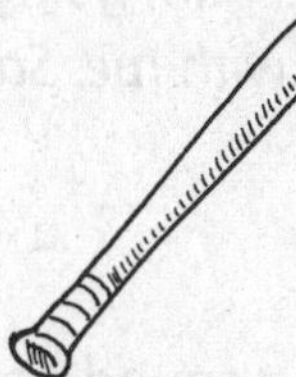

**3.**

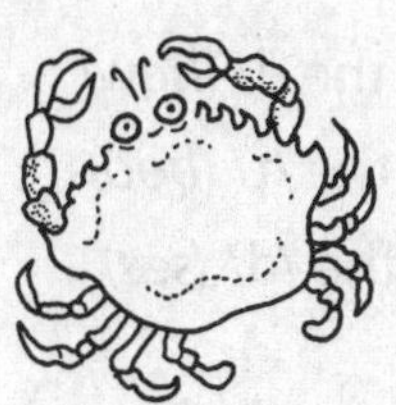

**4.**

# Final Sound Deletion

## TEACH/MODEL

**Introduce** Tell children that you will help them say a word sound by sound. Then you will help them take away the ending sound in the word. Explain that when you take away the sound at the end of a word you can sometimes make a new word.

Model breaking a word into sounds and deleting the ending sound. First, say the word *rope* sound by sound. Then take away the ending sound and say the sounds that are left. If children need help identifying sounds, use **Sound Boxes.** Have them drag one counter into a Sound Box for each sound in a word. Then have them delete the ending sound.

**Think Aloud** *We are going to say a word sound by sound. We will say each sound in the word. Let me try first. The word is* rope. *Listen: /r/ /ō/ /p/.* [Pause slightly between each sound.] *Now it's your turn. Say* rope *with me sound by sound. Ready? /r/ /ō/ /p/. I hear three sounds: /r/ /ō/ /p/. Next, we will take away the ending sound in the word* rope. *I am going to take away the /p/ from* rope. *The new word is* row. *Now you try with me. Say* rope *without the /p/. That's right,* row.

## GUIDED PRACTICE

Guide children in deleting the ending sound from words. Give the following directions: *Take away the /t/ from* meet. *What do you have left?* (me) Use the same routine with the following words. Provide corrective feedback.

*sheep:* take away the /p/ *(she)*
*wheat:* take away the /t/ *(we)*
*beach:* take away the /ch/ *(bee)*
*howl:* take away the /l/ *(how)*
*boot:* take away the /t/ *(boo)*
*seed:* take away the /d/ *(see)*

## APPLY

**Practice Reproducible** Help children cut apart the letter cards on **Practice Reproducible PA90.** Say the name of each picture, clearly pronouncing each sound: (1. cow, cat, comb 2. kite, king, key 3. pan, pie, pig 4. book, bear, ball). Then say the following words. Ask children to take away the ending sound, say each new word, and circle the corresponding picture in the row.

1. *couch*: take away the /ch/ *(cow)*
2. *keep*: take away the /p/ *(key)*
3. *pipe*: take away the /p/ *(pie)*
4. *bald*: take away the /d/ *(ball)*

Name ______________________________ Date __________



# Take Away a Sound

**Listen to each word your teacher says. Then take away the ending sound. Circle the picture of the word formed.**

**1.**

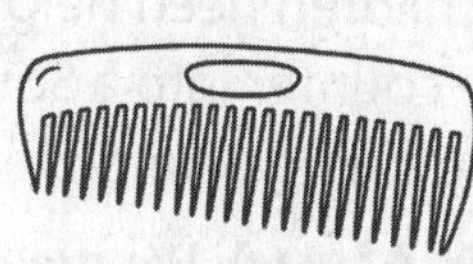

**2.**

**3.**

**4.**

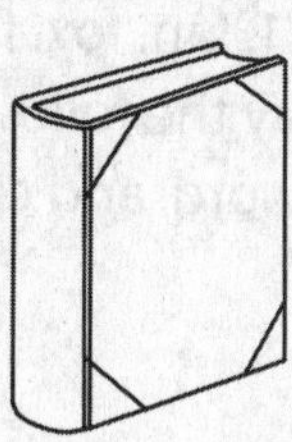

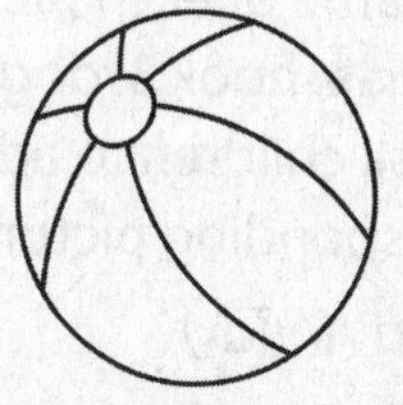

LESSON
91
Phonemic Awareness

# Phoneme Addition (Add an Initial Sound)

## TEACH/MODEL

**Introduce** Tell children that you will help them say a word sound by sound. Then you will help them add a new sound to the beginning of the word. Explain that when you do this, you can sometimes make a new word.

Model breaking a word into sounds and adding a beginning sound. First, say the word *it* sound by sound. Then add a beginning sound and say the new word. If children need help identifying sounds, use **Sound Boxes.** Have them drag one counter into a Sound Box for each sound in a word. Then have them add a beginning sound.

**Think Aloud** *We are going to say* it *sound by sound. Let me try first. Listen: /i/ /t/.* [Pause slightly between each sound.] *Now it's your turn. Say* it *with me sound by sound. Ready? /i/ /t/. Now we will add a new sound to the beginning. I will add /f/ to the beginning of* it. *Listen: /fff/ /i/ /t/. The new word is* fit. *Say* fit *with me sound by sound: /f/ /i/ /t/. The word is* fit.

## GUIDED PRACTICE

Guide children in adding the beginning sound in words. Give the following directions: *Add a /b/ to* at. *What word have you made?* (bat) Use the same routine with the following words. Provide corrective feedback.

*am:* add /r/ *(ram)*
*am:* add /h/ *(ham)*
*an:* add /m/ *(man)*
*an:* add /t/ *(tan)*
*ate:* add /h/ *(hate)*
*ate:* add /r/ *(rate)*
*eat:* add /s/ *(seat)*
*eat:* add /n/ *(neat)*

## APPLY

**Practice Reproducible** Have children complete **Practice Reproducible PA91.** Say the name of each picture, clearly pronouncing each sound: (1. fan, fox, fish 2. hat, horse, hook 3. dog, door, deer 4. goat, girl, guitar). Then say the following words. Ask children to add the beginning sound, say each new word, and circle the corresponding picture in the row.

1. *ox:* add /f/ *(fox)*
2. *at:* add /h/ *(hat)*
3. *ear:* add /d/ *(deer)*
4. *oat:* add /g/ *(goat)*

Name ______________________ Date __________



## Add a Beginning Sound

**Listen to each word your teacher says. Add the beginning sound. Circle the picture of the word formed.**

**1.**

**2.**

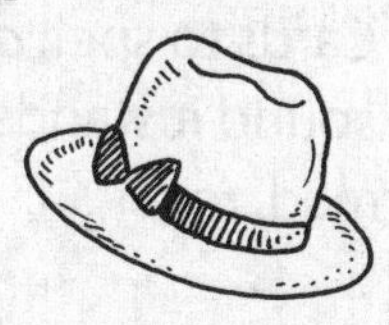

**3.**

**4.**

# Phoneme Addition (Add an Initial Sound)

## TEACH/MODEL

**Introduce** Tell children that you will help them say a word sound by sound. Then you will help them add a new sound to the beginning of the word. Explain that when you do this, you can sometimes make a new word.

Model breaking a word into sounds and adding a beginning sound. Say *an* sound by sound. Add a beginning sound. Say the new word. If children need help identifying sounds, use **Sound Boxes.** Have them drag one counter into a Sound Box for each sound in a word. Then have them add a beginning sound.

> **Think Aloud** *We are going to say* an *sound by sound. Listen: /a/ /n/.* [Pause slightly between each sound.] *Say* an *with me sound by sound. Ready? /a/ /n/. Now we will add the sound /r/ to the beginning. Listen: /r/ /a/ /n/. The new word is* ran. *Say* ran *with me sound by sound: /r/ /a/ /n/. The word is* ran.

**Letter Cards** Display the Letter Cards *a* and *n*. Identify the sound that each letter stands for. Have children repeat the sounds. Then use the Letter Cards to spell *an*. Model how to blend *an*. Show the Letter Card *r*, and identify the sound it stands for. Add the letter *r* to *an*, and model how to blend the word formed, *ran*.

## GUIDED PRACTICE

Guide children in identifying sound-spelling correspondences. Display the Letter Cards *a, p,* and *t*. Identify the sound that each letter stands for. Have children repeat the sounds. Then use the Letter Cards *a* and *t* to spell the word *at*. Model how to blend the word *at*. Add the Letter Card *p* at the beginning of the word *at*. Model how to blend the new word, *pat*. Continue using the Letter Cards to build the following words and add initial sounds. Help children read each word.

at, sat, bat    it, pit, sit    ad, bad, had

## APPLY

**Practice Reproducible** Help children cut apart the letter cards on **Practice Reproducible PA92.** Work through the following activity as a whole group or have children work in pairs. Say each of the following words. Ask children to add the beginning sound, say the new word, and build it with the letter cards. Have children read the words to confirm their answers. Provide corrective feedback.

| | | | |
|---|---|---|---|
| *it:* add /h/ *(hit)* | *at:* add /p/ *(pat)* | *at:* add /b/ *(bat)* | *ad:* add /b/ *(bad)* |
| *it:* add /b/ *(bit)* | *at:* add /s/ *(sat)* | *ad:* add /p/ *(pad)* | *ad:* add /d/ *(dad)* |
| *it:* add /s/ *(sit)* | *at:* add /h/ *(hat)* | *ad:* add /s/ *(sad)* | *ad:* add /h/ *(had)* |

# Letter Cards

**Cut out the letter cards. Use them to build and read words.**

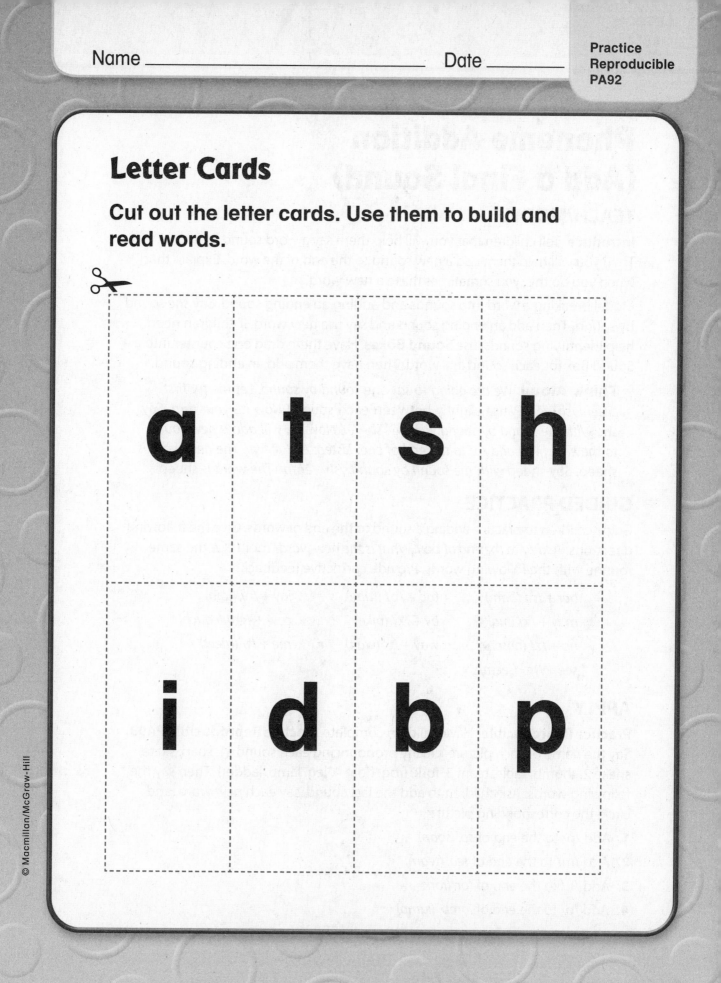

| a | t | s | h |
|---|---|---|---|
| i | d | b | p |

# Phoneme Addition (Add a Final Sound)

## TEACH/MODEL

**Introduce** Tell children that you will help them say a word sound by sound. Then you will help them add a new sound to the end of the word. Explain that when you do this, you sometimes make a new word.

Model breaking a word into sounds and adding an ending sound. Say *she* sound by sound. Then add an ending sound and say the new word. If children need help identifying sounds, use **Sound Boxes**. Have them drag one counter into a Sound Box for each sound in a word. Then have them add an ending sound.

**Think Aloud** *We are going to say* she *sound by sound. Let me try first. Listen: /sh/ /ē/.* [Pause slightly between each sound.] *Now it's your turn. Say* she *with me sound by sound. Ready? /sh/ /ē/. Now we will add a new sound to the end. I will add /p/ to the end of* she. *Listen: /sh/ /ē/ /p/. The new word is* sheep. *Say* sheep *with me sound by sound: /sh/ /ē/ /p/. The word is* sheep.

## GUIDED PRACTICE

Guide children to practice adding a sound to the end of words. Give the following directions: *Add /l/ to the end of* boy. *What is the new word?* (boil) Use the same routine with the following words. Provide corrective feedback.

*bar + /n/ (barn)* *too + /b/ (tube)* *joy + /n/ (join)*
*may + /k/ (make)* *by + /k/ (bike)* *cow + /ch/ (couch)*
*no + /z/ (nose)* *way + /t/ (wait)* *me + /t/ (meet)*
*see + /m/ (seem)*

## APPLY

**Practice Reproducible** Have children complete **Practice Reproducible PA93.** Say the name of each picture, clearly pronouncing each sound: (1. soap, skate, snake 2. thumb, table, team 3. fork, frog, float 4. leg, lamp, ladder). Then say the following words. Ask children to add the last sound, say each new word, and circle the corresponding picture.

1. Add /p/ to the end of *so. (soap)*
2. Add /m/ to the end of *tea. (team)*
3. Add /k/ to the end of *for. (fork)*
4. Add /p/ to the end of *lamb. (lamp)*

Name ______________________ Date __________



# Add a Sound

**Listen to each word your teacher says. Add the new sound you hear to the end of each word. Circle the picture of each word that is formed.**

# Phoneme Addition (Add a Final Sound)

## TEACH/MODEL

**Introduce** Tell children that you will help them say a word sound by sound. Then you will help them add a new sound to the end of the word. Explain that when you add a new sound to the end of a word you sometimes make a new word.

Model breaking a word into sounds and adding an ending sound. Say *toe* sound by sound. Then add an ending sound and say the new word. If children need help identifying sounds, use **Sound Boxes.** Have them drag one counter into a Sound Box for each sound in a word. Then have them add an ending sound.

**Think Aloud** *We are going to say* toe *sound by sound. Let me try first. Listen: /t/ /ō/.* [Pause slightly between each sound.] *Now it's your turn. Say* toe *with me sound by sound. Ready? /t/ /ō/. Now we will add a new sound to the end. I will add /d/ to the end of* toe. *Listen: /t/ /ō/ /d/. The new word is* toad. *Say* toad *with me sound by sound: /t/ /ō/ /d/. The word is* toad.

## GUIDED PRACTICE

Guide children to practice adding a sound to the end of words. Give the following directions: *Add /t/ to the end of* for. *What is the new word?* (fort) Use the same routine with the following words. Provide corrective feedback.

*see + /d/ (seed)* *way + /l/ (whale)* *shore + /t/ (short)*
*tea + /ch/ (teach)* *hi + /k/ (hike)* *zoo + /m/ (zoom)*
*ray + /k/ (rake)* *tray + /n/ (train)* *row + /z/ (rose)*
*too + /th/ (tooth)*

## APPLY

**Practice Reproducible** Help children complete **Practice Reproducible PA94.** Say the name of each picture, clearly pronouncing each sound: (1. ring, rake, rainbow 2. wig, watch, wave 3. girl, goat, guitar 4. peach, paint, pizza). Then say the following words. Ask children to add the last sound, say each new word, and circle the corresponding picture.

**1.** Add /k/ to the end of *ray. (rake)*

**2.** Add /v/ to the end of *way. (wave)*

**3.** Add /t/ to the end of *go. (goat)*

**4.** Add /ch/ to the end of *pea. (peach)*

Name ______________________ Date ____________

# Add a Sound

**Listen to each word your teacher says. Add the new sound you hear to the end of each word. Circle the picture of each word that is formed.**

1.

2.

3.

4.

# Initial Phoneme in a Blend Deletion

## TEACH/MODEL

**Introduce** Tell children that you will help them say a word sound by sound. Then you will help them take away the first sound in the word. Explain that when you take away the first sound in a word you sometimes make a new word.

Model breaking a word into sounds and deleting the first sound in an initial consonant blend. First, say the word *stop* sound by sound. Then delete the initial sound and say the new word. If children need help identifying sounds, use **Sound Boxes.** Have them drag one counter into a Sound Box for each sound in a word. Then have them delete the beginning sound.

> **Think Aloud** *We are going to say* stop *sound by sound. Let me try first. Listen: /s/ /t/ /o/ /p/.* [Pause slightly between each sound.] *Now it's your turn. Say* stop *with me sound by sound. Ready? /s/ /t/ /o/ /p/. Next, we will take away the first sound in the word* stop. *I am going to take away the /s/ from* stop. *The new word is* top. *Now you try with me. Say* stop *without the /s/. That's right,* top.

## GUIDED PRACTICE

Guide children to practice deleting the first sound from words with initial consonant blends. Give the following directions: *Say* snap *without the /s/. What word have you made?* (nap) Use the same routine with the following words. Provide corrective feedback.

*trail* without the /t/ *(rail)*
*spin* without the /s/ *(pin)*
*flake* without the /f/ *(lake)*
*stool* without the /s/ *(tool)*
*price* without the /p/ *(rice)*
*swell* without the /s/ *(well)*
*ground* without the /g/ *(round)*
*blast* without the /b/ *(last)*

## APPLY

**Practice Reproducible** Have children complete **Practice Reproducible PA95.** Say the name of each picture, clearly pronouncing each sound: (1. rug, rake, rope 2. lock, leaf, lamp 3. table, top, tub 4. rain, run, ring). Then say the following words. Ask children to take away the first sound, say each new word, and circle the corresponding picture in the row.

**1.** Say *brake* without the /b/. *(rake)*

**2.** Say *flock* without the /f/. *(lock)*

**3.** Say *stable* without the /s/. *(table)*

**4.** Say *bring* without the /b/. *(ring)*

Name ______________________ Date ____________

Practice Reproducible PA95

# Take Away a Sound

**Listen to each word your teacher says. Take away the first sound. Circle the picture of the word formed.**

**1.**

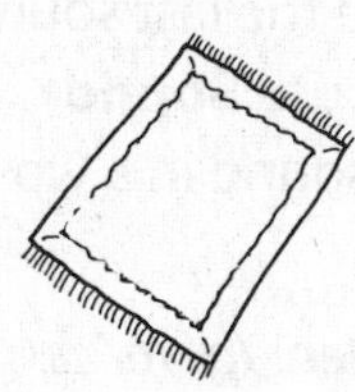

**2.**

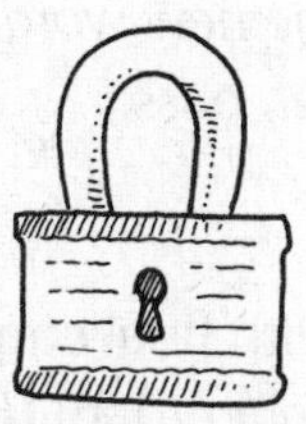
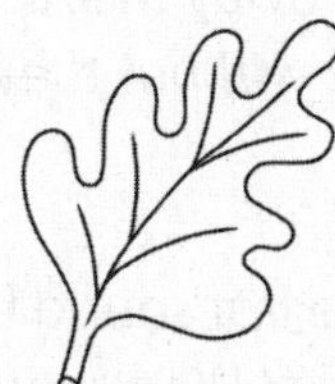

**3.**

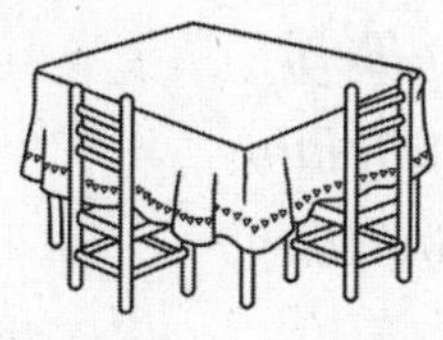

**4.**

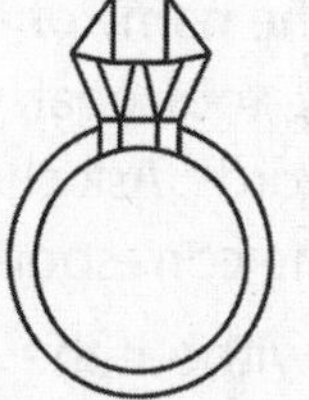

LESSON
96
Phonemic Awareness

# Final Phoneme in a Blend Deletion

## TEACH/MODEL

**Introduce** Tell children that you will help them say a word sound by sound. Then you will help them take away the last sound in the word. Explain that when you take away the last sound in a word you sometimes make a new word. Model breaking a word into sounds and deleting the last sound in a final consonant blend. First, say the word *past* sound by sound. Then delete the last sound and say the new word. If children need help identifying sounds, use **Sound Boxes.** Have them drag one counter into a Sound Box for each sound in a word. Then have them delete the ending sound.

**Think Aloud** *We are going to say* past *sound by sound. Listen: /p/ /a/ /s/ /t/.* [Pause slightly between each sound.] *Now it's your turn. Say* past *with me sound by sound. Ready? /p/ /a/ /s/ /t/. Next, we will take away the last sound in the word* past. *I am going to take away the /t/ from* past. *The new word is* pass. *Now you try with me. Say* past *without the /t/. That's right,* pass.

## GUIDED PRACTICE

Guide children to practice deleting the last sound from words with final consonant blends. Say: *Say* dent *without the /t/. What word have you made?* (den) Use the same routine with the following words. Provide corrective feedback.

*felt* without the /t/ *(fell)*
*guest* without the /t/ *(guess)*
*hold* without the /d/ *(hole)*
*mild* without the /d/ *(mile)*
*paint* without the /t/ *(pain)*
*bent* without the /t/ *(Ben)*
*plant* without the /t/ *(plan)*
*field* without the /d/ *(feel)*

## APPLY

**Practice Reproducible** Have children complete **Practice Reproducible PA96.** Say the name of each picture, clearly pronouncing each sound: (1. bell, whale, soil 2. tool, goal, yolk 3. can, ten, hand 4. drum, comb, ram). Then say the following words. Ask children to take away the last sound, say each new word, and circle the corresponding picture in the row.

1. Say *belt* without the /t/. *(bell)*
2. Say *gold* without the /d/. *(goal)*
3. Say *tent* without the /t/. *(ten)*
4. Say *ramp* without the /p/. *(ram)*

Name ______________________ Date __________

Practice Reproducible PA96

# Take Away a Sound

**Listen to each word your teacher says. Take away the last sound. Circle the picture of the word formed.**

1\.

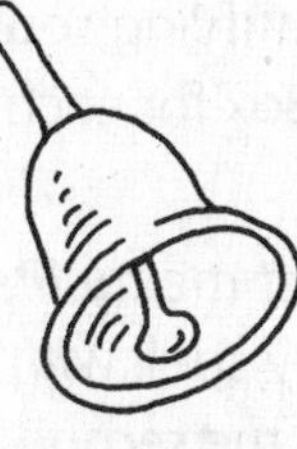

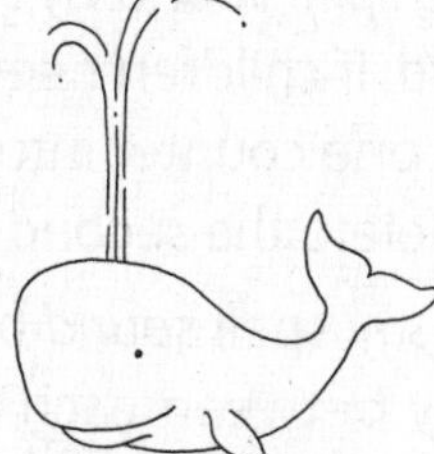

2\.

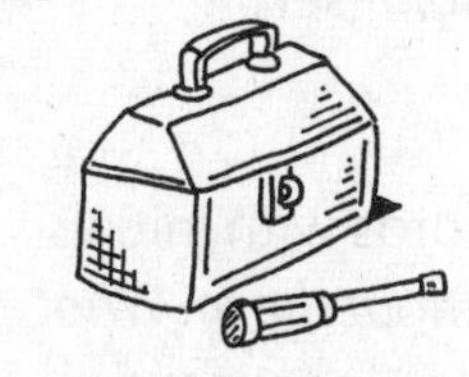

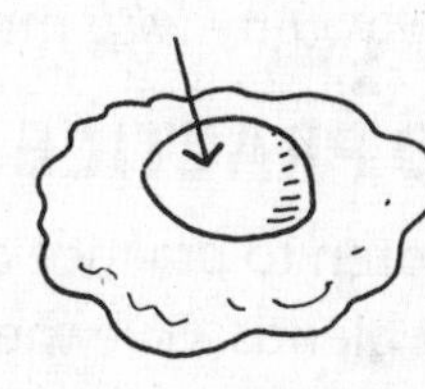

3\.

10

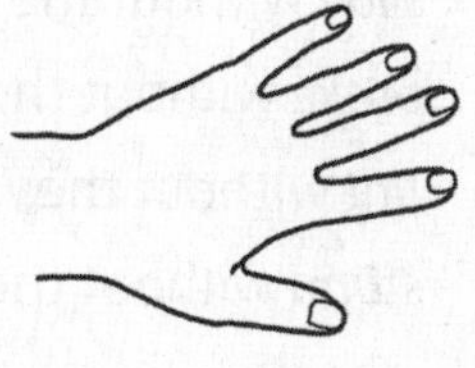

4\.

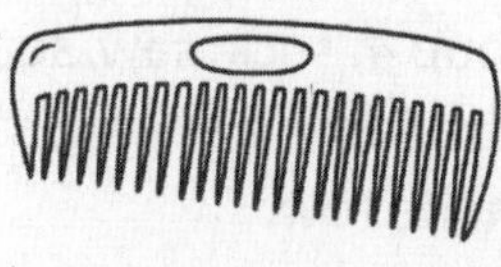

LESSON
97
Phonemic
Awareness

# Second Phoneme in a Blend Deletion

## TEACH/MODEL

**Introduce** Tell children that you will help them say a word sound by sound. Then you will help them take away the second sound in the word. Explain that when you do this, you sometimes make a new word.

Model breaking a word into sounds and deleting the second sound in an initial consonant blend. First, say the word *spell* sound by sound. Then delete the second sound and say the new word. If children need help identifying sounds, use **Sound Boxes.** Have them drag one counter into a Sound Box for each sound in a word. Then have them delete the second sound.

**Think Aloud** *We are going to say* spell *sound by sound. Let me try first. Listen: /s/ /p/ /e/ /l/.* [Pause slightly between each sound.] *Say* spell *with me sound by sound. Ready? /s/ /p/ /e/ /l/. Next w e will take away the second sound in the word* spell. *I am going to take away the /p/ from* spell. *The new word is* sell. *Now you try with me. Say* spell *without the /p/. That's right,* sell.

## GUIDED PRACTICE

Guide children to practice deleting the second sound from words with initial consonant blends. Give the following directions: *Say* drive *without the /r/. What word have you made?* (dive) Use the same routine with the following words. Provide corrective feedback.

*slide* without the /l/ *(side)*
*brake* without the /r/ *(bake)*
*flat* without the /l/ *(fat)*
*stand* without the /t/ *(sand)*
*trail* without the /r/ *(tail)*
*black* without the /l/ *(back)*
*skip* without the /k/ *(sip)*
*grass* without the /r/ *(gas)*

## APPLY

**Practice Reproducible** Help children complete **Practice Reproducible PA97.** Say the name of each picture, clearly pronouncing each sound: (1. bug, bear, book 2. four, fish, feet 3. six, sun, soup 4. sock, saw, soap). Then say the following words. Ask children to take away the second sound, say each new word, and circle the corresponding picture in the row.

1. Say *brook* without the /r/. *(book)*
2. Say *floor* without the /l/. *(four)*
3. Say *scoop* without the /k/. *(soup)*
4. Say *smock* without the /m/. *(sock)*

Name ______________________ Date __________

Practice Reproducible PA97

# Take Away a Sound

**Listen to each word your teacher says. Take away the second sound. Circle the picture of the word formed.**

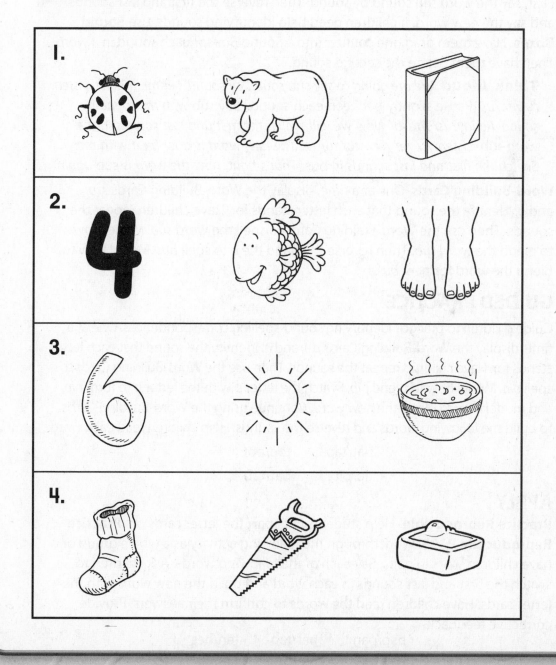

1.

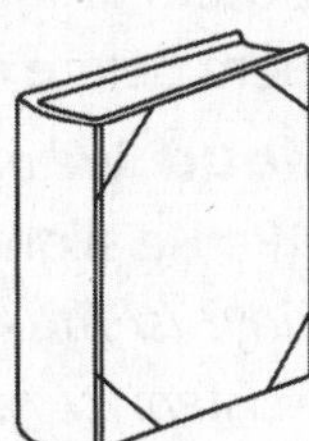

2.

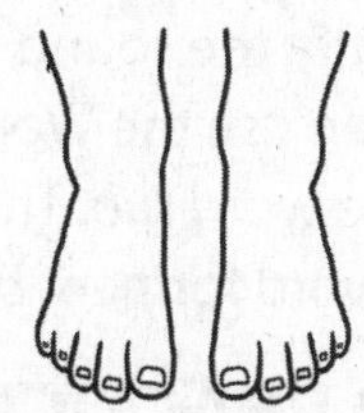

3.

4.

LESSON
98
Phonemic Awareness

# Phoneme Reversals

## TEACH/MODEL

**Introduce** Tell children that you will help them say a word sound by sound. Then you will help them switch the first and last sounds to make a new word. Explain that this will help them as they read and write words.

Model breaking a word into sounds and then reversing the first and last sounds. First, say the word *sub* sound by sound. Then reverse the first and last sounds and say the new word. If children need help identifying sounds, use **Sound Boxes.** Have them drag one counter into a Sound Box for each sound in a word. Then have them delete the second sound.

> **Think Aloud** *We are going to say* sub *sound by sound. Let me try first. Listen: /s/ /u/ /b/.* [Pause slightly between each sound.] *Say* sub *with me sound by sound. Ready? /s/ /u/ /b/. Now we will switch the first and last sounds in the word* sub. *Listen: /s/ /u/ /b/.../b/ /u/ /s/. The new word is* bus. *Try it with me. Switch the first and last sounds in* bus. *That's right, now the word is* sub *again.*

**Word-Building Cards** One at a time, display the Word-Building Cards *s, u,* and *b*. Identify the sound that each letter stands for. Have children repeat the sounds. Then use the Word-Building Cards to spell the word *sub*. Model how to blend the word *sub*. Then reverse the *s* and the *b* to spell *bus*. Model how to blend the word formed, *bus*.

## GUIDED PRACTICE

Guide children to practice identifying sound-spelling correspondences. One at a time, display the Word-Building Cards *p, i,* and *n*. Identify the sound that each letter stands for. Have children repeat the sounds. Then use the Word-Building Cards to spell *pin*. Model how to blend *pin*. Switch the letter *p* with the letter *n* to form *nip*, and model how to blend the new word. Continue using the Word-Building Cards to build the following words and reverse the sounds. Help children read each word.

pat/tap  top/pot
tip/pit  bat/tab

## APPLY

**Practice Reproducible** Help students cut apart the letter cards on **Practice Reproducible PA98.** Work through the following activity as a whole group or have children work in pairs. Say each of the following words. Ask children to switch the first and last sounds in each word and build the new word with the letter cards. Have children read the words to confirm their answers. Provide corrective feedback.

nap/pan  pat/tap  ten/net
pot/top  pal/lap  nip/pin

## Letter Cards

**Cut out the letter cards. Use them to build and read words.**

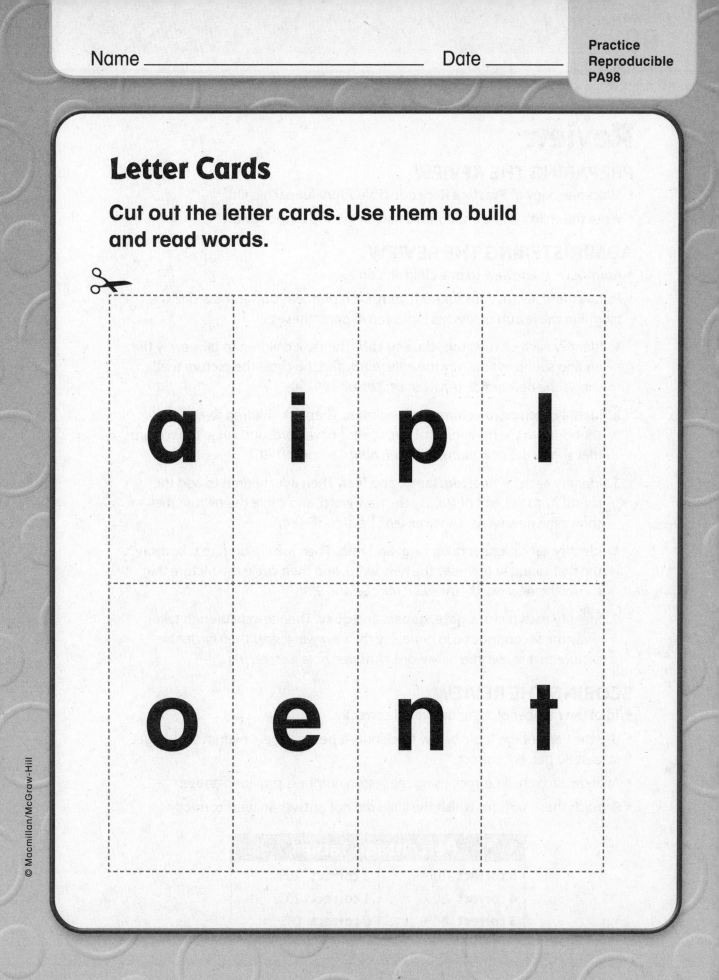

| a | i | p | l |
|---|---|---|---|
| o | e | n | t |

# Review

## PREPARING THE REVIEW

- Make one copy of **Practice Reproducible PA99** for each child.
- Write the child's name and today's date at the top of the review.

## ADMINISTERING THE REVIEW

- Administer the review to one child at a time.
- Follow these instructions for each item. Each phonemic awareness skill was taught in the lesson or lessons indicated in parentheses.

1. Identify each picture: **top, tie,** and **tub.** Then ask children to take away the ending sound in *time*, say the new word, and the circle the picture that shows the new word. (Answer: *tie*; Lessons 89–90)
2. Identify each picture: **ham, jar,** and **man.** Then ask children to add the sound /h/ to the beginning of *am*, say the new word, and circle the picture that shows the new word. (Answer: *ham*; Lessons 91–92)
3. Identify each picture: **log, lamp,** and **leaf.** Then ask children to add the sound /f/ to the end of *lea*, say the new word, and circle the picture that shows the new word. (Answer: *leaf*; Lessons 93–94)
4. Identify each picture: **rake, ring,** and **rain.** Then ask children to take away the first sound in *train*, say the new word, and then circle the picture that shows the new word. (Answer: *rain*; Lesson 95)
5. Identify each picture: **gate, goose,** and **goat.** Then ask children to take away the second sound in *grate*, say the new word, and then circle the picture that shows the new word. (Answer: *gate*; Lesson 97)

## SCORING THE REVIEW

- Total the number of items answered correctly.
- Use the Percentage Table below to identify a percentage. Children should get at least 80 percent correct.
- Analyze each child's errors, using the lesson numbers provided above.
- Reteach those skills for which the child did not answer an item correctly.

| Percentage Table | |
|---|---|
| **5 correct** 100% | **2 correct** 40% |
| **4 correct** 80% | **1 correct** 20% |
| **3 correct** 60% | **0 correct** 0% |

Name ______________________ Date __________



# Phonemic Awareness Review

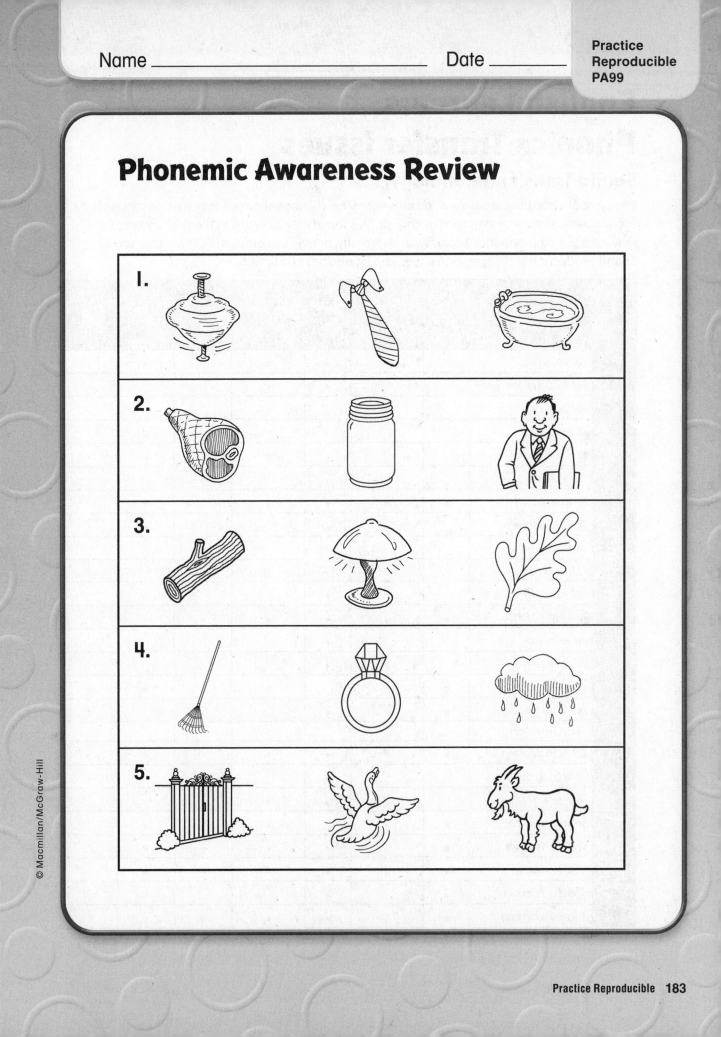

| | | | |
|---|---|---|---|
| 1. | 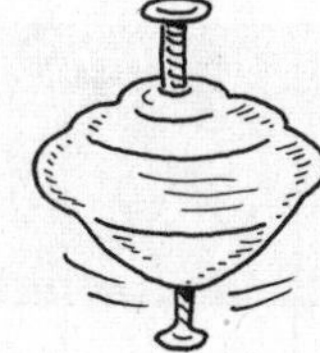 |  |  |
| 2. | 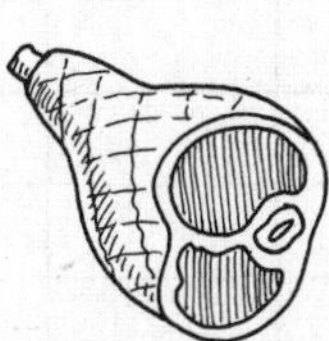 |  |  |
| 3. | 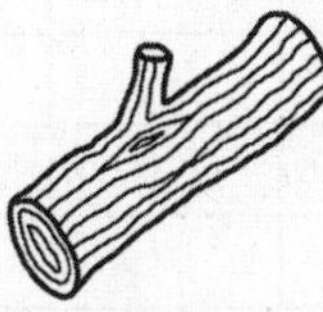 |  | 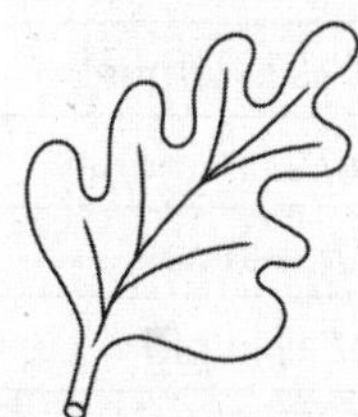 |
| 4. |  | 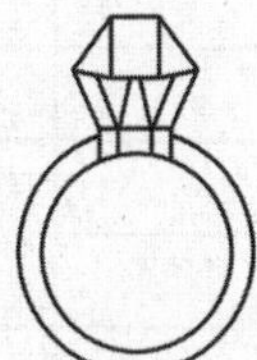 |  |
| 5. |  |  |  |

# English Learners: Phonics Transfer Issues

## Sound Transfer (Phonology)

The symbol • identifies areas in which these primary language speakers may have some difficulty pronouncing and perceiving spoken English. The sound may not exist in the primary language, may exist but be pronounced somewhat differently, or may be confused with another sound. Sound production and perception issues impact phonics instruction.

| | SOUND | SPANISH | VIETNAMESE | HMONG | CANTONESE | HAITIAN CREOLE | KOREAN | KHMER |
|---|---|---|---|---|---|---|---|---|
| Consonants | /b/ as in bat | | | • | • | | • | |
| | /k/ as in cat and kite | | | • | | | | |
| | /d/ as in dog | | | | • | | • | |
| | /f/ as in fan | | | | | | • | |
| | /g/ as in goat | | | • | • | | • | • |
| | /h/ as in hen | | | | | • | | |
| | /j/ as in jacket | • | • | • | • | | • | |
| | /l/ as in lemon | | | | | | • | |
| | /m/ as in money | | | | | | | |
| | /n/ as in nail | | | | | | | |
| | /p/ as in pig | | | • | | | | |
| | /r/ as in rabbit | • | | • | • | • | • | |
| | /s/ as in sun | | | • | | | | |
| | /t/ as in teen | | • | • | | | | |
| | /v/ as in video | • | | | • | | • | • |
| | /w/ as in wagon | • | | • | | | | • |
| | /y/ as in yo-yo | | | | | | | |
| | /z/ as in zebra | • | | • | • | | • | • |
| | /kw/ as in queen | | | • | | | | |
| | /ks/ as in X-ray | | | • | • | | | |
| Short Vowels | short *a* as in hat | • | • | | • | | • | |
| | short *e* as in set | • | | • | • | • | • | |
| | short *i* as in sit | • | • | • | • | • | • | |
| | short *o* as in hot | • | | • | | | • | |
| | short *u* as in cup | • | | • | • | • | • | |

| | SOUND | SPANISH | VIETNAMESE | HMONG | CANTONESE | HAITIAN CREOLE | KOREAN | KHMER |
|---|---|---|---|---|---|---|---|---|
| Long Vowels | long *a* as in date | | | • | • | | | |
| | long *e* as in be | | | | • | | • | |
| | long *i* as in ice | | | | • | | | |
| | long *o* as in road | | | • | • | | | |
| | long *u* as in true | | | | • | | • | |
| Vowel Patterns | *oo* as in book | • | • | • | | • | • | • |
| | *aw* as in saw | • | | | | | • | |
| Diphthongs | *oy* as in boy | | | • | | | | |
| | *ow* as in how | • | | | | | | |
| *r*-Controlled Vowels | *ir* as in bird | • | • | • | • | • | • | • |
| | *ar* as in hard | • | • | • | • | • | • | • |
| | *or* as in form | • | • | • | • | • | • | • |
| | *air* as in hair | • | • | • | • | • | • | • |
| | *ear* as in hear | • | • | • | • | • | • | • |
| Consonant Digraphs | *sh* as in shoe | • | • | | • | | | • |
| | *ch* as in chain | | • | • | | | | |
| | *th* as in think | • | • | • | • | • | • | • |
| | *ng* as in sing | • | | • | | • | | |
| Consonant Blends | *bl*, *tr*, *dr*, etc. (start of words) as in black, tree, dress | | • | • | • | | • | |
| | *ld*, *nt*, *rt*, etc. (end of words) as in cold, tent, start | | • | • | • | • | • | • |

# English Learners: Phonics Transfer Issues

## Sound-Symbol Transfer (Phonics)

The following chart identifies sound-symbol transfer issues for four languages that use the roman alphabet. (The remaining three do not.) The symbol • identifies symbols which do not represent the corresponding sound in the writing system of the primary language.

| | SOUND-SYMBOLS | SPANISH | VIETNAMESE | HMONG | HAITIAN CREOLE |
|---|---|---|---|---|---|
| Consonants | *b* as in bat | | | • | |
| Consonants | *c* as in cat | | • | • | • |
| Consonants | as in cent | | • | • | |
| Consonants | *d* as in dog | | | | |
| Consonants | *f* as in fish | | | | |
| Consonants | *g* as in goat | | | • | |
| Consonants | as in giant | • | | • | |
| Consonants | *h* as in hen | • | | | |
| Consonants | *j* as in jacket | • | • | • | |
| Consonants | *k* as in kite | | | • | |
| Consonants | *l* as in lemon | | | | |
| Consonants | *m* as in moon | | | | |
| Consonants | *n* as in nice | | | | |
| Consonants | *p* as in pig | | | | |
| Consonants | *qu* as in queen | • | | • | • |
| Consonants | *r* as in rabbit | • | | • | |
| Consonants | *s* as in sun | | | • | |
| Consonants | *t* as in teen | | | • | |
| Consonants | *v* as in video | • | | | |
| Consonants | *w* as in wagon | | • | • | |
| Consonants | *x* as in X-ray | | • | • | • |
| Consonants | *y* as in yo-yo | | | | |
| Consonants | *z* as in zebra | • | • | • | |
| Consonant Digraphs | *sh* as in shoe | • | | | |
| Consonant Digraphs | *ch* as in chair | | | | • |
| Consonant Digraphs | *th* as in think | • | | | • |
| Consonant Digraphs | as in that | | | | |

| Vowels and Vowel Patterns | SOUND-SYMBOLS | SPANISH | VIETNAMESE | HMONG | HAITIAN CREOLE |
|---|---|---|---|---|---|
| | *a* as in bat | • | | • | |
| | *aCe* as in date | • | • | | |
| | *ai* as in rain | • | • | • | • |
| | *ay* as in day | • | • | • | • |
| | *au* as in author | • | • | • | • |
| | *aw* as in saw | • | • | • | • |
| | *e* as in bet | • | | • | • |
| | *ee* as in seed | • | | • | • |
| | *ea* as in tea | • | | • | • |
| | *ew* as in few | • | | • | • |
| | *i* as in sit | • | | • | • |
| | *iCe* as in pipe | • | • | • | • |
| | *o* as in hot | • | | • | • |
| | *o* as in rode | • | | • | • |
| | *oo* as in moon | • | | • | • |
| | *oo* as in book | • | | • | • |
| | *oa* as in boat | • | | • | • |
| | *ow* as in row | • | • | • | • |
| | *ow* as in how | • | • | • | • |
| | *ou* as in sound | • | • | • | • |
| | *oi* as in boil | • | | • | • |
| | *oy* as in boy | • | | • | • |
| | *u* as in cup | • | | • | • |
| | *uCe* as in June | • | • | • | • |
| | *ui* as in suit | • | • | • | • |
| | *ue* as in blue | • | • | • | • |
| | *y* as in try | • | | • | • |
| | *ar* as in star | | | • | • |
| | *er* as in fern | • | | • | • |
| | *ir* as in bird | • | | • | • |
| | *or* as in torn | • | | • | |
| | *ur* as in burn | • | | • | |

# Notes on African American Vernacular English

Some of your students will be speakers of African American Vernacular English (AAVE). AAVE is a language system with well-formed rules for sounds, grammar, and meanings. Throughout the year you will help these students learn standard academic English by focusing on those places where AAVE differs from the standard and on those patterns that will have the most immediate impact on the students' reading and writing development.

| | |
|---|---|
| **/l/ Sound** | Many speakers of African American Vernacular English drop the /l/ sound in words, particularly in words with *-ool* and *-oal* spelling patterns, such as *cool* and *coal*, and when the letter *l* precedes the consonant *p, t,* or *k,* as in *help, belt,* and *milk*. These students will drop the *l* when spelling these words, as well. Provide additional articulation support prior to reading and spelling these words. |
| **/i/ and /e/ Sounds** | Many speakers of African American Vernacular English won't pronounce or hear the difference between /i/ and /e/ in words such as *pen/pin* and *him/hem*. Focus on mouth position for each vowel sound. |
| **/t/ Sound** | Many speakers of African American Vernacular English drop the /t/ sound when pronouncing the common words *it's, that's,* and *what's*. These words sound more like *i's, tha's,* and *wha's*. These students will need additional articulation support. |
| **/th/ Sound** | For many speakers of African American Vernacular English, the initial /th/ sound in words such as *this* and *then* is produced as a /d/ sound. In words such as *thing* and *through,* the /th/ sound is produced as a /t/ sound. At the ends of words and syllables, such as *bath* and *bathroom*, the /th/ sound is replaced by /f/. Provide articulation support. |
| **/r/ Sound** | Many speakers of African American Vernacular English drop the /r/ sound in words. For example, these students will say *sto'* for *store* or *do'* for *door*. Clearly pronounce these words, emphasizing the /r/ sound. Have children repeat several times, exaggerating the sound. |
| **/r/ Blends** | Many speakers of African American Vernacular English drop the /r/ in words with r-blends. For example, the students will say *th'ow* for *throw*. Clearly pronounce these words in the lesson, emphasizing the sounds of the r-blend. Have children repeat several times, exaggerating the sound. |

| Final Blends | Many speakers of African American Vernacular English drop the final letter in a consonant blend. For example, they will say *des'* for *desk*. Clearly pronounce the final sound in these words and have students repeat several times, exaggerating the sound. |
|---|---|
| **Final Blends** | Many speakers of African American Vernacular English will drop the first sound in a final blend when the blends *mp, nt, nk, lp, lt, lk* are used. These students will need additional articulation support. |
| **Plurals** | When the letter *-s* is added to a word ending in a consonant blend, such as *test* (*tests*), many speakers of African American Vernacular English will drop the final sounds, saying *tes'* or *tesses*. These students will need additional articulation support. |
| **Possessives** | In standard academic English, *'s* is added to a noun to show possession. For many speakers of African American Vernacular English, the *'s* is absent. However, the *'s* is regularly added to *mine*, as in *This is mines*. |
| **Contractions** | Many speakers of African American Vernacular English drop the /t/ sound when pronouncing the common words *it's*, *that's*, and *what's*. These words sound more like *i's*, *tha's*, and *wha's*. These students will need additional articulation support. |
| ***-ed* Ending** | Many speakers of African American Vernacular English understand the use of *-ed* to form the past tense but leave it out or add sounds when pronouncing the word, as in *pick* or *pickted* for *picked*. Students will need additional work with *-ed* in order to know when and where to use it in writing. |
| ***-ing* Ending** | Many speakers of African American Vernacular English will pronounce words with *-ing* as /ang/. For example, they will say *thang* for *thing*. Emphasize the /i/ sound in these words to help students correctly spell and pronounce them. |

# Screening Options

## DIBELS (Dynamic Indicators of Basic Early Literacy Skills), K–3

**What is the DIBELS screening assessment?** The Dynamic Indicators of Basic Early Literacy Skills measures reading acquisition skills. It provides an indicator of how proficient children are likely to be in their overall reading ability by the end of third grade. It identifies children who are at risk for reading difficulties before failure sets in and determines appropriate instructional support.

**How does it work?** Screening is administered to all children in the fall, mid-winter, and spring of each year, from kindergarten through third grade. All measures are individually administered and include special administration instructions. Each measure is timed for one minute, except for Initial Sounds Fluency. There are three or four short tasks at each grade level. Results help teachers identify skills, monitor progress, and intervene for children at risk.

| Reading First Component | DIBELS Measure | Grade |
|---|---|---|
| **Phonemic Awareness** | **Initial Sound Fluency** identifies a child's ability to recognize and produce the initial sounds in an orally presented word. | K |
| | **Phoneme Segmentation Fluency** identifies a child's ability to fluently segment three- and four-phoneme words into their individual phonemes. | K–1 |
| **Phonics** | **Letter Naming Fluency** identifies a child's knowledge of upper- and lower-case letters arranged in random order. | K–1 |
| | **Nonsense Word Fluency** identifies a child's knowledge of letter-sound correspondences and ability to blend sounds in words. | K–1 |
| **Fluency (Connected Text)** | **Oral Reading Fluency** identifies whether a child may need additional instructional support in fluency. | 1–3 |
| **Comprehension** | **Retell Fluency** identifies whether a child may need additional instructional support in comprehension. | 1–3 |
| **Vocabulary** | **Word Use Fluency** identifies whether a child may need additional instructional support with vocabulary strategies. | K–3 |

## Aligning DIBELS Phonemic Awareness Screening with *California Treasures*

**When do I screen for phonemic awareness?** You should test children's phonemic awareness skills in Kindergarten and Grade 1 only. Administer these tests three times a year, as shown below. The scores shown will help you interpret which of your children may be at risk for reading difficulties.

| Grade | DIBELS Measure | Beginning of the Year | Middle of the Year | End of the Year |
|---|---|---|---|---|
| **Kindergarten** | **Initial Sound Fluency** | **Start Smart**<br>***Goal: 8***<br>Low Risk: 8 or higher<br>Some Risk: 4–7<br>At Risk: Below 4 | **Unit 4**<br>***Goal: 25–35***<br>Established: 25 or higher<br>Emerging: 10–24<br>Deficient: Below 10 | **Unit 9**<br>Move to assessing Phoneme Segmentation Fluency |
| | **Phoneme Segmentation Fluency** | | **Unit 4**<br>***Goal: 18 phonemes***<br>Low Risk: 18<br>Some Risk: 7–17<br>At Risk: Below 7 | **Unit 9**<br>***Goal: 35 phonemes***<br>Established: 35–45<br>Emerging: 10–34<br>Deficient: Below 10 |
| **Grade 1** | **Phoneme Segmentation Fluency** | **Unit 1**<br>***Goal: 35 phonemes***<br>Established: 35–45<br>Emerging: 10–34<br>Deficient: Below 10 | **Unit 3**<br>***Goal: 35 phonemes***<br>Established: 35–45<br>Emerging: 10–34<br>Deficient: Below 10 | **Unit 5**<br>***Goal: 35 phonemes***<br>Established: 35–45<br>Emerging: 10–34<br>Deficient: Below 10 |

## TPRI (Texas Primary Reading Inventory), K–3

**What is the Texas Primary Reading Inventory?** The Texas Primary Reading Inventory (TPRI) is a teacher-administered assessment that quickly identifies children who are NOT at risk for reading failure. It is a predictive assessment that allows teachers to target their instruction and resources on those children who need further evaluation.

**How does it work?** The screening test is a series of short, student-friendly tasks. Each task lasts from three to five minutes.

- The Kindergarten screening is administered in mid-January and mid-April.
- The Grade 1 screening is administered in mid-September and mid-April.
- The Grade 2 screening is administered in mid-September.
- The Grade 3 screening is administered in mid-September.

| Reading First Component | TPRI Measure | Grade |
|---|---|---|
| **Phonemic Awareness** | **Blending: Onset and Rime, Phonemes** identifies a child's ability to identify, think about, and manipulate the individual sounds in words. | K–1 |
| **Phonics** | **Graphophonemic Knowledge** identifies a child's recognition of the alphabet and knowledge of sound-symbol correspondences. | K–1 |
| | **Word Reading** identifies a child's ability to identify words correctly. Children are identified as Developed or Still Developing. | K–3 |
| **Fluency (Connected Text)** | **Reading Accuracy and Fluency** identifies a child's ability to read connected text accurately, quickly, and automatically. | 1–3 |
| **Comprehension** | **Listening Comprehension** identifies a child's ability to understand what has been read aloud to him or her. | K–1 |
| | **Reading Comprehension** identifies a child's ability to understand what he or she has read. | 1–3 |